D0272915

Studies in Deprivation and Disadvantage

**Parenting Breakdown**

# Studies in Deprivation and Disadvantage

Studies in Deprivation and Disadvantage 14

# Parenting Breakdown

## The Making and Breaking of Inter-generational Links

*David Quinton and Michael Rutter*

## Avebury

Aldershot · Brookfield USA · Hong Kong · Singapore · Sydney

Published by
Avebury
Gower Publishing Company Limited
Gower House
Croft Road
Aldershot
Hants GU11 3HR
England

Gower Publishing Company
Old Post Road
Brookfield
Vermont 05036
USA

**British Library Cataloguing in Publication Data**

Quinton, David
    Parenting breakdown: the making and breaking
    of inter-generational links. — (Studies in
    deprivation and disadvantage; 14).
    1. Parent and child    2. Conflict of generations
    I. Title    II. Rutter, Michael    III. Series
    306.8'74        HQ755.85

**Library of Congress Cataloging-in-Publication Data**

Quinton, David.
    Parenting breakdown.

    (Studies in deprivation and disadvantage; 14)
    Bibliography: p.
    Includes index.
    1. Socially handicapped children——Great Britain.    2. Abused children——
Great Britain.    3. Intergenerational relations——Great Britain.    4. Parental
deprivation.    5. Family social work——Great Britain.    I. Rutter, Michael.
II. Title.    III. Series.
HV751.A6Q85    1988        306.8'74'0941        87—19585

ISBN 0 566 05582 1

Printed and bound in Great Britain by
Biddles Limited, Guildford and King's Lynn

# Contents

# Figures

Statistical significance in figures is as follows: * p < 0.05, ** p < 0.01, *** p < 0.001.

# Tables

# Acknowledgements

These two studies could not have been completed without the help and encouragement of many people. We would like particularly to thank Christine Liddle for helping in the development of measures, undertaking the bulk of the interviewing with David Quinton, and being an invaluably supportive colleague; Freda Sklair, Gerrilyn Smith and Maggie Winkworth for their help with the data collection; George Brown, Barbara Maughan and Janet Ouston for many helpful discussions on concepts and methods; Graham Dunn and Brian Everitt for invaluable statistical advice; and Roy King, Norma Raynes, Jack Tizard and Bill Yule for access to the records from their study of the two children's homes.

Thanks are also due to the two group general practices and their attached Health Visitors for allowing their patients to be approached for the retrospective study, and to the staff of the Borough Social Services Department and all the area teams for helping to identify and contact the families with children in care. The staff at the NHS Central Register were helpful and efficient in the tracing of subjects for the prospective study, and the local FPCs and GPs in making contact with them.

Jenny Smith and Joy Maxwell prepared the bulk of the manuscript, with help from Judith Coward and Nicola Billinton. Without their patient and expert help this volume could not have been completed.

The studies were generously supported by the DHSS/SSRC Joint Working Party on Transmitted Deprivation, and, during analysis and writing-up, by the William T. Grant Foundation.

Finally, our thanks are especially due to the families themselves for talking freely and openly about lives that had often been difficult and distressing. This book is dedicated to them in the belief that life, for those who are still unhappy and deprived, can, given the right circumstances, become rewarding and successful.

# 1 Introduction

Breakdowns in parenting are a distressingly common problem in modern society. Public concern is most readily roused by press reports of shocking cases of gross abuse or neglect that lead to a child's death; and whilst it is difficult to obtain accurate figures on the extent of such maltreatment, it is clear that the problem is a sizeable one. In Britain it has been estimated that each year 1.06 per cent of children under the age of fifteen — over 6000 children — suffer physical abuse (Creighton, 1984), and in America estimates are even higher, with 1.2 per cent of children experiencing abuse or neglect (Krug and Davis, 1981), and 3–4 per cent of the population reporting the experience of parental violence (Straus, 1979). But beyond these peaks of catastrophic failure lies a broader hinterland of parenting problems where parents find themselves unable to cope and where children suffer patterns of upbringing harmful to their physical, mental and emotional development. Thus, in addition to cases of overt maltreatment, there is a still larger proportion of children who experience temporary or permanent breakdowns in parenting for a variety of reasons. Recent figures indicate that currently there are approximately 97,000 children and young people in the care of local authorities in England and Wales (Berridge, 1985): just less than half the children being subject to a care order under the provision of the 1969 Children and Young Persons Act. Nearly half of these admissions are for neglect or ill-treatment, and the remainder because of the children's behavioural or educational problems. Of the two-fifths admitted voluntarily under section 2 of the Child Care Act 1980, 24 per cent come into care because of parental marital breakdown, 21 per cent because of unsatisfactory home conditions and 17 per cent because of illness in a parent or guardian.

These figures themselves suggest that parenting breakdowns happen for a wide variety of reasons. In the great majority of cases they occur in the context of major social and environmental hardships, to the extent that such hardships might themselves seem to be a sufficient explanation for breakdown. However, it is a common observation that marked parenting problems are often part of a wider cluster of psycho-social difficulties. In some cases these involve many members of the same family and seem to recur in the next generation. Oliver has provided several dramatic reports of families of this kind, in one case involving five generations of children (Oliver and Taylor, 1971; Oliver and Cox, 1973; Oliver, 1985). In these instances the familial aggregation tends to involve personality disorders, alcoholism and criminality as well as child maltreatment. On the whole, parents who injure their children are somewhat more likely to be of lower social status, to be of low average intelligence, to have their children at a younger age than most and to have larger families (Smith, 1978). However as compared with persons from comparable social groups, they differ much more strikingly in the very high frequency of marital disharmony and breakdown, high rates of premarital conception and illegitimate births, and high rates of psychiatric disorder, personality problems and criminality.

It was observations of this kind that, in 1972, led the Conservative minister, Sir Keith Joseph, to draw attention to the issue. In a speech to the pre-school play groups association he argued that: 'People who were themselves deprived in one or more ways in childhood become in turn the parents of another generation of deprived children.' Whilst he was not explicit on the processes involved, the implication seemed to be that poor parenting was one of the central mechanisms mediating the inter-generational transmission of family problems. This proposition involves several rather different scientific questions, but the starting-point was the query as to how often inter-generational continuity actually occurs.

### Frequency of the inter-generational transmission of parenting problems

At the time our studies began most of the evidence on inter-generational continuities derived from life histories taken from parents who were themselves involved in abusing or neglecting their children (Rutter and Madge, 1976). A variety of childhood antecedents of such abuse had been noted. Thus, men imprisoned for violence to children had been shown to come from large and disrupted families where abandonment or abuse by parents is common (Gibbens and Walker, 1956; Scott, 1973). Similar findings existed for women where child-battering was related to unhappy, loveless or traumatic childhoods (Lukianowitz, 1971). Although there was some evidence on continuities in battering itself (Oliver *et al.*, 1974), the majority of studies showed that abuse was linked to a wider range of severely adverse childhood experiences.

There was much less evidence on the degree of continuity in parenting difficulties *not* involving abuse or neglect. A substantial body of research showed that adverse early experiences were associated with a higher risk of later life-history features known to be associated with parenting problems; but the steps in the argument linking early experiences to later parenting difficulties involved inferences from one kind of data to another, with no *direct* measurement of parenting. For example, families with children in care experience a wide range of psychosocial problems including marital discord and breakdown (Lewis,

1954); coming from a home broken by discord increases the risk of conception early and outside of marriage (Ilsley and Thompson, 1961; Wolkind *et al.*, 1976); and the experience of parental divorce increases the risk of divorce for the children (Langner and Michael, 1963; Gurin *et al.*, 1969; Glenn and Skelton, 1983). Early conception, large family size, single-parent status, illegitimacy and receptions into care are all known to increase the risk of physical, behavioural and educational problems in the children (Davie *et al.*, 1972; Wadsworth *et al.*, 1984). However there was a lack of evidence on whether or not parenting provides the link between adverse early experiences, later life-history and problems in the children's health and development.

At the beginning of our study only the work of Frommer and O'Shea (1973a and b) had investigated this issue directly. In a study designed to identify variables predictive of women vulnerable for poor parenting, they examined the associations between childhood separations and parenting difficulties in 58 young mothers. The previously separated mothers were more likely to prop their babies with a bottle when feeding, more likely to wean them early and more likely to be over-anxious or lacking in care. By the one-year follow-up they were more likely to be pregnant again, to be depressed and to have marital and sexual problems. However, poor parenting at follow-up was much more likely when these marital or mental problems occurred. Therefore, although there was clear evidence for inter-generational influences on parenting behaviour, it could not be determined whether the link was via a greater vulnerability to depression — which is known to affect parenting; whether the *current* marital circumstances were the most powerful influence; or whether parenting *itself* was directly affected by the earlier experiences.

In sum, when our studies were begun, the evidence for continuities in parenting problems to a great extent rested on the evidence from studies of gross parenting failure. From these studies the inference could be drawn that an important mediating mechanism in the inter-generation transmission of these particular problems lay in the association between early disrupted family experiences and deviant personality development. This inference was warranted because of the very high rate of personality disorders in the samples studied. On the other hand, the evidence for continuities in parenting problems not involving abuse or neglect was largely lacking. There were suggestions of possible connections across the generations but also evidence of an association between parenting difficulties and *current* social hardships. Moreover, the extent of continuity in parenting difficulties between one generation and the next had not been systematically studied. A further range of issues therefore needed to be tackled. These involved questions concerning the best research design, the appropriate variables on which to seek continuity, the concept and measurement of parenting, and the concept of continuity itself.

## Issues in the inter-generational transmission of parenting problems

### Retrospective or prospective evidence

The first issue concerned the need for a combined retrospective/ prospective design for examining inter-generational parenting links. The great majority of studies had been retrospective, and most commonly were of the sort where the childhoods of a group *currently* experiencing parenting problems of one sort or another are studied to see whether they experienced similar problems in their own childhood. There are a number of reasons why such evidence is likely to overstate the degree of continuity. First, restrospective studies of parenting problems necessarily start with a child in difficulty. However, since there are usually several children in one family, at least two and quite often several parental figures, the likelihood of finding a history of childhood adversity in at least one of the parents is obviously greater than in a prospective study where the start is made with just one individual at risk because of childhood experiences. He or she may not have any children at all at the time of follow-up or may have several children, the majority of whom will not have problems. For this straightforward statistical reason it is likely that, ordinarily, continuities looking backwards will be stronger than those looking forwards. Further, if the retrospective evidence is based on clinic or social work samples one is by definition dealing with *unsuccessful* outcomes from early experiences. This will mean that all those who had an adverse childhood, but who are now functioning well, will remain unidentified. In order to understand the linking processes we need to know the reasons for *discontinuities* as well as for continuities, and also to know the extent to which severe parenting problems arise anew in each generation unconnected with childhood experiences.

The most straightforward design for the investigation of intergenerational links is the long-term longitudinal study, in which a sample is identified and followed until the next generation has reached the same point in the life-cycle. If such studies are representative of the whole population they can be used to answer these questions. However, such studies are very expensive and take decades to complete; moreover unless they are specifically designed to examine intergenerational questions they are likely to lack data on key variables. An alternative is the prospective investigation in which a group on whom systematic records exist from some time in the past are recontacted for further study. This can be a particularly effective method when the original data are directly relevant to the type of continuity of interest, as was the case in Robins' study of sociopathic personality (Robins,

1966) or Kolvin's follow-up of the Newcastle Thousand Families Study (Miller *et al.*, 1985). Such studies can answer questions concerning the outcome from particular behaviours or experiences but, unless there are adequate comparison samples, they cannot explain the full range of the *current* expression of a problem, since they are likely to omit links due to *other* background variables and also to omit current cases where problems do not have an inter-generational component.

A third approach is the retrospective study in which a sample identified through the current occurrence of some characteristic is chosen and life-history data collected to examine inter-generational links. This approach has immense advantages in that the sample can be chosen on the basis of the *outcome* variable of interest and the data on the previous generation collected with a specific research question in mind. However, this method can provide an estimate of the strength of an inter-generational link only if the selected sample is representative of the full range of outcomes on the variable of interest. In addition, on its own it is likely to be a risky procedure for the study of inter-generation processes unless it can be assumed that a particular characteristic is also well distributed in the previous generation. If this is not the case, an excessively large sample may need to be drawn in order to obtain a satisfactory number of cases on certain childhood variables.

These problems of prospective and retrospective approaches when used on their own make a two-stage strategy particularly efficient. In this approach two samples are taken. In one, the characteristic of interest is sampled as a *dependent* variable, with the inter-generational features measured retrospectively; in the other the characteristic is sampled as an *independent* variable with the inter-generational component measured prospectively. This strategy allows an estimate both of the inter-generational component in the *current* manifestation of the characteristic and of the *risk* of this outcome if the characteristic is a feature of the parental generation. This approach permits the use of relatively small samples and therefore the use of data collection methods capable of reliably assessing a number of key variables such as psychiatric disorder, marital relationships and parenting skills, as well as the use of flexible interview techniques to minimise distortions in long-term recall.

A second reason for a retrospective/prospective design arises because of the influence of secular trends on the apparent strength of inter-generational links. For example, if the number of children in care increases across a number of generations many more children currently in care will have parents who had been in care than was the case in the previous generation. The impression of an increasing inter-generational continuity may be largely an artefact resulting from secular trends or policy changes.

### Single or multiple indicators

A second issue concerns the use of single or multiple indicators in investigating inter-generational links. That is, are we to assume that continuities are to be sought only in terms of like leading to like — for example, physical maltreatment leading to physical maltreatment; or receptions into care leading to receptions into care — or should continuities be sought across a wider range of different but interconnected problems (Berthoud, 1983)? An important question here is whether the interest is narrowly focused on providing an estimate of the strength of continuity across generations, or whether the interest is in understanding the nature of the links. On their own single-indicator estimates of continuity are not very informative because secular trends and policy changes can obscure both continuities and discontinuities in underlying processes (Quinton, 1985). Since the study of inter-generational links needs to focus on the process of linkage it is necessary to examine not only whether a particular family feature or experience is an antecedent of the *same* behaviour in the next generation but also to see what other childhood experiences are precursors of the current difficulties. The data on the antecedents of child abuse made this clear, and this has been substantiated by more recent prospective research on parenting problems.

### Inter-generational continuities in parenting problems: Looking forwards

Prospective investigations of parenting problems have adopted two strategies (Rutter, 1986a). First, there are investigations that start with general population or high-risk samples at the time of pregnancy and follow them through the early years of child-rearing (Altemeier *et al.*, 1982, 1984; Wolkind and Kruk, 1985). In these studies, data on the parents' childhood experiences are collected from their own retrospective accounts. Secondly, there are studies that follow general population or high-risk samples from childhood through to their child-bearing years (Wadsworth, 1985; Elder *et al.*, 1985). These studies have the advantage of contemporaneous data on childhood experiences but have the disadvantage that parenting behaviour was not a focus of the investigations when they were begun.

The prospective study by Altemeier and his colleagues (1982, 1984) followed 1400 young women from the time of pregnancy until their children were between 21 months and four years of age. Within this group 23 mothers abused their children. These mothers were more likely to have experienced substitute care, to have had bad relationships with their parents, or to have experienced parental marital breakdown, and to report severe unfair punishment. On the other hand, the majority of women with these adverse experiences did not abuse their children. The continuities were greater if failure to thrive and other serious parenting difficulties were included, but still the majority of women with adverse experiences were, so far, parenting 'well enough'.

Wolkind and Kruk (1985) followed from pregnancy two high-risk groups selected (i) on prior residential care experiences, and (ii) on prolonged separations from parents because of family disharmony, but not involving receptions into care. These were compared with a random sample of non-separated women: all three groups being followed until the children were aged 42 months. Parenting outcome was assessed both by interview and direct observation. The institutionalised group were less likely to hold their baby for feeding and less likely to experience the baby as enjoyable. At 3½ their children were more likely to show behavioural problems, to have had accidents or to have been into hospital. None of these problems was significantly increased in the high-risk but non-institutionalised group. The difference in the style of feeding in the mothers who had been in care reflects Frommer and O'Shea's (1973a and b) finding discussed earlier.

The high-risk prospective study by Egeland and his co-workers (1984) examined the parenting outcome from three types of parenting experience (a) where mothers were emotionally supported as children; (b) where mothers did not have clear support in childhood but there was no abuse; and (c) where there was abuse, neglect or foster-home placement. The three groups differed markedly in rates of maltreatment of their own children (3, 9 and 34 per cent) but there were no differences with respect to other parenting difficulties. Expressed the other way round, of the 24 children who were maltreated, 16 were being reared by mothers who had themselves experienced abuse or neglect and only one by a mother who experienced emotional support during childhood.

Few data directly concerning parenting are yet available from the major British cohort studies. Findings from the British National Survey of a stratified sample of individuals born in one week in 1946 indicate that there is some association between the experience of early family disruption and the probability of divorce or separation in adulthood. Also, unhappy recollections by those with these early adversities were in turn associated with a somewhat higher rate of reserved relationships with their first-born children (Wadsworth, 1984, 1985).

Much the most substantial body of data on inter-generational continuities in general population samples is provided by the follow-up by Elder and his colleagues of a group of subjects whose childhoods spanned the Great Depression. Data are available not only on the individuals themselves but also on their parents, their grandparents and their children (Elder, 1974; Elder *et al.*, 1985). Psychological instability and marital tension in the grandparental generation were associated with hostility to the subjects as children. These parenting patterns in the first generation were in turn associated with similar negative parenting qualities in the second generation. The children reared in this aversive family environment were more likely to show disturbed behaviour in childhood, to show lack of self-control as adults and to have discordant and unstable marriages. The inter-generational correlations were clear although not large. The authors therefore cautioned that the outcome from poor experiences is very variable with many turning-points and breaks in the inter-generational cycle of parenting difficulties. This led them to raise the question of what factors buffered children from the adverse effects of poor parenting and what factors led to a break in the cycle — questions that are central to the investigations with which this volume is concerned. However, before the possible processes and mechanisms are discussed it is necessary to consider the two other central issues in inter-generational links: the concept of parenting and the concept of continuity.

## The concept of parenting

It is important to consider what is involved in parenting in order to determine what might be affected when parenting fails (Rutter, 1975, 1986a; Rutter *et al.*, 1983). A growing literature has begun to delineate a number of dimensions involved in a person's behaviour as a parent, and to underly the growing field of parent education (Harman and Brim, 1980). Thus, parenting is now understood not only to involve what parents do with their children and how they do it, but also to be affected by the quality of the parents' relationships more generally, by their psychological functioning, by their previous parenting experiences both with other children and with a particular child, and by the social context in which they are trying to parent.

Concepts of the requirements of good parenting have changed over the years. Of course, the debate between the advocates of a free and unpressured approach to child-rearing and the devotees of the careful structuring of the environment from infancy onwards — which goes back to Rousseau and Locke — still continues. But the focus of discussion has shifted from arguments over types of discipline, toilet-training or demand-feeding to an emphasis on reciprocity, to doing things *with* children rather than *to* them, to communication and problem-solving, and to security and continuity in parent–child relationships (Maccoby and Martin, 1983).

### Parenting as a task

Parenting as a task is concerned with the provision of an environment conducive to children's cognitive and social development (Rutter, 1985b and c). Thus, parenting requires certain 'skills' appropriate to the handling of children's distress, disobedience or social approaches, as well as the resolution of conflicts and interpersonal difficulties (Shure and Spivack, 1978). These skills are reflected in the parents' sensitivity to children's cues and their responsiveness to the needs of different phases of development; in helping with social problem-solving and coping with stresses; in knowing how to play with and talk to children; and in the use of disciplinary techniques that not only achieve their aim but also do so in a way that results in and increases the child's *self*-control.

## Parenting as a social relationship

Parenting is more than a set of skills and techniques; it is also a particular kind of social relationship. It has its own peculiar qualities and characteristics but nevertheless it is related to a broader set of social qualities. The implication of this is that the upbringing of children needs to be considered in terms of the enduring 'relationship' aspects of parent–child interaction. It is possible, therefore, that inter-generational links in parenting difficulties may apply either to aspects of skill or to the quality of relationships or to both.

## Effects of parental psychological state

Parenting also reflects the mother's and father's current psychosocial functioning. Thus Cox and his colleagues found that mothers with recurrent or chronic depressive disorders tended to be less appropriately responsive to their children, less likely to sustain positive interactions, less able to put their children's experiences into a personal context, and more often involved in unsuccessful attempts to control them (Mills *et al.*, 1985; Pound *et al.*, 1985). Adverse effects have also been found for manic-depressive illness (Davenport *et al.*, 1984), and schizophrenia (Naslund, 1984). On occasions even lethal abuse may be a consequence of parental emotional disturbance rather than any inherent lack in parenting skills or relationship qualities (Troisi and D'Amato, 1984).

## Parenting and parenting experience

Current parenting can be influenced by previous experience as a parent in two ways. First, it can be an outcome of the experience of bringing up previous children. It is known, for example, that parents tend to respond differently to their first-borns than they do to their subsequent children (Rutter 1981a). Secondly, parenting may be influenced by earlier experiences with the same child. This possibility has been dramatically highlighted by Klaus and Kennell's (1976) claim that mother–infant bonding was dependent on skin-to-skin contact during the neo-natal period. This claim has *not* been supported by empirical findings (see Goldberg, 1983), but it may be that *prevention* of parent–infant interaction in hospital may impair parenting (Wolkind and Rutter, 1985). It may also be that current difficulties in the inter-actions between a parent and a particular child may depend on the mishandling of some event much earlier in the child's life, such as disturbance following the child's return from hospital, or the arrival of a new sibling in the family (Dunn and Kendrick, 1982). Finally, parenting involves a two-way interaction that is affected by the charac-teristics of the child as well as of the parent (Maccoby and Martin,

1983). Such interactions may lead to vicious cycles that lead to increased parenting difficulties associated with greater problem behaviour in the children.

### Parenting and social context

Lastly, parenting must be seen as just one relationship within a broader social network. This means that parenting is affected by the quality of the parent's other social relationships, and also that parenting behaviour varies according to who else is present. For example, the pattern of mother–child interaction has been shown to alter depending on whether the father is there (Clark-Stewart, 1978). Also, when several children are present adults tend to be more peremptory and prohibitive and more likely to ignore children's approaches (Schaffer and Liddell, 1984). It is, however, the *quality* of relationships in the parent's social circle that seems most implicated in parenting difficulties. For example, parenting seems to be less adequate when the marital relationship is discordant or when the parent lacks the support of a spouse altogether (Hetherington *et al.* 1982; Wallerstein, 1983). Moreover, parenting tends to be affected by the presence or absence of effective social supports, perhaps especially at times of stress or when dealing with a difficult child (Belsky, 1979; Crockenberg, 1981; Werner and Smith, 1982; Crnic *et al.*, 1983).

These findings imply that parenting must be seen in an *ecological* perspective that recognises the family as a functional system, the operation of which will be altered by its internal composition and by external forces (Bronfenbrenner, 1979). This means that parenting must be assessed in terms of the emotional resources available to the parent, together with the material resources that can be drawn on and the physical environment in which parenting is taking place. Of course, social support is not only a feature of what is available in the environment, it also reflects personality factors that elicit or attract support (Cohen and Syme, 1985; Rutter, 1986b). Nevertheless, the ecological perspective means that attention must be paid not only to individual characteristics but also to the social and environmental contexts in which people are parenting. The observed behaviour will be an outcome of the complex interaction between these factors.

In conclusion, it makes no sense to view parenting as a unidimensional variable or as a personal attribute. To be sure, some people parent better than others under similar circumstances, but this does not justify the conclusion that inter-generational continuities arise through impacts of early experiences on parenting capacities or qualities *per se*. They might equally arise through psychiatric disorders, or lack of social support, or adverse living conditions. The demonstration of inter-generational continuities is a necessary starting-point, but does not presuppose any particular processes of transmission.

**Concepts of continuity**

A number of writers have recently criticised the lack of precision in the use of the concept of continuity (Kagan, 1980; Wohlwill, 1980). There is, of course, little dispute over the existence of meaningful and predictable links from earlier experiences and behaviour to later functioning, or that development goes through a number of predictable stages. Rather, the dispute concerns the nature of these links and whether they reflect the *influence* of what has gone before on later behaviour or rather whether one stage simply replaces another. Further, if continuity does in part reflect influences over the course of development, to what extent are the effects of earlier experiences reversible later?

Rutter (1984a) has reviewed the different ways in which the concept of continuity has been used. A number of these concern specific psychological issues that need not concern us here. However, three different meanings need to be kept in mind. First, there is the question of stability in ranking compared with other people. That is, are we concerned with whether individuals stay in the same position on some variable relative to others, or are we concerned with absolute changes in their own behaviour? For example, individuals usually retain their ranking on IQ scores over their lifetime but the *level* of their IQ increases markedly over the course of development. With regard to parenting, we need to be clear whether the interest is in detectable influences of early experiences on later behaviour, or whether the main concern is whether poor experiences lead to *poor* performance. This decision will have implications for the measurement of parenting.

Secondly, there is the question of whether the interest is in continuity in underlying process or whether it is in the surface form of behaviours. For example, the presence of supportive relationships may have a similarly protective effect at all ages although the way in which support is provided may vary.

Thirdly, the concept of continuity is used to refer to the cases in which particular patterns of family environment or experience increase or decrease the risk of particular forms of psychosocial outcome. Unlike other uses of the term, this meaning of *continuity* carries no necessary implication that the continuities occur through processes at the individual level. To the contrary, the links may be made entirely through environmental variables beyond the influence of the individual herself although the more likely route is through some interaction between personal and environmental factors. This meaning of 'continuity' is the one most relevant to the inter-generational links in parenting problems that are the subject of the studies reported here. Further aspects of the process of linkage are considered in the last section of this chapter.

The data deriving from our studies focus on continuities within a single generation. That is, they provide information on the processes linking the *experience* of poor parenting in childhood with parenting difficulties *shown* in early adulthood. Nevertheless, the same data necessarily concern continuities in parenting behaviour across two generations — that is, poor parenting provided by parents and poor parenting provided by their children. Accordingly, the findings shed light both on developmental issues and on inter-generational questions. Whether or not our conclusions on the factors involved in linkages across two generations would apply equally to continuities across three or four generations must remain uncertain.

### Individual differences

One of the most important conclusions to come from risk research over recent years is that even with the most glaring adversities it is unusual for more than half the children to succumb (Rutter, 1979). The same observation has been made on the development of depression in adults following stressful life-events. Although the risk of depression following losses and rebuffs is increased, it is usual for people *not* to become depressed in spite of the stressful experiences (Paykel, 1978). Nor is it sufficient to attribute these individual differences in resilience to constitutional factors alone (Rutter, 1985a). Temperamental features reflect both experiential and genetic factors (Plomin, 1983) and genetic factors themselves may help create or select the environments an individual experiences (Scarr and McCartney, 1983). Thus the susceptibility to stressors at one point in time may be determined either by previous experiences or by constitutional factors or by a subtle interaction between the two. The likelihood that more complex models are needed to explain individual differences in response to stress — and therefore to explain inter-generational discontinuities in parenting difficulties — is reinforced by the failure of simple additive models to explain much of the variance. That is, the evidence does not support the view that people succumb because the sum of accumulated risks is greater than the sum of positive experiences (Rutter, 1986b), rather we need to consider the question of protective factors and interactive *processes* over time (Rutter, 1983).

### *Protective factors*

Protective factors are influences that modify, ameliorate or alter a person's response to some environmental hazard (Rutter, 1985a). Such factors need not be pleasurable and, unlike positive experiences, may have no detectable effect in the absence of any subsequent stressor. That is, they serve to modify later responses not to foster normal development. For example, programmes to prepare children and their families for hospital admission successfully reduce rates of disturbance in hospital (Wolkind and Rutter, 1985) but may have no detectable effects on children's responses to other stressful experiences. In addition, protective factors may not refer to experiences at all; they may concern a quality of the individual as a person. Thus girls seem less vulnerable to many psychosocial adversities than boys (Rutter, 1970, 1981c). However, this is not simply a question of constitutional differences. There is also evidence that females are less likely to elicit damaging behaviour from others. For example, when parents are in severe conflict they are more likely to quarrel in front of their sons than their daughters (Hetherington *et al.*, 1982). Nor need such protective personal characteristics be pleasant or appealing. Several investigators have noted that those who are immune to stress are often more self-centred and shallow in their relationships (Rutter, 1981b).

Two experiences stand out amongst those likely to foster resilience in the face of adversity (Rutter, 1985a): secure stable affectional relationships; and success, satisfaction and achievement in activities that are felt to be personally important. The appropriate successful taking on of responsibilities may be protective but so too may be a degree of distancing oneself from adversities or stigmatising circumstances that cannot be altered. However, the limited available evidence suggests that these experiences are *not* mainly effective through their creating some feeling of happiness or contentment. Rather, it seems that their effectiveness resides in their impact on people's sense of self-esteem and self-confidence; on beliefs about their self-efficacy and ability to deal with life's challenges; and on the acquisition of a repertoire of social problem-solving approaches. It matters greatly *how* people deal with adversities and life stressors — perhaps not so much in the particular coping strategies employed but in the fact that they do *act* and not simply react. It appears that the promotion of resilience does not lie in an avoidance of stress, but rather in encountering stress at a time and in a way that allows self-confidence and social competence to increase through mastery and appropriate responsibility. The strong implication is that resilience must be viewed in developmental terms of changes over time, not just in some 'chemistry' of a supportive or protective effect that operates at one point.

## Processes of transmission

We need, finally, to consider the range of processes that might mediate inter-generational continuities or discontinuities in parenting problems. The association might simply reflect genetic mechanisms. Alternatively, it might reflect environmental processes by which the experience of poor parenting leads a person to become a poor parent him or herself. This might arise either through a direct impact on the capacity to parent or through a more general effect on personality development. Here parenting would be harmed in so far as personality difficulties involved parenting amongst the various relationships affected. On the other hand, none of these explanations might hold. Instead, the links might be due to processes outside the individual altogether. In this case continuities would be mediated by factors such as social disadvantage or stressful life experiences. Finally, continuities might stem from the tendency of societal institutions to treat individuals according to family 'labels' deriving from either the behaviour or social position of family members in the previous generation.

### Genetic factors

The possible importance of genetic factors arises particularly because inter-generational links are most apparent with severe failures in parenting and because these in turn are associated with major psychiatric and personality problems (Smith, 1978). A genetic component is now well established for personality disorders, criminality and alcoholism (Bohman *et al.* 1981; Cloninger *et al.* 1981; Crowe, 1983; Rutter and Giller, 1983), as well as for schizophrenia (Kety *et al.*, 1974; Kendler and Gruenberg, 1984; McGuffin *et al.*, 1984), and major affective disorders (Gershon, 1983), although not for a milder range of depressive and neurotic conditions (Torgersen, 1983). However, a number of cross-fostering and adoption studies have suggested that although genetic factors are important in the transmission of these problems, environmental factors may have a substantial influence on whether or not these problems occur. For example, Hutchings and Mednick (1974) have shown that criminal behaviour in adopted-away offspring was markedly increased only if both biological and adoptive fathers were criminal. Neither children of criminal fathers in non-criminal homes nor children of non-criminal fathers in criminal homes showed an increased risk of deviant behaviour. A somewhat similar interactive effect in the development of criminality has also been shown by Crowe (1972, 1974), and it is possible that genetic–environment interactions may operate in the case of schizophrenia (Tienari *et al.*, 1985). This may be the case also for personality disorders where parental disorders appear to increase the risk of emotional or behavioural disturbance in children only if the parental problems lead to overtly hostile family relationships (Rutter and Quinton, 1984). When this occurs there is a suggestion that the risk to children whose parents have personality problems is greater than when family discord occurs in their absence. However, in both cases, the current environment seems to be the most potent influence.

### Direct effects

The marked overlap between parenting and other problems means that it is difficult to determine whether direct or specific effects exist. The best data for examining the question come from studies of non-human primates. Harlow's early experiments clearly showed that infants reared in social isolation failed in adolescence and adult life to show normal mating behaviour (Harlow, 1965) or parenting (Seay *et al.*, 1964; Arling and Harlow, 1967). Such isolates were more rejecting of their babies than normally-reared mothers, and were sometimes so abusive that the infants died. However, these rearing experiences were so extreme as to make any extrapolation to the human situation difficult. A better parallel is the parenting of the *offspring* of these isolates. In their case their social behaviour is nearer normal than that of their parents but both as infants and juveniles they were exceptionally violent (Sackett and Ruppenthal, 1973). In general, the evidence from these studies suggests that the devastating effects of markedly adverse early experiences apply to social relationships generally, rather than specifically to parenting capacities.

### Effects on personality development

It is clear from the above discussion that major parenting difficulties are frequently accompanied by serious problems in psychosocial or personality functioning. Does it not, then, follow that intergenerational continuities in parenting deficits are a consequence of deviant personality development? The answer to this depends in part on whether the behavioural continuities that exist are relatively resistant to environmental changes. This is hard to determine in the case of serious parenting problems because of the overlap between psychosocial adversity and parenting difficulties; the continuities in parental functioning might be maintained by the persisting social disadvantage. It seems likely that both situational and individual characteristics are important in determining behaviour. This is so because although there is marked variation in individual behaviour from situation to situation, individual differences are responsible for variations in people's responses to similar circumstances (Rutter, 1984a). This view does not imply that individual characteristics are immutable features of personality, only that they are relatively stable ways of responding that have consistency over a variety of situations.

Traditionally, deviant personality development resulting from abuse, neglect or deprivation in early childhood has tended to be thought of in terms of some environmental damage to the 'structure' of personality, with the implication that the effects are necessarily permanent. That view has increasingly been called in question as a result of the evidence of change and adaptation during the developmental process, together with the finding that personality functioning may be affected by environmental circumstances even in adult life (Rutter, 1984c). This shift of view has been reflected in the altered thinking about the ways in which insecure parent–child attachments may lead to later problems in social relationships (Bretherton and Waters, 1985). Thus, it has been suggested that the early attachment relationships lead to an internal cognitive and affective 'model' of the self and of relationships with others. In other words, poor parenting may lead to personality difficulties not so much because of an irremediable damage to the capacity to form relationships but because the experience of rejection, insecurity and lack of affection has led to a set of expectations about how other people behave and hence to a self-protective, but maladaptive, style of interacting with others that does not involve reciprocal affection and trust. Whether or not that is so remains uncertain but the possibility requires that personality development be studied from a perspective that allows the examination of both continuities and discontinuities, stability and change.

### Environmental continuities

The above discussion has highlighted the difficulty in choosing between an environmental or constitutional explanation for continuities in parenting problems. The relative stability of environments means that it is difficult to assess how far individuals would change in their be-haviour if circumstances were different. The most satisfactory way to tackle this problem is to examine those cases where marked environ-mental changes have occurred. When this is done the potential for marked recovery of normal functioning even from extremely adverse experiences is apparent, at least with respect to cognitive functioning. This is shown in the single case studies of children reared in markedly depriving circumstances such as in darkened rooms or cellars in their early years without any normal human interaction (Clarke and Clarke, 1976; Skuse, 1984a and b).

The most satisfactory data on recovery of interpersonal functioning come from the follow-up studies of previously institutionalised children by Tizard and her colleagues (Tizard and Rees, 1974, 1975; Tizard and Hodges, 1978). At two years of age the institutionalised children were more clinging and less discriminating in their attachments than children brought up in ordinary families. At four years they remained less deeply attached and were, in addition, attention-seeking and in-discriminately friendly with strangers. At the age of eight they continued to show the combination of affection-seeking behaviour and lack of close attachments together with unpopular behaviour at school. Particularly important data concern those children from the residential nurseries who were adopted after the age of four. At eight the adoptive parents reported that almost all the children had developed good stable affectionate relationships with them and showed few behaviour problems at home. Evidently marked changes in environments can cause marked changes in behaviour. However, the late-adopted children continued to show problems at school similar to those shown by the children who remained in the institution. Most recently the same children have been followed up again at the age of 16 (Hodges and Tizard, in press). Two findings stand out. First, for the majority of behaviours *current* family circumstances were most relevant. Thus, the children who left the residential nursery and were returned to their *own* parents experienced much more family discord and disadvantage than those who were adopted. This was associated with a much higher rate of delinquency and conduct disorder in this 'restored' group. Secondly, even a dozen years after the adoption the adopted children continued to be more indiscriminately friendly and to have more problems in peer relationships. In this they were more like the children who were restored or who stayed in the institution than children reared from infancy in a family environment. It seemed that, in spite of generally good home circumstances throughout the school years, the institutional experience had left some mark on the style and quality of their relationships.

These data suggest that although there are some continuing behavioural impacts in childhood and adolescence of early adverse parenting experiences, *current* circumstances are heavily implicated in more serious behavioural difficulties. The consequences of early hardships for continuities in parenting problems may therefore depend on whether later environments exacerbate or ameliorate the vulnerabilities caused by the early childhood adversities.

There are virtually no studies reporting the adjustment in adulthood of institutionalised or severely deprived children who later experienced radically improved environments. Skeels (1966) followed up 25 children placed at birth in long-stay institutions. Thirteen of these later received 'mothering' in hospital by high-grade mentally subnormal women and were later adopted. All the offspring of these children were tested and found to be normal. In comparison, of a contrast group from the same institution who had not been adopted, four were still in state institutions, one had died, and the remainder had significantly lower occupational and educational achievements than the adopted children. Although there are serious concerns about the comparability of the two groups (Longstreth, 1983), the study clearly demonstrates the possibility of satisfactory adult outcomes from severe early deprivation if later experiences are good.

### Continuities in social disadvantage

The fact that such marked improvements in functioning can occur suggests that observed continuities in parenting problems are indeed related to continuities in social disadvantage; disadvantage involving not only economic or material deprivations but also lack of supportive relationships. It is necessary to ask how this continuity in disadvantage might be maintained. It is clear that socio-structural factors beyond the control of the individual are responsible for the overall level of poverty, unemployment and bad housing in the community. In that those who experience major childhood adversity are likely to come from families who are the worst placed as far as access to income, work or housing are concerned a substantial proportion of the inter-generational continuity is likely to be due to inequalities in opportunity (Atkinson *et al.*, 1983). However, substantial discontinuities in disadvantage also occur (Rutter and Madge, 1976), and the existence of structural factors does not preclude the operation of individual factors in determining *which* families show continuity. It is important to consider whether the interest is in continuities in overall ranking in some particular disadvantage or in the absolute level. For example, in McDowell's (1983) study of transmitted housing deprivation the rapid changes in the quality of the housing stock during the 1960s meant that very few children, even from the most disadvantaged backgrounds, experienced the poor housing conditions that were common in the previous generation. However, children tended to keep the ranking of their parents with respect to housing disadvantage and those now in the poorest conditions came from families with similar hardships when these people were children.

Over the lifetimes of the subjects in the two studies reported in this volume inter-generational continuities in major social disadvantages in the population as a whole were not high (Rutter and Madge, 1976). If continuities are stronger in the study families, we shall need to ask why this is so. Recourse to an overall explanation in terms of the structure of society alone is not sufficient, since this will not account for *discontinuities*. Instead more complicated model-building will be called for in which the links are traced not only through social hardships but also through the actions of the children themselves and the actions of others towards them in the overall context of their life chances and opportunities.

*Societal actions*
Lastly, there is the possibility that the inter-generational linkages stem from societal actions rather than from any effects on the individual. The strongest continuities tend to be seen with overt parenting breakdown and it could be suggested that the continuity arises less from parenting difficulties as such as from social agencies' greater propensity to remove children from families if there is a family history of previous removal of children into care or if it is known that one of the parents was also reared in an institution. Certainly, there is evidence that administrative factors, both deliberate and inadvertent, markedly affect children's care careers (Rowe, 1985; Millham *et al.*, 1986; Vernon and Fruin, 1986; Packman *et al.*, 1986). However, the greatest weight of evidence is on the way such factors influence how long children remain in care, and on maintenance or loss of links with the family, rather than on the initial decision that children need to go into foster or institutional care. It is clear that those children who go into care usually come from families with multiple psychosocial problems (Shaffer and Shaffer, 1966; Wolkind and Rutter, 1973), so that it is most unlikely that prejudiced societal actions could account for the inter-generational continuities. Nevertheless, the findings emphasise the need to consider parenting difficulties and parenting breakdown as two separate, albeit associated, phenomena. It is possible that societal

actions play some role in the translation of parenting difficulties into parenting breakdown.

## Conclusions

The evidence available at the time we started our studies indicated that there was something important to account for and investigate. In some instances there were striking inter-generational continuities in parenting breakdown; equally, however, it was clear that some individuals exposed to severely adverse patterns of child-rearing did *not* go on themselves to become poor parents. Both continuities *and* discontinuities needed to be explained. It was necessary to account for the role of childhood experiences in the genesis of parenting difficulties, for the processes involved in vulnerabilities deriving from exposure to poor parenting, and for the mechanisms responsible for resilience in the face of adversity and the breaking of inter-generational cycles. The existing evidence did not point clearly to one set of factors rather than another as responsible for the inter-generational links. Accordingly, our studies were designed so that competing explanations could be examined.

# 2 Research design and methodology

## Research questions

The issues in the study of inter-generational continuities in parenting problems discussed in Chapter 1 can be rephrased as a number of specific research questions. First, are current severe parenting problems usually related to the experience of poor parenting in childhood, or do they occur anew in each generation because of current social disadvantage or other factors? Secondly, how strong is the link looking forwards: that is, what proportion of children who experience poor parenting in their own childhood are themselves poor parents when they have children? Thirdly, what are the processes or mechanisms involved in continuities *and* in discontinuities? In particular, do the inter-generational links occur primarily through continuities in social disadvantage — a sociological explanation; do they occur through the effects of prior experiences on personality functioning and parenting capabilities — a psychological explanation; or are problems transmitted through biological inheritance — a genetic explanation. Knowledge on the origins of parenting difficulties is important in its own right: society must be concerned to prevent the tragedies that ensue when parenting fails badly (as with serious child abuse and neglect). However, from the viewpoint of research methodology a focus on parenting problems also has particular advantages for the examinations of rival hypotheses regarding the inter-generational transmission of psychosocial adversities more generally. This is because, depending on which generation is being considered, parenting is both an *independent* (or input) variable — a particular kind of social environment that serves as a possible causal influence on the child's development — and a *dependent* (or output) variable — an aspect of adults' social functioning that may be related to previous experiences *and* to current circumstances. For the child it is a set of experiences, but for the parents a facet of their behaviour. It is therefore possible to study the extent to which the *experience* of poor parenting can lead to the *behaviour* of poor parenting towards the next generation. Secondly, as discussed in the previous chapter, research findings show that parenting is influenced by a wide range of variables that include aspects of individual functioning (as with parental depression or other forms of mental disorder); of prior experiences (as with the efforts of raising a previous child); of the immediate family context (as with the effects of marital discord or the particular family constellation that is present at the time); and of wider social circumstances (as with housing conditions). However, while it is known that parenting may be influenced by these factors, it is *not* known which factors are relevant with respect to inter-generational continuities and discontinuities. That question provides the main focus of our studies reported here. Because parenting as a varaible has these qualities it is neutral as to whether a psychological, sociological or genetic explanation of transmission is to be preferred, whilst allowing all three to be investigated. We examine the possibility of genetic effects but the adequate testing of genetic hypotheses requires a different research design and our main emphasis is on the examination of different forms of environmental transmission.

### The choice of an index of parenting

In order that both retrospective and prospective strategies could be used, it was necessary to choose an index of parenting problems that could satisfy the following criteria: (i) it must reflect severe and persistent parenting difficulties; (ii) such difficulties must be reasonably common in the general population; (iii) they must be of a kind known substantially to increase the risk that the children develop disorders of psychosocial development; and (iv) the index must be able to be employed on an epidemiological basis both to identify families currently experiencing parenting difficulties and to identify individuals who had experienced similar parenting problems in their own childhood.

The admission of children into the care of a local authority because the parents were no longer able to cope with child-rearing was the most appropriate index that met all four criteria. Several studies have shown the very considerable difficulties in relationships and in child-rearing experienced by the parents of children admitted to care — even when the ostensible reason for admission is the mother's confinement or physical illness (Schaffer and Schaffer, 1968; Wolkind and Rutter, 1973); about 2 per cent of seven-year-old children in Britain have been in care for some period of their lives (Mapstone, 1969); and follow-up studies have been consistent in showing a marked increase in emotional and behavioural problems among children taken into care (Yule and Raynes, 1972; Wolkind and Rutter, 1973; Lambert *et al.*, 1977) with differences often persisting into adulthood (Wolkind, 1977).

Although the criterion of admission to care is a satisfactory indicator of the occurrence and the experience of parenting difficulties the sampling requirements for a retrospective study and a prospective study are somewhat different. When looking backwards the only concern is that families with children admitted to care are selected in such a way as to provide a representative epidemiologically-based sample. For such a study the *type* of residential care is not important provided that for the group selected the admissions to care are associated with parenting difficulties rather than with family problems that do not include any impairment of parenting. Since reception of children into care is often associated with problems in child-rearing even when the given reasons for admission are predominantly for other family difficulties, sampling cannot be based solely on the reasons for admission given on RIC forms. Instead an alternative approach should be used in which *multiple admissions* of children to care is taken as the indicator of likely parenting problems. Of course, the extent to which this approach is justified needs to be examined.

Different considerations arise for a prospective study. Three points are of particular importance. First, we need to be sure that the admission of children to an institution is for reasons of parenting breakdown rather than because of problems in the children themselves. Secondly, we need to show that the substitute care does not constitute an entirely satisfactory alternative form of parenting. And thirdly, it is necessary that the form of institutional care is of a reasonably homogeneous type so that the interpretation of inter-generational processes is not complicated by a multiplicity of early adversities. The first requirement can be met by sampling from children admitted early in their lives — although even here the assumption of parenting difficulties rather than problem in child behaviour needs to be tested. The second and third requirements can be met by sampling from institutions with known characteristics and providing for children with similar 'in-care' careers. Children's homes vary greatly in size, purpose and child-care approach. Although the numbers of children in residential homes has declined in recent years there remain 1600 such establishments in England and Wales catering for some 18,000 children. Berridge (1985) has shown that the majority of these homes now cater for adolescents, and that there has been a shift in function from long-term placement to short-term reception cases or the management of adolescent behaviour problems. Children remaining in homes are more likely to be awaiting long-term family placements or to have experienced particularly disrupted in-care careers. His study of 20 children's homes highlighted the variety of institutional provision from family-group homes to adolescent hostels and multipurpose establishments, but he concluded that it is difficult to correlate residential styles with the problems and the needs of children. Moreover, in many cases staff lack professional training and are trying to cope with a variety of problems many of which need a specialist approach.

At the time the subjects in our prospective study were placed in care the picture was somewhat different. Many more children were then being placed in long-stay institutions early in their lives and remaining there until discharge from care in their teenage years. We were particularly fortunate to be able to sample from the children placed in two large long-stay homes of this kind serving the Inner London area during the 1960s. These two homes had been intensively studied by

Tizard and his colleagues in 1964 and we therefore had both systematic evaluations of the quality of the care received by the children and also data on their behaviour and adjustment whilst in the institutions (King *et al.*, 1971). It is important to emphasise, however, that the subjects were sampled in this way in order to select a group who had experienced less than adequate parenting of a reasonably homogeneous type. The purpose was *not* to evaluate a particular kind of care provision nor to draw conclusions on the consequences of in-care experiences in general. In so far as the subjects in this study are an epidemiologically-based sample of children, conclusions are warranted as to the outcome from this kind of placement. However, one purpose of these studies was to raise questions on what might be meant by 'outcome' and how it is mediated. It would be quite wrong to conclude on the basis of the assessments of functioning in these subjects' mid-twenties that the 'outcomes' observed are an inevitable consequence of the institutional experience *per se*. The reasons for this caveat will become clear during the course of the analysis.

## Outline of the two studies

An outline of the two studies can now be given. In both studies the samples selected on the criterion of having children in care or having experienced institutional care are compared with groups from the general population. These do not constitute 'control' groups in a strict scientific sense (in that they were chosen as representative of the general population rather than matched in detail) and therefore the label *comparison group* has been generally preferred. However, for stylistic reasons the phrases *control group*, *comparison group* and *contrast group* are used interchangeably throughout this volume. The sampling and sample sizes are given here as part of an overview of the research design and methodology. A fuller account of sampling procedures is given in Appendix A.

### *The retrospective study*

The sampling for the retrospective study was relatively straightforward. One Inner London borough generously allowed us to seek the co-operation of all families from their area who had children admitted to care and who met the sampling criteria. This 'in-care' group consisted of a consecutive sample of 48 families with European-born parents who had children admitted to residential care by one Inner London borough during a continuous eight-month period. In order to exclude cases in which admission had occurred because of some short-term crisis, the series was confined to families for whom this was at least the second time a child had been taken into care. Selection was further restricted to those with a child between the ages of 5 and 8 years living at home prior to admission, so that comparable assessments of parenting could be made. This group is referred to as the *in-care* sample. The comparison group consisted of 47 families with a child in the same age group living at home with its mother, but in which no child in the family had ever been taken into care by a local authority. This sample was drawn randomly from the age-sex registers of two group general practices in the same Inner London borough. It was possible to interview over 90 per cent of mothers in both samples.

### The prospective study

The prospective study consisted of a follow-up into early adult life of 93 young women who, in 1964, were in one or other of two children's homes run on group cottage lines. A parallel follow-up of boys from the two homes and a comparison sample is being completed and the results will be reported separately. The children had been admitted to institutional care because their parents could not cope with child-rearing, rather than because of any type of disturbed behaviour shown by the children themselves. During their time in care the children's behaviour at school had been assessed by means of a standardised questionnaire (the Rutter B scale: Rutter, 1967). The sample was restricted to children identified as 'white' (on Tizard's original record sheets); and was defined in terms of those aged between 21 and 27 years on 1 January 1978. Of the 93 'ex-care' women, four had died by the time of follow-up. Eighty-one of the 89 women (91 per cent) still living were interviewed (including one in Germany and three in Australia). This group is referred to as the *ex-care* sample.

The contrast group of 51, comprised a quasi-random general population sample of individuals of the same age, never admitted into care, living with their families in the same general area in Inner London, and whose behaviour at school had been assessed at approximately the same age by means of the same questionnaire. The group was originally studied because they constituted the control group for a study of the children of parents with some form of psychiatric disorder (Rutter and Quinton, 1981, 1984). The contrast sample was similarly followed to age 21 to 27 years using methods of assessment identical to those employed for the 'ex-care' sample. Of the 51 female controls, 41 (80 per cent) were interviewed, five could not be traced and five did not agree to be seen.

## Interviewing methodology

### Interviewing techniques

In both studies, women and cohabiting spouses were interviewed in their homes for some 2½–5 hours about their childhood, their subsequent history, their current psychiatric state, the nature and quality of marital relationship, the background characteristics of previous co-habitees, and their own parenting behaviour. The interviewing methods used were based on techniques developed by Rutter and Brown and their colleagues (Brown and Rutter, 1966; Rutter and Brown, 1966; Graham and Rutter, 1968; Quinton *et al.*, 1976) and tested in a series of naturalistic and experimental studies of interviewing (Cox and Rutter, 1985). All interviews in the retrospective study were undertaken by DQ who is highly experienced in the methods used. The reliability and validity of the assessments of marital relationships, psychiatric state and social contacts are well established (see also Walker *et al.*, 1984). Although no formal tests of reliability were possible in the retrospective study, since only one interviewer was used, the rates of psychiatric disorder in the comparison group were very similar to those obtained in epidemiological studies of families in similar Inner London areas (Rutter *et al.*, 1975b; Brown *et al.*, 1975). Moreover, the mothers' rating of their own current state on a symptom inventory known to distinguish between those with and without psychiatric problems (Rutter *et al.*, 1970) closely paralleled the rates of disorder obtained from the more detailed interview data (see Chapter 3). In the prospective study, four additional interviewers were used and were trained to criterion levels on these established measures.

## The assessment of parenting by interview

Interview measures of parenting were newly developed for this research. The approach used was identical in both studies. The assessments concentrated on obtaining a detailed account of the child's behaviour and the parent's response to it — for example, on *how* they dealt with issues of discipline or responded to their child's distress — rather than just whether they employed a particular technique. Parents were encouraged to talk freely about the child and to describe the child's life and their own style of coping in detailed and specific terms. They were asked to describe the child's daily routine, including the regularity and timing of waking, of meal-times, and of bed-times, as well as the parents' handling of any problems associated with these. The major part of the parenting assessment dealt with the parent–child interactions over issues of control, peer and sib disputes, and fears and anxieties. The parent was first asked to describe the child's behaviour in these areas, and to report in detail the most recent incident. This involved specification of precipitants, of the child's behaviour and of the methods used by the parent to gain control, calm distress, settle disputes and allay fears or worries; giving as full an account as possible of the sequence of events. The frequency and typicality of such interactions were established as well as the frequency of less often occurring parenting issues or parenting techniques. For example, the most common control sequence might involve a parent at first ignoring the behaviour, then trying to distract the child and finally raising her own voice. The parent would then be asked if she ever used different methods or if the sequence ever extended further than this, perhaps to the child being smacked or sent to his room. An important part of the rating concerned the way in which the dispute (or episode of distress) terminated. In particular, codings were made of the proportion of control sequences that ended in a 'reconciliation' or re-establishment of a positive relationship through overt behaviours of contrition and acceptance. In addition the balance of power between parent and child was assessed as reflected in the proportion of control episodes in which the parent established her own authority when she tried to do so.

In this way, a detailed day-to-day picture of parenting style was developed from a wide range of individual ratings. In addition to these handling characteristics, information was systematically obtained on the frequency of parent–child interaction in play. This was rated in the prospective study on a number of categories such as reading, imaginative (role) play, rough-and-tumble play, involvement in household tasks or watching television. Finally, in the second study the parent was also asked to describe the previous day's activities in detail so that scores of the amount of concentrated, continuous, available and separate activity could be rated.

Overall ratings of parenting style and consistency were made taking all the information into account. These included the level of expressed warmth, the sensitivity shown in the handling of the child, the style, effectiveness and consistency of control, and of the management of anxieties and fears. These overall ratings allowed the interviewer to make summary assessments of parenting qualities using information from a number of features of parenting and parenting contexts. For example, difficulties in one area such as feeding or sibling relationships could be balanced against positive features such as anticipatory actions to reduce anxieties or the use of rewards for good behaviours (as defined by the parent).

The reliability of such overall judgements has been shown for a number of ratings used in these studies both of adult relationships such as marriage (Quinton *et al.*, 1976), the level of tension in the home and the amount of warmth and criticism expressed to the spouse and children (Brown and Rutter, 1966; Rutter and Brown, 1966). These approaches were extended to aspects of parenting to cover the overall style, consistency and effectiveness of control and the handling of anxiety and distress. The criteria for those ratings were established in the retrospective study. In the prospective study interviewees were trained to reliable levels, and overall team reliability was maintained by team discussions of tape-recorded case examples.

### The assessment of parenting by direct observation

Interview assessments can give a reliable overall picture of the style and quality of parenting. However, since parenting outcome was a key variable in these studies it was necessary to use additional approaches to measurement in order to check on some of the problems and biases that may occur with interviews, and to examine features of parenting that cannot be reliably assessed by them. The possibility of bias arose both because interviewers would inevitably know the childhood background of the subjects and because the interview measurement relied on the parents' account of their own behaviour and of their children's characteristics. Such accounts might be affected by a number of factors including the parents' mental state, fear of the consequences of reporting parenting difficulties or a tendency to give socially desirable answers. Features of parenting inaccessible to measurement by interview include details of the sequence of parent–child interactions, accurate counts of the occurrence of behaviours such as the child's approach to its mother, or the content and quality of their conversations. For all these reasons it was decided to include in the prospective study direct home observation of the interactions between mothers and children. This had the double advantage that observers could be kept blind to the mother's background and that the specifics of parenting and the sequences of mother–child interactions could be measured. The rationale for and details of the observational scheme are presented in Chapter 8. Observational measures were not used in the retrospective study because in that investigation the principal outcome variable was the fact of parenting breakdown, not finer-grained assessment of parenting behaviour. In that study, the interview measures are used to check whether the parenting breakdown was indeed associated with more general problems in the handling of the children and also to see whether in these families parenting problems occur in all aspects of parent–child relationships, what the overlap is between problems in one area of parenting and another and whether there are very consistent differences in child-rearing patterns between the families with children in care and the comparison group.

## The issue of long-term recall

One further methodological issue needs to be discussed before the findings from the two studies are presented: the issue of long-term – or retrospective – recall. Both studies rely heavily on the subjects' memories of their childhood as the major source of life-history data. Such data are often considered to be unreliable, particularly with respect to the evaluation of experiences and relationships. The best-known evidence against the retrospective method is the study by Yarrow and her colleagues (1970) which compared mothers' reports of their children's development with systematic clinic and nursery school records; the reports being given up to 30 years after the children's births. In general, correlations between maternal reports and clinic records were low. More importantly, systematic biases were found with mothers reporting fewer problems in their children's development than appeared in the records and also overestimating their children's abilities. These reports were influenced by the child's developmental history and by current child-rearing fashions.

However, before accepting that retrospective reports are necessarily flawed we need to consider the possible sources of error and how these might be minimised. The first point to make is that in examining the reliability of reporting it is necessary to be sure that the data against which recall is being tested are themselves reliable. This assumption cannot usually be made except where the events recorded have a particular significance or finality — for example a date of death. Variations in the quality of records are well illustrated in a recent study of mothers whose daughters were exposed *in utero* to the sex hormone diethylstilboestrol (Tilley *et al.*, 1985). Data in that study were collected by questionnaire from the mothers and from physicians where clinic records did not exist. Data were also collected from clinics the mothers had attended ten years earlier. Some of these had a relatively homogeneous record-keeping system and in others there were several physicians keeping their own records. The mailed questionnaires from doctors had most missing data and the homogeneous clinic records least, with the heterogeneous clinics in between. But there was also evidence that, *within* the homogeneous clinic group, missing data (according to research workers' abstracts) showed systematic biases with more missing information amongst the group exposed to the hormone. In general, mothers' reports and the records agreed well on such items as birth-weight and the number of previous pregnancies, but particularly badly on whether the mothers had ever had X-rays of the trunk or had been given particular drugs. Because these variations exist in the quality of most criterion data for assessing the accuracy of reporting, agreement between people and records can usually be taken as an indication of the reliability of accounts but not of their validity.

The majority of studies that have compared subjects' reports with written records have used hospital or clinic data. Two general conclusions can be drawn from these investigations. First, that reliable recall is more likely for events that carry some importance for the individual. In the study discussed above, for example, data from the mothers were most complete for pregnancies, miscarriages and children's birth-weight. These data also agreed best with the records. Recall was worst for routine clinical investigations such as X-rays. This is consistent with Cannell's earlier finding that prolonged hospital admissions or those involving surgery are more likely to be remembered than minor contacts (Cannell *et al.*, 1961; Cannell, 1977). Secondly, *whether* events have happened is more accurately recalled than *when* they occurred. This can be so even for major happenings. For example, approximately 20–30 per cent of women in two separate studies were more than one year out in the reporting of the data of an hysterectomy (Bean *et al.*, 1979; Paganini-Hill and Ross, 1982). In the dating of events there is a tendency for time-periods, ages and quantities to be rounded. This process involves both interviewer and respondent effects (Baddeley, 1979).

A second issue is whether we are concerned with *recall* or with *reporting*. For many variables in life-history research the main concern is with whether a subject can report the occurrence of some event accurately — for example, whether they went into hospital early in their lives or their age at the time their parents split up. For such factual material it usually does not matter whether they remember the event or whether their information comes from someone else. However, if the interest is in their *reactions* to the event then it is necessary to rely on their recall. As yet no studies have been published that assess recall of family relationship or of reactions to events against systematic criterion data. As a consequence it is not possible to estimate the extent of unbiased forgetting. It may be that there are quite major losses of information in retrospective studies due to such processes, although it seems likely that saliency rule will apply here also: that is, people will remember the more personally important events in their lives.

Support for this comes from studies that have addressed the third issue in reporting: namely, whether there are *systematic* biases in recall. Here the question is whether a person's current circumstances or mental state affect the events and relationships they remember or report. Some data suggest that this is the case. Wolkind and Coleman (1983) found that women currently suffering from depression or anxiety reported conflict between their parents more frequently than did women who had previously been depressed or anxious but were now well. Robins (1966) found that adverse childhood events (as noted in clinic records) were more reliably reported by those with current psychosocial problems than by those who were now well. However in a more systematic evaluation of the recall of childhood environments 30 to 50 years later by sibs with and without current psychiatric problems Robins has not replicated this biasing effect of current mental state (Robins *et al.*, 1985). Agreement between siblings was good for factual data such as the number of homes they had lived in, schools attended and family socio-economic circumstances. Agreement was also good for parental behaviours such as marital disputes or involvement in community activities. Robins drew the important conclusion that what might be thought to involve 'forgetting' is attributable to the fact that what concerns us about family histories are feelings and attitudes that are intrinsically dependent on individual interpretation and assessment of behaviour.

A number of important issues concerning retrospective recall still remain to be investigated. Amongst the most important of these is the question of the comparison of accounts of family relationships and of feelings against good criterion data, and the extent to which differing interview approaches are effective in improving recall. However, the overall level of agreement between sibs and the lack of major biases established by the Robins study makes the method acceptable for scientific studies. However, until the question of individual experiences, memories and reactions to childhood experiences are better understood it is preferable to place most weight on discrete events located within broad time-periods; to place more weight on clear descriptions of events and relationships rather than on generalised recollections, and to use the reconstructive nature of memory (Bartlett, 1932) to locate events within a coherent life-history framework.

# 3 The retrospective study: Current circumstances and parenting

In the retrospective study we sought to examine the extent to which serious current family and parenting problems were associated with the experience of poor parenting in the parents' own childhood and how often they arose anew in each generation in the absence of childhood adversities. We begin with the findings on the current circumstances and parenting skills of the in-care and comparison samples; but it is necessary first to ask whether the criterion of multiple admissions of children to residential care *is* an adequate indicator of parenting problems. That is, do parents with children admitted to care have more difficulties in their day-to-day relationships with their children and in their handling of them?

**Multiple admissions to care and parenting problems**
The justification for using multiple admissions to care as an indicator of current parenting difficulties may be examined first, by considering the reasons for admission; and secondly, by comparing the two groups on the interview measures of parenting.

*Reasons for admission*
The reasons for admission were taken from the reception into care (RIC) forms, since these gave the social workers' judgement on the most pressing justification for placement. The reasons were divided into three categories: (1) those stressing environmental factors or parental hospital admission for physical conditions; (2) those involving parental psychiatric or marital difficulties but not directly mentioning parenting difficulties as such; and (3) those including statements referring to parenting problems. Examples of each group are given in Appendix B. Of the 48 cases, 9 per cent were in group one, 27 per cent in group two and 64 per cent in group three. Thus, nearly all the admissions involved situations in which parenting problems were mentioned, or in which major family problems known to have adverse effects on parent-child relationship were present.

*Interview measures of parenting*

*Mother–child relationships*    Figure 3.1 summarises the findings with respect to various aspects of parent–child relationships and positive interactions. In all these main areas the in-care group mothers showed

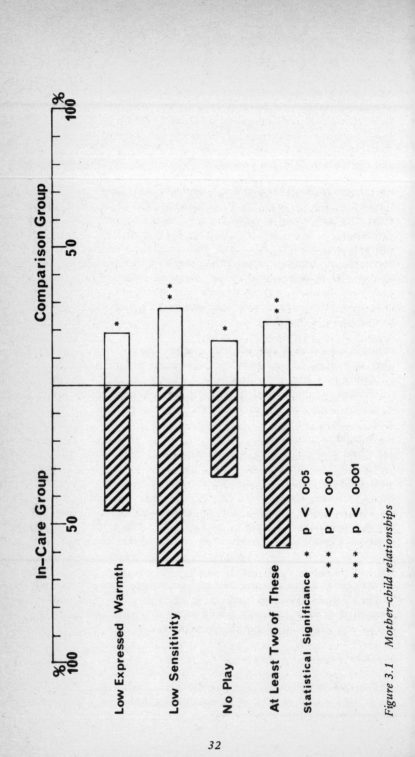

Figure 3.1  Mother–child relationships

greater difficulties in parenting. Nearly half the mothers in the in-care group were low in expressed warmth to the child, nearly two-thirds appeared insensitive to the child's distress or worries and a third did not play with their child. In each case, the proportions were about twice those in the control group. When two or more of the individual indicators were considered together, much the same pattern was seen. Well over half the in-care group mothers showed problems in their personal relationships and interactions with their children, a rate more than double that in the control group. All of these differences were statistically significant. Significance levels are conventionally presented in terms of the times out of 100 that a difference of the magnitude found between groups might have occurred by chance. Thus a significance level of 0.05 (the 5 per cent level of significance) means that the observed difference will occur by chance only five times in 100. This is the usual level that is taken to mean that the possibility of the difference having occurred by chance is sufficiently low that we may conclude that the difference is significant or reliable. Obviously, the clinical — as distinct from the statistical — significance or the meaningfulness of the difference for practice or policy will depend on other additional considerations.

For most straightforward comparisons between the groups we have used the chi-square test ($\chi^2$). This is simply a way of determining numerically the size of the difference between the frequencies (numbers) actually observed and those that would be expected if there were no association between the variables. The figure obtained for the chi-square can then be compared with statistical tables to determine the frequency with which the difference could have arisen by chance. For technical reasons, when the expected frequencies in the table are low it may be preferable to use Fisher's exact test. Here, as its name implies, the statistic is used to calculate the exact probability distribution of the observed frequencies. As ordinarily employed, the exact test gives the departure from chance in a specified direction. Everitt (1977) has provided an excellent straightforward account of these techniques.

*Maternal discipline*   In both groups a high proportion of mothers used disciplinary techniques that were aggressive in style, involving slapping or hitting the children or frequent severe shouting. This was so for 62 per cent of the in-care sample and 42 per cent of the comparison group, a non-significant difference. The extensive use of such techniques is in keeping with other evidence concerning disciplinary methods in families of similar social class (Newson and Newson, 1968). However, the style of discipline may be of less importance than its effectiveness or its consistency, and in both of these respects the in-care mothers were also much more likely to be having difficulties (Figure 3.2). Twice as many of this group were involved in disciplinary

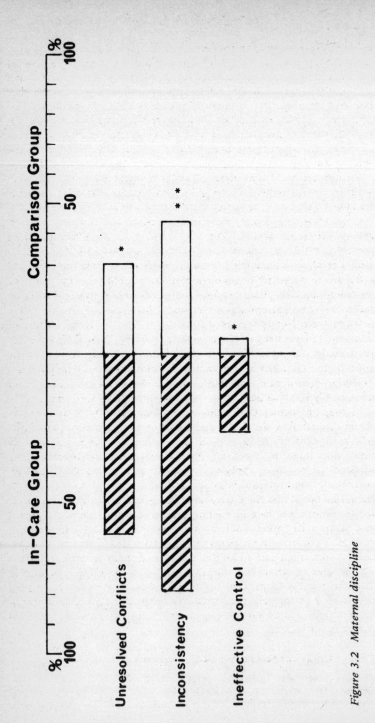

Figure 3.2  Maternal discipline

episodes in which the control attempt was unsuccessful or the conflict remained unresolved. Resolution of conflicts was regarded as having occurred if there was any form of reconciliation between the child and the parent, either through direct apologies or through actions that provided clear signals that the relationships had been re-established (for example, by giving each other a hug or starting some joint activity). In general, these reconciliations involved some indication that the nature of the original dispute had been recognised and that the nature of the rules or procedures governing that type of activity had been reaffirmed.

Inconsistency of discipline (meaning control episodes that were arbitrary or unpredictable either in terms of the particular child behaviours reacted to, or in terms of the strength or nature of the parental response) was considerably more frequent in the in-care group. An even greater difference was evident with respect to the effectiveness of control (a rating of the extent to which the parents were able to maintain control when they tried to do so). Ineffectiveness in this sense was a feature of a quarter of the care mothers but only 5 per cent of the control group. When these various indicators were considered together much the same pattern was seen. Nearly twice as many in-care group mothers were having serious difficulties in two or more aspects of discipline (72 per cent v. 40 per cent; $p < 0.05$). These differences are particularly striking if they are viewed the other way round. In the control group families 37 per cent of the mothers showed no problems in any aspects of parenting at all, but this was so for only 10 per cent of in-care group mothers; thus, as anticipated from the definition of the group, parenting difficulties were substantially more frequent in the in-care families. To find that 1 in 10 of the mothers with children in care showed no marked problems in parenting does not necessarily mean that there had been an absence of parenting difficulties. The measures of parenting applied only to the present situation and only to the one child selected who was at home and aged 5 to 8 years. It should be noted that there were no differences according to the reasons for admissions into care in the proportions of mothers in who reported two or more parenting problems in the areas of either relationships or control. Two or more problems in one or both areas occurred in 66 per cent of admissions said to be due to external environmental factors, in 77 per cent of admissions due to the parents' psychiatric or marital difficulties and in 75 per cent of admissions said to stem from parenting problems. It is apparent that, whatever the mediating mechanisms may be, multiple admissions to care were strongly related to reported parenting difficulties.

## Current family circumstances and characteristics

### Family structure

The family structure and circumstances of the two groups were

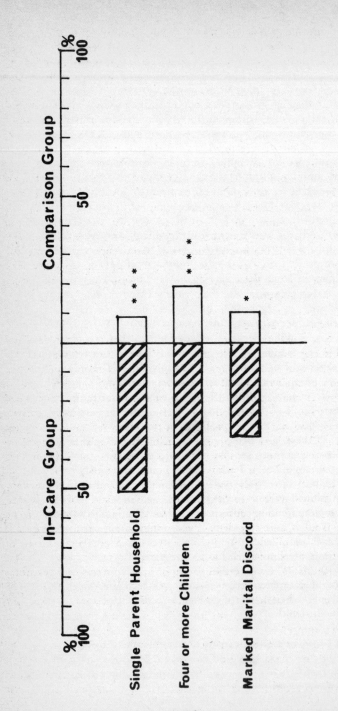

Figure 3.3   Family circumstances

markedly different (Figure 3.3). Whereas over 90 per cent of the control group mothers were in a stable cohabitation (in almost all cases with their legal spouse) this was so for only half (49 per cent) of the in-care families. Indeed, only a third of the latter were living with men to whom they were married. Moreover, of the half living with a male partner of some kind the proportion who had a markedly discordant relationship was several times that in the control group (one third versus one tenth). The parenting burden on the in-care families was also much greater in that three-fifths of them had at least four children compared with only one in five of the control families.

These circumstances had important implications for the parentage of the children. In 93 per cent of the control families, all the children had the same father, whereas this was so in only 43 per cent of the in-care families. Furthermore, in a high proportion of cases none of the children was living with his or her biological father. Not only, therefore, were just over half the in-care families single-parent households lacking any father figure, but even amongst the half with two parents, in a third of the families the mothers' current cohabitee was not the father of any of her children.

### Social status and housing

Figure 3.4 summarises some of the main features of the families' current social conditions. The majority of the in-care families were of low social status and half were living in rather crowded conditions (a reflection of their considerably larger families). Although social status was partly determined by their single-parent status, the difference between the groups remained when the in-care mothers had a current cohabitee. However, over 90 per cent of all the families in both samples were in local authority or private trust housing. Much the biggest difference between the groups lay in the proportion who had been in their present accommodation for less than a year. This applied to half the in-care families but to only one in ten of the control group. Frequent housing moves were a particularly prominent feature of the in-care families. Despite these differences it was apparent that many of the control families were themselves disadvantaged. Thus two-fifths of the fathers had unskilled or semi-skilled jobs — a proportion over twice that in the general population as a whole.

Nevertheless, a more detailed study of housing circumstances at the time of admission into care shows the greater disadvantage experienced by the in-care families (Quinton and Rutter, 1984a). Although this group was somewhat worse off in respect of basic household facilities, the disadvantages were more striking in other aspects of housing. For example, in over a quarter of the in-care families the child had to share a bed with its parents or sibs, or had to share the parental bedroom, compared with only one in 20 of the control group. None of the latter relied on paraffin heaters or electric-bar fires for their household

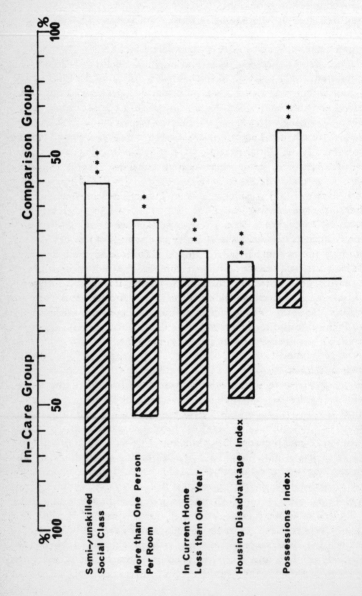

Figure 3.4 Current social circumstances

heating but nearly half the in-care families did so. Conversely, nearly half the control group had central heating whereas this was so for only one in ten of the in-care sample. These differences are a reflection of the fact that the control group were much more likely to be in new or newly-renovated local authority housing. Many in-care families were in older flats or patch-repair dwellings. This accounts for the paradoxical fact that nearly one-quarter of them had a garden, or some private play space for their children, whereas this was the case for only 7 per cent of the control group.

The housing differences are even more apparent if assessed in terms of an overall housing disadvantage index. Nearly half the in-care families either lacked one of the three basic housing facilities (toilet, bathroom or kitchen with hot water) or had unsatisfactory sleeping arrangements for their children (such as sharing beds) or had housing with severe problems with damp or other structural defects, compared with only 7 per cent of the control group (47 per cent v. 7 per cent).

The greater material disadvantage of the in-care families was also evident in terms of their household possessions at the time of admission. Less than half of them, compared with four-fifths of the control sample, had a washing machine, despite their greater number of children, and very few had a car (5 per cent v. 30 per cent) or a telephone (12 per cent v. 58 per cent) and they were thus much more restricted in communications with family or friends. An overall score of housing possessions, based on the exclusive or shared use of a television, washing machine, refrigerator, telephone and car brings out the differences between the groups. Three-fifths of the control group (a disadvantaged sample) had a score of eight or more on possessions compared with only one in nine of the in-care cases. (The possessions score is the sum of scores on the above items where 0 = not available, 1 = shared use, and 2 = exclusive use.)

## Psychiatric disturbance

Figure 3.5 gives the main features of the psychiatric history and current adjustment of the two groups of mothers. The rates of disorder and deviance amongst the control group mothers are comparable with those obtained in previous general population studies of mothers in Inner London (Brown *et al.*, 1975; Rutter *et al.*, 1975b). In sharp contrast, the rates in the in-care group mothers were several times higher on all indices, with the differences most marked in terms of indicators of severe psychiatric disorder. Thus, nearly two-thirds of the in-care group mothers had been under psychiatric treatment at some time and no less than two-fifths had been admitted to a psychiatric unit or mental hospital. In both cases the proportions were very much higher than those for the control group. Moreover, over three-quarters of in-care group mothers were assessed on interview data as having some form of current handicapping psychiatric problem. In most cases this took the

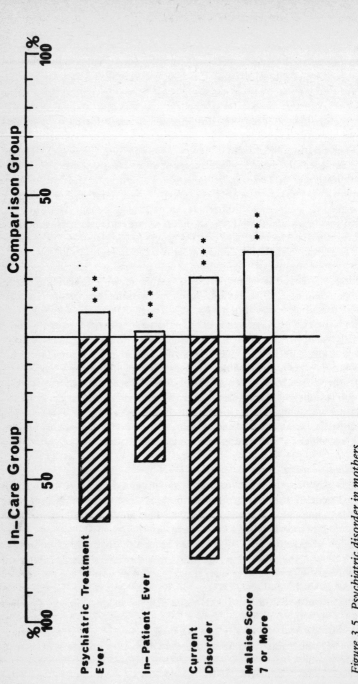

Figure 3.5  Psychiatric disorder in mothers

form of an affective condition involving depression or anxiety, but frequently it was associated with personality disorder, i.e. a long-standing maladaptive pattern of behaviour existing from the individual's teenage years or earlier.

The rate of current psychiatric disorder in the in-care group mothers was four times that in the control group. Not only was psychiatric disorder rated very much more frequently but also many more of the mothers rated themselves as having emotional disturbance much more often than did mothers in the control group. The difference between the two groups with respect to the proportion with a score over 7 or more on the malaise inventory (the cut-off that discriminates people with psychiatric disorder: Rutter *et al.*, 1970) was closely similar to that for interview ratings for psychiatric disorder.

*Characteristic of cohabitees*
As noted earlier, half of the in-care group mothers had no current cohabitee. Also it proved impossible to interview approximately one-quarter of those men who were currently part of the family, and therefore the resulting small numbers make statistical comparisons between the fathers in the two groups inappropriate. More information was available when the mothers' account of the current *or* previous spouse was considered and these data are presented in Figure 3.6.

It is apparent that the spouses of the in-care mothers were generally more socially deviant than those in the control group. This was most striking with respect to the proportion who had been put on probation or been in prison. This applied to over half the cases but to only 13 per cent of the control group. The difference between the two samples with respect to any convictions was much less, as a consequence of the high proportion of fathers in the control group who had been found guilty of less serious offences, including driving offences (speeding and parking offences were excluded) and drunk or disorderly, or who had only transitory involvement in crime. The in-care group husbands were somewhat more likely to have current psychiatric disorder and were substantially more likely to be diagnosed from interview data as having long-standing personality problems (this rating was based on persistent and handicapping difficulties in relationships and in life functioning generally; it was by no means synonymous with having a criminal record). It is noteworthy that the rate of disorder in the comparison sample was much higher than that we found in an overlapping but somewhat less deprived working-class area (23 per cent v. 12 per cent). The difference on personality problems was even greater (15 per cent v. 2 per cent). The reasons for this are not known but it seems likely that poor circumstances were implicated. However, in contrast with the in-care sample, the comparison husbands were much more likely to seek help from their general practitioner or from psychiatric services (11 per

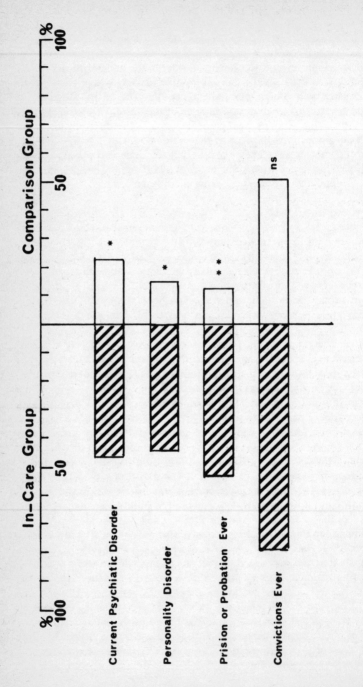

Figure 3.6 Deviance and disorder in spouses

42

cent v. 21 per cent) and for this reason the impact of their illness on the family may have been less.

## Mothers' social relationships and support

Very few (7 per cent) of the in-care group mothers reported current close relationships with their own fathers compared with half of the control group mothers (approximately the same proportions in each group had fathers who were still alive). The same trend for a lower rate of close relationships for in-care group mothers also applied to relationships with their own mothers (31 per cent v. 50 per cent) and to those with their sibs (31 per cent v. 40 per cent) but these differences fell short of statistical significance. A close relationship in this connection meant that there was fairly frequent contact, that positive feelings were expressed towards the person and that the respondent said she would confide in him or her about problems or worries. Strained relationships with all categories of close relatives were many times more common in the in-care sample than in the control group but again the difference was most marked with respect to fathers (36 per cent v. 4 per cent) but was also substantial for mothers (34 per cent v. 9 per cent) and sibs (43 per cent v. 12 per cent), all differences being statistically significant. Strained relationships were rated as present when contact was avoided or when the respondent adopted a markedly critical attitude towards the relative's current behaviour or personality. The control group mothers were twice as likely (51 per cent v. 23 per cent) to see their parents at least weekly and they were more than twice as likely (67 per cent v. 28 per cent) to report that they felt that their family was a close one. Altogether it was clear that the in-care group families were considerably less likely to have close relationships with near relatives, and considerably more likely to have strained relationships with them. On the other hand, over half the in-care group mothers (54 per cent v. 72 per cent) reported that they had a confiding relationship with someone, including either a spouse, a relative or a friend, to whom they could turn, or with whom they could talk over personal worries or difficulties. The difference between the groups on this measure was not statistically significant.

*Practical help*   In both groups most of the mothers had received some help from kin or friends over the previous three months. However, the in-care group mothers were rather less likely to have received any help with the children either in looking after them or collecting them from school, and were more likely to have borrowed money. Moreover, the majority of the in-care group mothers said that in the past three months they had wished there was someone they could turn to for help with practical matters but there was no one available, a marked difference from the control group (71 per cent v. 15 per cent). Clearly this was a reflection of their less satisfactory primary group relationships, their

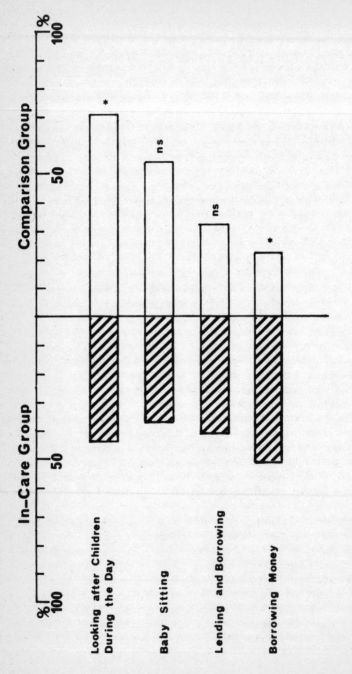

Figure 3.7 Practical help

greater need for emotional and practical support and probably also a function of their frequent moves of housing, which prevented the development of helping relationships with neighbours.

## Discussion

The parents with children multiply admitted to care were twice as likely as a socially disadvantaged control group to be experiencing parenting difficulties with a young school-aged child. Nevertheless, not all mothers with children in care showed difficulties on our parenting measures and a considerable proportion of the control group mothers also exhibited some problems in parenting. The finding of substantial overlap between the two groups has implications for concepts of parenting. Two conclusions may be drawn from these data.

First, it is apparent that 'parenting' is neither a unitary phenomenon nor an intrinsic attribute of individuals that is independent of circumstances. A few of the in-care group mothers were coping reasonably well with their 5–8 year olds, and rather more had only mild or moderate difficulties, even though they may have had more problems in the past or have current difficulties with other children. In addition, the problems in parenting in one area did not necessarily imply that deficits existed across the board. Thus although 89 per cent of the in-care group mothers were either low in expressed warmth to their child or had unreconciled disputes with them, only 19 per cent had both problems at the same time. Also, a substantial minority of control group mothers were also having significant parenting difficulties although there was no question of their children going into care.

Clearly, parenting difficulties associated with reception into care cannot be seen as something that is independent from other aspects of life. The in-care families were distinguished as much by *other* kinds of family difficulties as by parenting problems *per se*. They constituted a multiple problem group and not just one with parenting difficulties. The impact of poor parenting on the child or of a difficult child on the parents' ability to cope has to be considered in the context of the family's general emotional and physical resources. Thus a secure relationship with one parent may attenuate the effects of a poor relationship with the other (Rutter, 1981), and a good marital relationship may make it easier to cope with a difficult child even if parenting techniques are not particularly skilled.

The second conclusion is that the parenting problems of the in-care group mothers were more a reflection of general problems with interpersonal relationships than of deficiencies in specific techniques. Thus the differences between the groups were less marked with respect to smacking or shouting than they were in the general sensitivity with which parents perceived and dealt with their children's worries and upsets, or in the consistency with which they pursued their control attempts to some firm conclusions. This conclusion is consistent with the much higher rates of both psychiatric and marital problems in the in-care group families. Similar difficulties were also apparent in their relationships with their relatives; this pattern has also been reported amongst other groups experiencing severe disadvantage (Wilson and Herbert, 1978) or having children taken into care because of the mother's confinement (Schaffer and Schaffer, 1968). The extent to which all these problems represent continuities between childhood experiences and current circumstances is considered in the next chapter.

# 4   The retrospective study: Inter-generational continuities

As discussed in Chapter 3, the current disadvantage of the in-care families was very striking even in comparison with a relatively disadvantaged social group. The majority faced a variety of psychosocial problems. About half were single parents; a high proportion of the mothers' cohabitees had a criminal record; and their marital relationships tended to be disrupted and discordant. Many mothers were coping on their own with large families in unsatisfactory and overcrowded housing. Over recent years a large proportion had moved frequently from one set of unsatisfactory housing conditions to another.

If these data are considered cross-sectionally the parenting difficulties of these families might be interpreted as being either a direct reaction to social disadvantage or secondary to the resulting stress and psychiatric problems experienced by the parents. Nevertheless, it is not possible to conclude from this evidence alone that current social disadvantages constitute a sufficient explanation for the differences between the groups with respect either to parenting problems or psychiatric disorder. Questions remain on why some disadvantaged families have children taken into care whereas others do not, and on how families come to be in poor social circumstances. Both issues are considered further in this chapter in relation to the findings on the parents' childhood experiences. The quality of these experiences and the main features of the parents' life-histories are considered first. The question of how these experiences relate to or explain the later parenting breakdown can then be approached. Before this, however, it is necessary to consider the appropriate dependent variable for this analysis.

## Measures of parenting difficulties

In the analysis of factors associated with serious parenting difficulties either admission into care (as an index of parenting difficulties) or the direct interview measures of parenting might be chosen as the main dependent variable. The former has been selected for two main reasons. First, it provides the better index of *serious* parenting problems in that, by definition, at least one child had had to be admitted to care because the parents could not cope at the time. Secondly, it would be misleading to rely on the one-off parenting measures as best representing the differences between the two groups. A lack of problems on the interview measures in the control group probably meant that there were no serious parenting difficulties, but obviously this could not be so in the 'in care' group, as the admission into care meant that there had been some kind of breakdown in parenting. The in-care/control group contrast itself provided the best means of comparing families with and without serious problems as parents. It was not possible to examine the antecedents of parenting as assessed at interview by pooling the samples, because of the major differences between the two groups both as regards background variables and current family characteristics. Such a procedure would confound between-group differences with within-group correlations. However, the interview measures *were* useful as a means of *within-group* comparisons. Accordingly, for some purposes, comparisons have been drawn between good and less satisfactory parenting (as assessed from interview) within the in-care group, and separately within the control group.

### Parents' childhood experiences

*Mothers' social background*
The in-care and control groups differed little in their social background. In both samples, about half the mothers came from a sibship of at least four children (64 per cent v. 49 per cent) and about half came from families in which the father held an unskilled or semi-skilled job (60 per cent v. 47 per cent). It is clear from these findings that the proportion of mothers in both groups who had socially disadvantaged childhoods was considerably greater than in the population as a whole, but the two groups did not differ significantly between themselves on these variables. The in-care mothers seemed somewhat more likely to have been immigrants to London (50 per cent v. 33 per cent), but again this difference was not statistically significant.

*Deviance and disorder in mothers' parents*
The differences were somewhat greater with respect to parental deviance and disorder as reported by the mother. Psychiatric problems in the mothers' mother, as evidenced by known visits to the family doctor or hospital contacts were similar in the two groups (38 per cent v. 29 per cent), but reports of paternal criminality or drinking problems were significantly more common for the in-care group mothers (20 per cent v. 5 per cent). In all, half of the latter reported having a parent with psychiatric, drink or criminal difficulties, compared with a third of the comparison group, the difference falling short of statistical significance.

*Family relationships in mothers' childhood*
The differences between the two groups were much more striking with

respect to family disruption and harsh parenting during the mothers' childhood (see Figure 4.1). Thus, a quarter of the in-care mothers had been in care themselves, compared with only 7 per cent of the control group; 44 per cent of the former had been separated from one or both parents for at least one month as a result of family discord or parental rejection, as compared with 14 per cent of the control sample; and three times as many had suffered harsh discipline from one or both parents. Discipline of this severity involved frequent physical punishment, often including beatings with sticks, shoes or other objects, being repeatedly locked in cupboards or cellars — or in one case, being tied in the bagwash — amongst the regular methods of punishment. Of all the background factors, it was discordant and aggressive family relationships that most clearly differentiated the two groups.

The high levels of early stresses experienced by the mothers in both groups can be illustrated by considering the overlap of a range of adversities that have frequently been shown to be associated with a variety of psychological difficulties in childhood (Davie *et al.*, 1972; Wedge and Prosser, 1973; Rutter and Quinton, 1977). These include: in-care experiences, prolonged hospitalisations, persistent parental discord, separations from parents through discord, hard or harsh discipline, large family size, low social class, and psychiatric or criminal histories for the parents. Sixty-one per cent of 'in-care' mothers experienced *four* or more of these adversities compared with 16 per cent of the control group. Almost as striking, however, is the fact that nearly two-thirds of the latter sample (65 per cent) experienced *two* or more of these hardships.

### Mothers' teenage difficulties

The two groups of mothers also differed markedly in the frequency of teenage problems. Marked unhappiness at school and persistent truancy were reported for some one half of the in-care mothers (a rate double that in controls), and discordant relationships with one or both parents were four times as frequent (56 per cent v. 14 per cent). The meaning of these childhood difficulties is discussed below.

The difference between the two groups was equally marked with respect to difficulties in the later teenage period. More than twice as many in-care group mothers had left home by their nineteenth birthday (65 per cent v. 26 per cent), more than twice as many were already pregnant by this age (61 per cent v. 23 per cent), and nearly three times as many (92 per cent v. 33 per cent) had left home for negative reasons — meaning that the reason concerned a wish to escape from the existing situation rather than any positive desire for the new one. Rejection by their parents or a wish to get out of intolerable circumstances were the commonest 'negative' reasons (premarital pregnancy in itself was not considered to be a negative reason if the relationship with the future father was a positive one in which marriage or regular

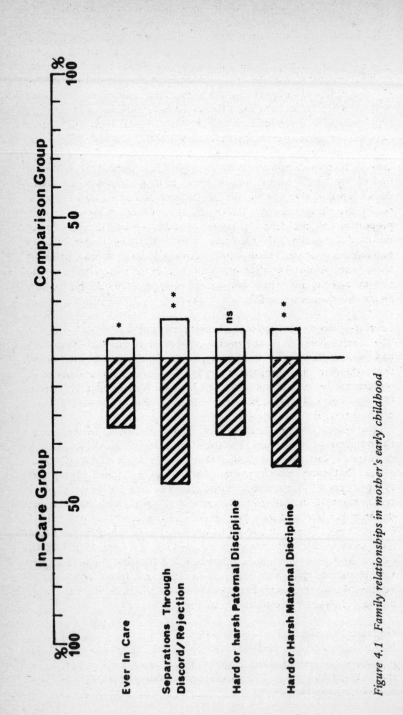

Figure 4.1 Family relationships in mother's early childhood

cohabitation was already planned). Following, and perhaps as a consequence of these disturbances, three-quarters of the in-care group mothers began their first marriages or cohabitations for negative reasons, compared with less than one-third of the comparison women (74 per cent v. 29 per cent), and the majority set up their first home with spouses from similar adverse backgrounds or with current problems of a psychiatric or criminal nature. All these differences between the groups were statistically significant.

Only limited data were available on first spouses. However, 63 per cent of first spouses in the in-care sample had a discordant childhood or had psychiatric or criminal problems in their teens compared with 39 per cent of the first spouses of the comparison women — a non-significant difference. As shown in the previous chapter, a high proportion of the first marriages of the 'in-care' mothers broke down. At the time of the study, only about one-quarter lived in harmonious marital relationships, compared with three-quarters of the control group. The data on current cohabitees suggested that the overlap of early adversities and current deviance may have been much greater for the in-care sample.

## Characteristics and background of current cohabitees
The current 'fathers' of the in-care children were more likely to have had deviant histories and to have current psychiatric disorders than the fathers in the comparison group. This was most striking with respect to the proportion who had been on probation or in prison (55 per cent v. 13 per cent), or who had current psychiatric disorder on the interview evaluation (58 per cent v. 18 per cent).

The comparison of social background and childhood adversities for the husbands showed many similarities to the comparison between the mothers — thus the two groups of men were similar in social background but there were consistent differences in in-care experiences (31 per cent v. 11 per cent), harsh discipline (53 per cent v. 19 per cent), parental discord (50 per cent v. 19 per cent) and paternal deviance (33 per cent v. 8 per cent) and criminality (20 per cent v. 6 per cent). These data should be treated with caution, since the number of in-care husbands in the analysis was small (14–18 v. 35–38), due to high proportions of single-parent families and the lower interviewing success rates. Some of these differences fell short of statistical significance. Nevertheless, the consistency in the differences for both mothers and their husbands is noteworthy.

## Overview of parents' childhood experiences
It is clear from these findings that the childhood experiences of the parents in the in-care group differed sharply from those of parents in the comparison group. The in-care group mothers and fathers were somewhat more likely to have had parents who had shown deviance or

disorder themselves; they were much more likely to have experienced serious adversities in early childhood; they were much more likely to have suffered seriously strained family relationships in the early teens; twice as many left home early in the later teenage years, often becoming pregnant or marrying to escape family tensions; and far more married (or cohabited with) men from a similarly disadvantaged background who showed deviance or disorder themselves. It is not difficult to create a coherent story linking this unhappy string of adversities and stressful experiences. Indeed, it is scarcely surprising that with this background of deprivation, disadvantage and discordant relationships that the women grew up to experience difficulties in parenting their own children.

However, the threads tying these variables together are more difficult to unravel. On the one hand, the marked overlaps over a wide range of past adversities and current personal and social handicaps in the in-care families, means that explanations of parenting problems *solely* in terms of current social disadvantage are likely to be inadequate. On the other hand, two features of the findings suggest that explanations for continuities solely in terms of 'deviant personality development' are also unsatisfactory. First, although all manner of childhood adversities were more frequent in the in-care group, they were also surprisingly common in the comparison sample. The question therefore arises as to why the latter did not suffer parenting breakdown (only one family was excluded from the comparison group because a child had been in care) or show current handling difficulties as assessed from the interview measures, to anything like the same extent. Was it simply because they experienced less adversity overall, or was it that they had experienced important protective factors? Secondly, the in-care families were currently living in circumstances that were socially and materially much less satisfactory than those in the comparison group. This observation raised the question of the extent to which childhood adversities were important not primarily because they predisposed to a deviant or handicapped personality development, but rather because they made it more likely that, as adults, individuals would be living in seriously disadvantaged circumstances.

The remainder of this chapter will discuss the extent of the continuity in parenting and in associated family problems when viewed retrospectively, and attempt to disentangle some of the social and psychological threads tying these problems together across generations.

### Inter-generational continuities in parenting problems: Looking backwards

The analysis of the current adjustment and circumstances of the two groups showed that the in-care families were characterised as much by a complex of family, psychiatric and environmental difficulties as by parenting difficulties as such. There was, however, a clear excess of current parenting problems among the mothers in the care group. They showed more current difficulties and also had a range of family problems associated with recurrent parenting breakdown. Although limitations in parenting skills are likely to be involved in breakdown, and although particular problems are likely to be associated with current adverse parenting contexts, it is helpful to keep parenting breakdown and handling problems distinct when considering inter-generational continuities.

In examining the transmission of parenting problems in the in-care sample, we are in practice examining the transmission of a wide range of family difficulties. For example, the backgrounds of the in-care parents were characterised as much by difficulties *between* their parents as by behaviours directed towards the children. Although parenting skills themselves are almost certainly affected by childhood experiences, the extent of difficulties manifest in adult life may be determined as much by the overlap of concurrent personal and social disadvantages as by these early adversities. The contribution of current stresses to handling problems is discussed below.

The central questions with respect to the transmission of parenting problems are therefore: (1) the extent to which parenting *breakdown* was associated with early family adversities; (2) the mechanisms involved in continuity and discontinuity; (3) the extent to which current handling problems were related to childhood stresses; and (4) the role of current family and environmental hardships in perpetuating or attenuating difficulties.

### Early experiences and parenting breakdown

In considering the relationship between early adversities and parenting breakdown, it is necessary to take into account the backgrounds of both mothers and fathers. This is because it is not only the transmission of parenting problems that is being considered, but also the family environments in which parents, especially mothers, are operating. The role of fathers and husbands in both these aspects of transmission is considered later.

For the analyses of inter-generational continuities with respect to parenting breakdown, the information on fathers refers to the current cohabitee (where there was one) but, where there was no spouse at the time of interview, information on the previous cohabitee has been used. In all cases, ratings apply to only one 'father' in each family. Information was available on 27 fathers in the in-care group and 39 fathers in the control group.

No firm conclusions can be drawn about the families where information is lacking, but there are reasons for assuming that the rates of childhood adversities were at least as high as in the families where information was available on both parents. First, the missing information was predominantly amongst the in-care group husbands. The first cohabitees of the mothers in this group are known to have higher rates of earlier adversity or teenage problems than the control group, and this applies particularly to those cases in which information on the current or most recent cohabitee is missing. Secondly, among those cohabitees for whom information existed, the rates of early adversity were much higher amongst the cases than among control husbands. It is known that people who cannot be contacted or who refuse to participate in surveys generally have higher rates of various problems than those who take part (Cox *et al.*, 1977); hence, it is likely that the fathers not contacted had more problems than those included in this analysis. The childhood background variables used in this comparison were those that most strongly differentiated the two groups. Early adversity was rated as present if there were at least *two* adversities before the age of 16 involving admissions to care, harsh parenting, parental marital discord (including separations), and parental deviance or psychiatric disorder.

The findings for those families for whom information was available are presented in Figure 4.2. Four conclusions can be drawn from these data. First, as already noted, a surprisingly high proportion of control group parents had experienced childhood adversities — in two-fifths of families one or both parents had experienced two or more. It is thus apparent that despite quite serious adversities in childhood, individuals can become ordinarily well-functioning adults, or at the very least be in little danger of having a child admitted to care. Secondly, the differences between the two groups were most striking with respect to childhood adversities in *both* parents. Thirdly, in cases when only one parent had suffered childhood adversity, the difference between the in-care group families and the control group appeared to apply to mothers only, although this difference between the parents fell short of statistical significance. Finally, there were only three in-care group families in which neither parent had experienced two or more of the defined childhood adversities. Even in these cases it is apparent that their childhoods contained definite hardships. Details of these families and of the 'no adversity' families in the comparison group are given in Appendix C1. It is clear that in terms of the familial antecedents of parenting breakdown inter-generational continuity looking backwards was virtually complete. This conclusion requires that comparable rates of maternal adversity were also found in those in-care cases omitted from the analysis because no data were available on husbands. This information is given in Appendix C2. It is clear that these mothers also suffered considerable childhood stresses.

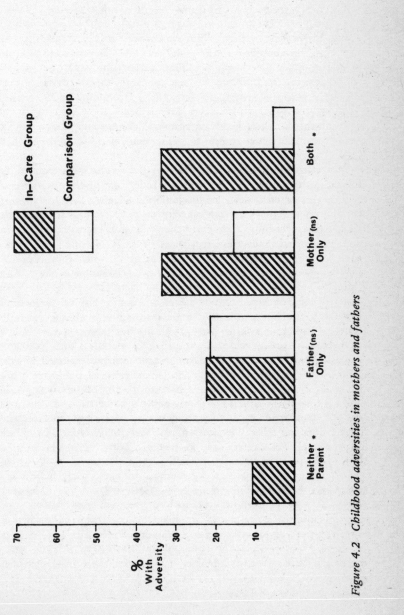

*Figure 4.2   Childhood adversities in mothers and fathers*

## Processes of transmission

*Relative importance of parental deviance and adverse childhood experiences*   Both parental deviance and adverse experiences have been shown to be more common during the childhood of the mothers in the in-care group. Not surprisingly, these two background variables tend to be associated, and the biggest differences between the two groups concerned mothers who experienced neither adversity or both. For this analysis early adversity was rated as present if any *one* of: in-care, hard or harsh parenting, parental marital discord and separations occurred before the age of 16. Parental deviance was defined as: treated psychiatric disorder, alcoholism or conviction for indictable offences, in either parent. Thus, three times as many of the in-care mothers had both parental deviance and adverse family experiences, and three times as many control group mothers had neither background factor (Figure 4.3).

The relative importance of these two factors can be examined by considering the cases where there was only one of the two adverse features (i.e. parental deviance *or* childhood adversity). It was striking that the control mothers recalled parental deviance or disorder *on its own* significantly more frequently than did mothers with children in care. In contrast, adverse experiences such as reception into care, family discord or disruption or harsh parenting, when they occurred without parental deviance, were much more common in the in-care group.

It may be concluded that it was not a family history of parental criminality, alcoholism or psychiatric disorder as such that directly put the mother at risk for later parenting breakdown; rather it was the personal experiences of a disruptive or stressful kind. It seems that such parental deviance was important largely because it greatly increased the likelihood of these adverse experiences; but when it did not do so, it did not substantially increase the risk of parenting break-down. These findings make a purely genetic explanation for the links between childhood experiences and major parenting problems un-likely, although they do not mean that hereditary factors are unimportant. These data are consistent with the cross-fostering studies discussed in Chapter 1 which suggest that one way in which some hereditary influences may work is to make individuals more susceptible to stresses of various kinds. Genetic factors may, in part, determine who is likely to succumb to environmental stresses, but to an important extent the environmental factors determine whether or not genetically-based problems will be manifested. The findings from the retrospective study are consonant in their implication that, compared with a family history of parental deviance, personal experiences of adversity are more strongly associated with the risk of later parenting breakdown.

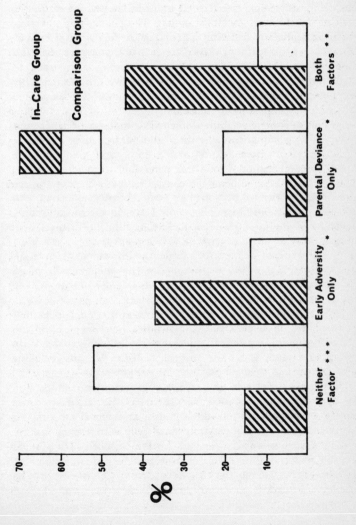

Figure 4.3  Adversity and deviance in mothers' background

*The role of teenage difficulties*   It has been shown that the rates of both early adversities and problems during the early teenage years were much higher in the in-care group. The question therefore arises whether this provides evidence that continuities are due to disturbed personality development.

The teenage difficulties considered here involved marked unhappiness at school, persistent truancy from before the final year and markedly negative relationships with one or both parents. Only 9 per cent of the in-care group mothers were free of any of these problems compared with nearly three-fifths (58 per cent) of the control group. School problems on their own occurred in about a quarter of mothers in both groups and seemed of little importance in leading to parenting breakdown. Poor relationships with parents in the absence of school difficulties were twice as frequent in the in-care group (19 per cent v. 9 per cent) although this difference failed to reach statistical significance. The differences were much more marked with respect to problems both at home *and* at school. These were experienced by 43 per cent of the in-care sample but only 7 per cent of the comparison group — a highly significant difference.

It was uncommon for teenage problems involving poor relationships with parents to occur in the absence of *some* early family discord or disruption (one or more of: admission into care, hard or harsh parenting, parental marital discord, or separations through discord or rejection). Thus, 71 per cent of the control sample with such teenage problems had experienced one or more early adversity compared with 22 per cent without such problems. Similarly, in the in-care group, 92 per cent of mothers who had had relationship difficulties with parents had one or more adversities before their teenage years compared with 56 per cent without such difficulties. However, the question remains whether there was an association between childhood adversities and parenting breakdown that was *not* mediated through marked teenage problems. This is examined in Figure 4.4.

For this analysis marked teenage problems were rated as present if there were *two* or more teenage difficulties involving marked unhappiness at school, persistent truancy and discord with parents. Early adversities were rated as for the analysis in Figure 4.2, but excluding problems occurring only during the secondary school years. The biggest differences between the two groups lay in the proportion with both problems or without either. However, when early adversities or teenage problems occurred on their own a statistically significant difference between the groups was present only with respect to early adversities. This suggests that isolated teenage problems such as these are of little importance on their own as a precursor of later parenting breakdown, and that adverse experiences in childhood may be associated with marked parenting problems even when there are no overt behavioural or emotional problems during adolescence itself.

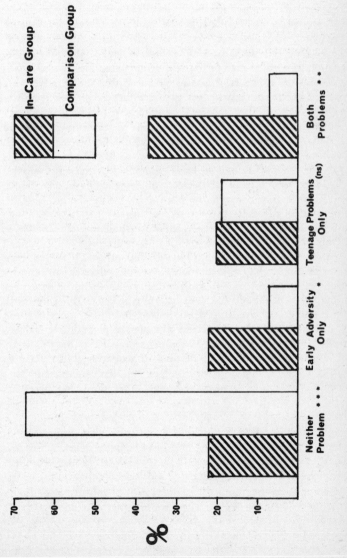

Figure 4.4  Early adversities and teenage problems of mothers

Continuity in parenting difficulties cannot therefore be explained simply by measurable direct effects on personality development. However, necessarily this suggestion must be somewhat tentative in the absence of systematic contemporaneous measures of behaviour obtained during adolescence. The issue is reconsidered in the prospective study, in which such data were available (see Chapters 10 and 11).

*The role of fathers and husbands*   As discussed above, when background adversities in only one parent were considered, a difference between the two groups occurred only with mothers. It seems likely, therefore, that the background and functioning of the mother are more important than that of fathers when parenting *breakdown* is being considered. However, this does not mean that mothers are more affected by childhood experiences than are fathers, or that the latter are unimportant in the transmission of severe parenting problems. In the first place, the in-care group husbands also had much increased rates of early adversity and of current deviance. In the second place, it has been shown that an excess of deviance or disorder in the parents of both mothers *and* fathers in these samples occurred only amongst their own *fathers*. Finally, the effects of deviance have been shown to operate primarily through the associated family discord and disruption. Taken together, these findings suggest first, that although parenting breakdown is closely related to the mother's ability to cope, this greater maternal vulnerability to stress may be determined to a considerable extent by childhood disruptions in which their fathers play a key part; and secondly, that when deviance or disorder in husbands form part of the context in which deprived mothers are parenting, the likelihood of breakdown is considerably increased.

Interestingly, the available data showed few differences between the in-care and control group fathers in current parenting techniques and skills (Quinton and Rutter, 1984a). It seems likely that this is due to the much more restricted repertoire of parenting skills that men are called upon to deploy with younger children, rather than to a lack of a connection between childhood adversities and parenting in men.

*Housing problems*   Chapter 3 showed that the in-care group families were much more likely than the controls to be living in poorer housing as evidenced by lack of basic facilities, major structural defects or the need for children to share beds or to share a bedroom with parents. Nearly half had major problems of these sorts compared with 7 per cent of the comparison group. The question therefore arises whether the continuities between early adversities and parenting breakdown operated only through links with current disadvantages.

This issue could be examined through a multivariate analysis that enabled us to ask whether the links between early adversities and outcome remain when we also took current circumstances into account. That is, is the association merely a consequence of the fact that those people who suffered early adversities were more likely to be in poorer social circumstances in adulthood, so that it is the poor circumstances alone that explain their current parenting problems? Because parenting breakdown is used as the main outcome variable and the numbers in each outcome group are therefore fixed by the design of the study, it is statistically simpler to test this model the other way round. That is, we can treat the fact of outcome (i.e. in-care or control group) as an *independent* variable and ask whether early adversities can be predicted from this once current circumstances are taken into account. We can similarly ask whether the addition of current hardships as a factor intervening between early adversities and parenting breakdown improves the completeness of our explanation or whether the occurrence of early adversities is a sufficient explanation for parenting breakdown on its own. Equally, we may reach the conclusion that some combination of both early and current hardships is necessary to explain the associations.

In statistics this process is usually called 'model fitting'. The procedures involved attempt to fit explanations proposed by the investigator to the frequencies observed in the data. The methods outlined above for the chi-square test may be thought of as a simple example of model fitting. In that case we were asking whether the observed frequencies might have arisen by chance. In more advanced model fitting techniques the investigator can ask more sophisticated questions of the data both because it is possible to take more variables into account at the same time, and because it is possible to ask whether any particular combinations of variables adds anything to the explanation.

An appropriate technique for data with a dichotomised dependent variable is linear logistic analysis. In this and other related techniques (see Everitt, 1977; Feinberg, 1977; Dunn, 1981; Gilbert, 1981) the analysis attempts to explain the observed data in the simplest or most parsimonious way; that is, by specifying as few variables and interactions as possible. The techniques proceed in the opposite direction from normal significance testing. Since the model specified tries to 'fit' the data, the analyst is looking for a non-significant 'scaled deviance' for the model (a statistic that can be thought of as similar to chi-square). If this is achieved the data observed can be said to be consistent with (or to 'fit') the model of relationships between the variables proposed by the investigator. In similar fashion, the contribution by any one variable or interaction to the fit of the model can be examined by seeing whether adding it to the variables currently included in the analysis improves the fit. This is determined by whether the addition reduces the scaled deviance of the previous model by a

*Table 4.1  Group selection, current disadvantage, and early adversity: linear logistic analysis*

| Model | | Model fitted | | | Comparison of models | | | |
|---|---|---|---|---|---|---|---|---|
| | | Deviance | df | P | Term added | Improvement in fit | df | P |
| A. | Constant | 22.95 | 7 | 0.001 | | | | |
| B. | Marital circumstances only | 14.84 | 6 | 0.05 | B to A | 8.14 | 1 | 0.01 |
| C. | Housing problems only | 17.13 | 6 | 0.01 | C to A | 5.85 | 1 | 0.02 |
| D. | Group selection only | 5.66 | 6 | ns | D to A | 17.32 | 1 | 0.001 |
| E. | Marital problems and housing | 9.72 | 5 | ns | E to A | 13.16 | 2 | 0.01 |
| F. | Group, marital and housing | 2.37 | 4 | ns | F to A | 20.61 | 3 | 0.001 |
| | | | | | E to D | 3.29 | 2 | ns |
| | | | | | D to E | 7.35 | 2 | 0.05 |

statistically significant amount. Of course, in complicated multivariate tables a number of models may fit the data equally satisfactorily and a choice between them must be made on theoretical grounds or in connection with findings from other studies.

This approach can now be illustrated in the analysis of these data. For this, early adversities were defined as for the analysis for Figure 4.2. The intervening variables were housing, as defined above, and marital circumstances. These were rated as unsatisfactory if the woman was either a single parent or had a spouse with current criminality or psychiatric disorder, and as satisfactory otherwise.

The results from this analysis are clear-cut. The model-fitting group selection (i.e. that based solely on the in-care v. control group comparison) on its own (model 3) reduced the overall deviance for the whole table (constant = 22.95) to a non-significant level. This was not true of the models fitting the housing or marital variables. Although both these models improved the fit to the data significantly (22.95 – 14.84 = 8.14 for marital circumstances, and 22.95 – 17.14 = 5.85 for housing) they both left a significant amount of the variance in the data unaccounted for. This shows that the association between early adversities and parenting breakdown could not be wholly explained through the association between early adversities and later social circumstances. That is, parenting breakdown was not just a consequence of current troubles. However, it would be incorrect to infer that current social circumstances were unimportant. The combination of current marital and housing problems without taking into account the in-care v. control group distinctions, also reduced the overall deviance to a non-significant level (model 4). We may judge the relative importance of childhood v. current influences by noting that the addition of the group criterion (in-care v. control distinction) to this model produced a further significant reduction in the deviance (9.72 – 2.37 = 7.35) whereas the addition of housing and marital circumstances to the model fitting group selection only did not.

We may conclude from this analysis that disadvantaged current circumstances were related to adversities in childhood but that these links were insufficient to explain the association between such adversities and parenting breakdown. Although these simple additive models fit the data well, the question of interactions between early adversities and later circumstances must remain open because of the small numbers and the range and definition of indicators used.

*Psychiatric disorders*    The above analyses suggest that current disadvantages are important mediating variables in the links between early adversities and parenting breakdown but they do not provide any evidence on the *processes* that lead from the one to the other, nor on the nature of their current impact. The differences between the two samples both on major psychiatric problems in the past and on present disorders were very striking and it seems likely that this was one important linking factor. Unfortunately, the overlap between psychiatric disorder and other problems in the in-care sample was so great and the rate of disorder so high as to preclude examination of the issue.

### Current problems in parenting

The analyses so far have been confined to a discussion of the antecedents of parenting *breakdown*. This was necessary both because multiple breakdown was likely to be a better indicator of parenting difficulties than a one-off interview assessment and because data from the prospective study suggested that the antecedents and correlates of mild to moderate problems might differ from those for more severe parenting difficulties (see also Egeland *et al.*, 1984). However, it was possible to make some preliminary analyses of the contribution of current circumstances to day-to-day parenting problems. Because of the marked difference in the frequency and severity of current problems between the two samples, these analyses were necessarily restricted to within-group comparisons.

*In-care mothers*    Since virtually all the in-care mothers had suffered marked early adversities, the question of the *independent* effect of current circumstances is redundant. Nevertheless, the effects of housing problems and/or lack of marital support as defined above on current handling can be considered against the background of adverse childhoods. Current parenting problems were rated as present if the mother had two or more problems in the areas of control and/or responsiveness. Figure 4.5 shows the rate of parenting problems according to the presence or absence of housing disadvantage and/or a lack of marital support.

The first point that emerges from this analysis is that only 11 per cent of the in-care mothers were free of both types of current adversities. Secondly, it is apparent that this minority subgroup showed a rather low rate of parenting problems. Difficulties in parenting were substantially and significantly increased if mothers suffered the combination of housing disadvantage and lack of marital support. The data suggest that parenting may be impaired when either of these disadvantages occurred on their own without the other, but the numbers with single disadvantages were small and the differences fell short of statistical significance. The findings re-emphasise the observation from previous studies that adversities rarely occur in isolation (Rutter, 1979); the frequency of overlap makes it very difficult (often impossible) to determine whether specific adversities have effects that are independent of their association with other risk factors.

The multiplicity of difficulties in the in-care families made it

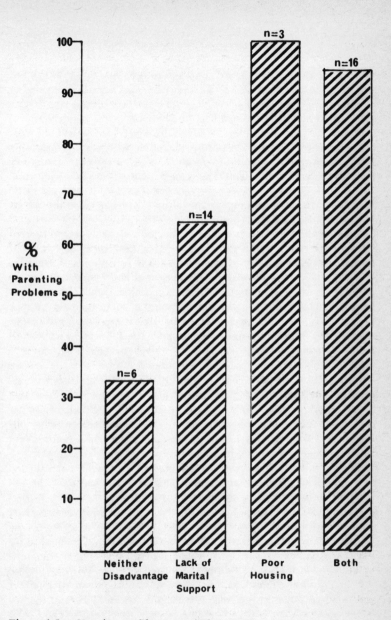

Figure 4.5   *Housing problems, marital support and parenting
(in-care mothers)*

impossible to tease out the factors influencing current parenting problems. However, the matter could be re-examined in the control group.

*Control group mothers*   The data on the control mothers (who had not had children taken into care) showed that quite severe adversities in childhood did not usually lead to later parenting breakdown. Is this attenuation of influences also true of day-to-day parenting difficulties?

When the strict definition of childhood adversities applied in earlier analyses was used there was no association with current parenting problems within the control group. Thus 19 per cent of mothers without parenting problems had experienced such adversities compared with 18 per cent with parenting difficulties. It remains to be seen whether the parenting problems in this group were influenced by current disadvantages.

Because the control group were better housed, the impact of current circumstances had to be examined using a less severe definition of housing disadvantage than that used for the in-care sample. In this case 'housing difficulties' were rated as present if the family had *one* or more of the following: major structural problems; children sharing a bed; lack of a kitchen, bathroom or toilet; or more than 1.5 persons per room. Housing difficulties were also rated if the family had *two* or more of the following: some overcrowding (1.1–1.4 persons per room), lack of washing machine and lack of telephone. The definitions of marital problems and handling difficulties are as for the in-care mothers. It was found that current housing disadvantage was significantly related to parenting problems. Thus, mothers in poorer housing were twice as likely to have current handling problems (64 per cent v. 28 per cent). However, before concluding that housing disadvantage itself impeded parenting we need to take into account any association between poor housing and marital problems. Figure 4.6 presents this analysis for the control group in a form comparable to that employed for the in-care sample (Figure 4.5), except for the less strict definition of housing difficulties.

As in the in-care group, housing disadvantage was strongly associated with lack of marital support; it occurred on its own in only 9 per cent of cases. As with the in-care mothers, current disadvantage significantly increased the risk of parenting problems only when both housing difficulties and lack of marital support occurred together. However, unlike the findings in the in-care sample, there was no suggestion of an effect when either disadvantage was present on its own. This difference between the in-care and control groups may have been a function of chance variations due to small numbers, but also it may have been a consequence of the lower level of housing disadvantage in the control group (or of the association of poor housing with other risk factors in the in-care sample).

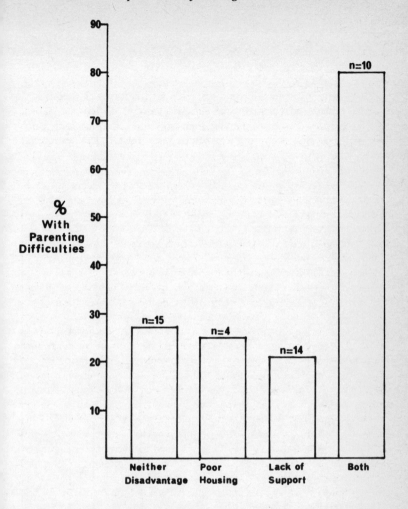

*Figure 4.6*    *Housing difficulties, marital support and parenting (comparison mothers)*

In that connection, it may be relevant that whereas nearly all of the in-care mothers had experienced serious adversities in their own childhood, this was so for a minority of the control group mothers. Possibly the more stable childhoods of the latter group had rendered them less vulnerable to the effects of disadvantage in adult life. Figure 4.7 examines this possibility using lack of marital support as the current disadvantage variable (because the housing difficulties were not comparable with those in the in-care sample). Childhood adversity was rated if any *one* of the indicators of early family disruption was present, i.e. admission into care, separation through discord, marital discord or hard or harsh parenting before the age of 16. Note that necessarily this was a lesser degree of early adversity than that in the in-care sample.

Although one third of mothers with satisfactory childhoods and good current marriages had some current parenting difficulties, lack of marital support seemed to increase their likelihood. In this sample early adversity and lack of marital support were not related. Lack of marital

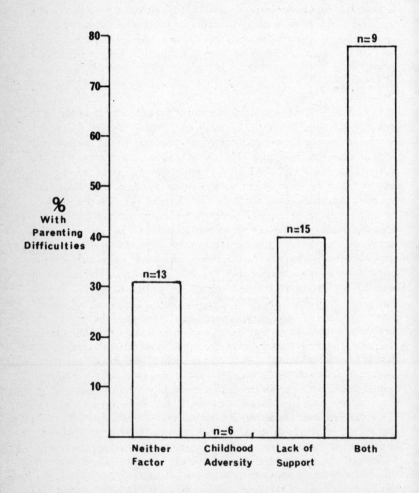

*Figure 4.7    Childhood adversity, marital support and parenting (comparison mothers)*

support was as common for mothers without childhood adversities as it was for those with them. Interestingly, in the few cases where mothers with adverse childhoods were currently in satisfactory marriages there were no parenting problems. The rates of parenting difficulties seemed most markedly increased when current disadvantage was associated with childhood adversities. The numbers were too few, however, to allow formal statistical appraisal of these findings and accordingly they should be treated with extreme caution. Nevertheless, the data suggest that a stable childhood may provide mothers with a greater capacity to cope under stress and conversely that the effects on later parenting of moderate childhood difficulties may be principally manifest when these lead to or are associated with disadvantageous circumstances in adult life. It is not known whether the same would be true for multiple childhood adversities such as those in the in-care group.

## Discussion

It is evident that when multiple parenting breakdown has occurred in a family it is usual for one or both parents to have experienced serious adversities in their own upbringing in childhood. Such breakdowns seldom occurred in response to current disadvantage *alone*. On the other hand, the in-care families were strikingly disadvantaged in many ways — in their living conditions, marital problems and their own psychiatric disturbances. Not only was the parenting breakdown part of a much more widespread pattern of psychosocial difficulties, but also the breakdowns occurred in the context of current social disadvantage. The within-group analyses were consistent in showing that such current disadvantage (in the form of lack of marital support and poor living conditions) increased the rate of parenting difficulties as assessed at interview. In other words, any explanation of serious parenting difficulties must include the effects of *both* childhood adversities and current psychosocial disadvantage. The two most straightforward models that have been proposed in the past can be rejected. The first suggests that the causal mechanism concerns the direct effects of current disadvantage, with childhood adversities associated only incidently through their connection with social hardships. This model cannot account for parenting breakdown because it almost never occurred in the absence of childhood adversities; clearly, the childhood experiences must play a more central causal role than allowed by that model. It is possible that less serious parenting difficulties that do *not* lead to overt parenting breakdown may arise from current disadvantage in the absence of childhood adversities. Our study was not designed to investigate the origins of these milder, less pervasive parenting difficulties. However, the control group data are relevant in two respects; first, they suggest that it is the *combination* of marital discord and housing difficulties that puts parenting at risk rather than poor living conditions on their own; and secondly, they suggest that, even with these lesser parenting problems, there may be an interaction between childhood adversities and current disadvantage. Our numbers were insufficient for adequate testing of this possibility but the suggestion warrants further exploration.

The second model proposes that serious adversities in childhood lead to abnormal personality development which in turn is associated with poor parenting. With this model any associations between parenting breakdown and current social disadvantage should be artefactual, arising only because mentally disordered individuals get themselves into social difficulties. In its strong form, this model too must be rejected if only because current psychosocial conditions were significantly associated with parenting difficulties *within* both the in-care and control groups. The findings suggested an effect from current social circumstances that was not simply an artefact of patterns of upbringing.

A third model must be introduced to account for the findings. It requires several different elements. First, the pattern in the control group is important in showing that: (a) mild-to-moderate parenting difficulties are relatively common in the general population, but it is unusual for them to lead to a breakdown of parenting; (b) such difficulties frequently occur in the *absence* of personality disorder and without problems in other areas of psychosocial functioning; (c) these isolated parenting difficulties are associated with current psychosocial adversities, but the adversities that put parenting at risk tend to be multiple with some combination of marital disturbance and poor living conditions; (d) even with these isolated parenting difficulties, childhood adversities may play a minor role in contributing to a vulnerability to current psychosocial stress.

Secondly, the rather different pattern in the in-care group shows that most instances of parenting *breakdown* (as distinct from parenting difficulties) are associated with widespread psychosocial problems that extend far beyond parenting skills and qualities and usually arise in individuals with a markedly adverse upbringing. The implication is that parenting breakdown should not be seen as synonymous with serious parenting difficulties. It is true that breakdown usually involves such difficulties but it seems that the difficulties lead to breakdown, not so much through their severity, as through their association with problems in many other aspects of the parents' lives — in their marital relationship, in their interactions with people outside the family, in work, and in housing, as well as in their own mental functioning. A further implication is that the origins of isolated parenting difficulties (as seen in the control group) may well be different from the origins of serious psychosocial disturbances that includes but extends far beyond parenting problems.

We may infer that parenting is a multifactorial function that is reliant on a range of personal, material and social resources. These include the time available; the person's own emotional state; the presence of other life stresses and problems; the qualities of the spouse; the extent to which child-rearing is shared; the existence of other satisfactions and achievements apart from parenting (as in a job outside the home); the availability of adequate social supports; and housing conditions.

Thirdly, the model for parenting breakdown must take account of the demonstrated effects of both childhood adversities and current psychosocial disadvantage *and* the strong association between these two hazards. Several alternatives have to be considered. One possibility is that the main influence stems from the childhood adversities. It could be suggested that these lead directly to a disorder of personality functioning, a disorder that predisposes to marital discord and also to employment difficulties. These in turn mean that the people are likely to suffer poor housing: all of which adult circumstances make parenting more difficult. According to this model, the main mediating variable would be a personality disorder, with current psychosocial circumstances playing only a minor contributory role. The retrospective data do not allow an adequate testing of this model but the moderate strength of the effect on parenting of marital discord and housing disadvantage raise doubts about its validity. The relatively satisfactory parenting of some of the mothers who had had children taken into care raises even more doubts because of its suggestion that the quality of parenting may vary greatly by social context and circumstances.

An alternative possibility is that the adverse childhood experiences operate as a risk factor by several rather different routes — through a disturbance in personality functioning; through one set of environmental hazards making others more likely (hence, increasing the rate of social disadvantage in adult life); through the creation of a mental set of helplessness leading the women to make poor choices (as of marriage partner); and through processes leading to a greater vulnerability to environmental stressors. Obviously, such a model requires a prospective study for its testing, both through the need to examine linkages over time and its implicit assumption of individual variations in responses to adversity.

The likelihood of such individual variation is also shown by the frequency with which a history of childhood adversities was apparent in the control group. The strong implications that many women develop normally in spite of seriously adverse experiences in childhood. This possibility cannot be examined adequately through retrospective data. Rather it requires a follow through into adult life of a total sample of children exposed to these environmental hazards. With these considerations in mind we need to turn to our prospective study of girls reared in institutions for much of their childhood years.

# 5 The prospective study: Samples and sources of information

The prospective study starts with a sample of girls who had been admitted into the care of a local authority and placed in one or other of two children's homes. These homes had been studied by King and his colleagues (1971) during the mid-1960s. The rationale for this choice of sample was that the girls' experiences in childhood directly paralleled that of the second generation in the retrospective study. That is to say, parenting had broken down primarily because of family difficulties rather than because of the child's deviant behaviour. However, it should be noted that as most of the children had spent several years in the children's home, the potential environmental risk factors involved both the parenting breakdown and factors leading to it (mainly parental mental disorder and gross family discord), and also the experience of an institutional upbringing. There were three main reasons for choosing the King *et al.* (1971) sample rather than any other group of young people in residential care. First, their study of the children's homes provided direct contemporaneous assessment of the children's upbringing in the institutions. Secondly, standardised questionnaire data were available on the children's behaviour and emotional adjustment while in the children's home. Thirdly, the same teachers' questionnaire data were available on a general population sample of similar aged girls for the same time period, thus we had available a suitable control group studied in the same way from the same age.

## Samples

Thus, the prospective study involved two samples. The first — ex-care — group comprised 93 girls who had been raised in one of the two children's homes. This group included all those who were recorded as 'white' on King *et al.*'s original record sheets and who were aged between 21 and 27 years on 1 January 1978. This age criterion was applied in the expectation of obtaining a substantial sample of subjects with young children. Selection was further restricted to those (the great majority) with questionnaire data because of the importance of this independent measure of the girls' functioning during childhood. However, in order to increase the sample of sibling pairs in the study, the sibs of those children fitting the main selection criteria, but for whom behavioural data were missing, were also included. Further details of sampling are given in Appendix A. Since the two homes served as long-stay institutions for the whole of Inner London, they provided an epidemiologically-based sample of Inner London children experiencing this form of substitute care. The majority of the children had been admitted into care before the age of 5 years and spent much of their school years there.

The comparison sample of 51 girls was drawn from the classroom controls for a study of the children of psychiatric patients who were living in one Inner London borough during the late 1960s (Rutter and Quinton, 1984c). It is thus a quasi-random sample of the general population of schoolchildren from this area (it departs from randomness in terms of the requirement that the children be in the same school classes as the children of parent-patients). The sample met the same criteria as the institution-reared group except that, of course, they had never been admitted to care.

Interviews were conducted both with the subjects and with their current spouses. In all, 91 per cent of female ex-care subjects were traced and all of these were interviewed. The tracing losses for female controls were somewhat higher but 89 per cent of those traced were also interviewed, with an overall success rate of 80 per cent. Approximately, two-thirds (63 per cent) of the spouses of the ex-care subjects and three-quarters (73 per cent) of comparison group spouses were interviewed. Basic life-history data were collected from the women on those husbands who were not seen.

## Measures

### Data on the children's homes
Our data on the children's homes derived from those obtained by King *et al.* (1971). Their detailed systematic study involved both qualitative and quantitative findings based on observations, interviews with staff and material from records. The material on life in the homes is more fully described in Chapter 6.

### Social service case notes
Social service case notes were available for about half of the originally selected sample. Social services cases notes were available for nearly half of the originally selected sample of girls (42/93). Data were missing for 46 cases because boroughs could not find the notes or because they had gone astray in the transfer of files back to the placing boroughs in 1965 following reorganisation of services: 23 of these files being the responsibility of two of the ten boroughs placing children in these homes. One file was not seen because a borough refused access, two because one borough allowed access only with the written permission of the subjects and we were unable to trace them (permission was freely given by all traced subjects), and in two cases the Greater London Council records department could not identify the boroughs to whom the records had been returned. The abstracting of data from social services case files was

undertaken by all team members. Despite the fact that such records included a number of statutory record forms concerning the child's reception into care and his or her subsequent progress and history, systematic evaluations of any aspects of family life and circumstances were lacking. The records provide some indication of the *most pressing* justification for reception into care but not necessarily details of other adverse features such as parental psychiatric problems or criminality. As a result, piecing together the reasons for admission and the child's subsequent in-care history and adjustment was a laborious task. Interviewers generally dictated key features of the child's life from the notes, paying particular attention to evidence of family discord, psychiatric or criminal history, neglect or abuse, poor circumstances and the adjustment of the child. Care was taken that wherever possible the interviewer who saw the subject was blind to the contents of that person's files.

A number of important areas could not be determined from the notes. For example, there were no consistent data on parental visiting; changes of cottage within the homes were not systematically logged, and there were no records of changes of houseparents. Finally, no systematic record appears in the notes of the children's educational progress or their emotional or behavioural development. Such assessments only appear when a child was referred to psychological services because of problems of one sort or another. The notes did contain painstaking and conscientious handwritten accounts by child care officers of their contacts with the families but these were of limited use in assessing the lives and progress of the children.

## Delinquency and crime records

Individual data from the Criminal Records Office on court appearances for convictable offences were supplied for both samples by the Home Office. In many cases a single criminal episode can involve a number of separate offences. This is the case, for example, with the taking and driving away of motor vehicles where separate offences concerning insurance, dangerous driving, driving under age, as well as other charges may occur. In Chapter 7, these data are presented both in terms of the overall *number* of court appearances in order to show the persistence of criminality, and in terms of each separate offence in order to show the predominant *type* of crime.

## Behavioural questionnaires

Rutter 'B' questionnaires completed by teachers were available for both samples of children when they were in their late primary or early secondary school years. The questionnaire has 26 items, each describing some observable behaviour of the child (such as 'frequently cries on arrival at school' or 'not much liked by other children'), and the teacher has to code whether the statement 'definitely applies', 'applies somewhat' or 'doesn't apply' to that particular child (scored '2', '1' and 'O', respectively). The item scores are summed to produce a total score. The questionnaire has a satisfactory retest and inter-rater reliability (see Rutter, 1967, for details), and high scores have been found to differentiate psychiatric clinic attenders from non-attenders and to agree well with independent assessments of children's emotional and behavioural problems from parental interviews (Rutter, 1967; Rutter *et al.*, 1970; Rutter *et al.*, 1975a).

The 'A' questionnaire is a parallel version for completion by parents (but with a few additional items on behaviours, such as sleep difficulties, that would not be observable at school). It was completed in 1964 for all the children in the institutions, but was not available for the control group.

### Interview data

The interview format used in the prospective study was developed from the retrospective study schedule during a six-month pilot period. The interviewing was undertaken by David Quinton, one full-time and three part-time interviewers.

The assessments of current family relationships and social functioning followed the measures developed in earlier studies (Brown and Rutter, 1966; Rutter and Brown, 1966; Quinton *et al.*, 1976; Rutter and Quinton, 1984c). New interviewers were trained to satisfactory levels of agreement. In addition, two major new sections of the interview were developed to cover features of individual life-history and parenting. These sections focused on obtaining a detailed and event-oriented account of what had happened to the subjects, and on how they handled their children.

Because of pressure of time and because two of the interviewers were employed for only one year, no formal tests of inter-rater reliability were possible on these new interview sections. Comparability of ratings was monitored in two ways. First, weekly team meetings were held in which problems were discussed and ratings agreed. Secondly, extensive cross-checking of interviews was carried out. Thus, prior to the transfer of interview data to computer coding sheets the interview was read and checked by another team member who raised queries about codings and checked the evidence upon which ratings were based. The final transfer of data for the computer always involved one of the two senior interviewers as the checker.

### Home observation of parenting

Experience from the retrospective study had suggested that interview-based measures of parenting provide a satisfactory assessment of current parenting within broad categories of performance. Interview measures were also essential for recording data on parenting history. However, interview data may not be sufficient on their own for an adequate assessment of parenting. This is particularly so because parents are unlikely to be aware of the ways in which parent–child interactions develop over time; because it is difficult to keep inter-viewers blind to the childhood background of subjects; and because parental accounts as well as interviewer judgements may be biased by current circumstances or by psychological problems. These difficulties can be circumvented in observational studies. Current circumstances and problems may still affect parental behaviour, but here these are the variations one is trying to detect.

Direct home observations of mother–child interactions were under-taken for 21 ex-care mothers with children aged 2–3½ years, and 23 comparison mothers who had children in the same age group. The observational methodology is described in detail in Chapter 8 and the outcome on parenting according to both to interviews and observations in Chapter 9.

### Summary of sources of information

In the analyses that follow, variations commonly occur in many of the table numbers (Ns). To a minor extent, this is due to missing data on individual interview items — for example, because a subject could recall

*Table 5.1　Samples and sources of information*

|  | Ex-care sample | Comparison sample |
|---|---|---|
| Number selected | 93 | 51 |
| Number interviewed | 81 | 41 |
| Maximum N used | 82 | 45 |
| *Of those interviewed* | | |
| Child(ren) aged two or over | 49 | 32* |
| Assessment of current parenting made | 42 | 27* |
| Assessment of overall parenting made | 48 | 27* |
| Teacher questionnaire (B scale) | 68 | 40 |
| Teacher and/or parent questionnaire | 68 | – |
| Current parenting assessment *and* B scale | 34 | 13 |
| Overall parenting assessment *and* B scale | 39 | 13 |
| Social Service records:　Interviewed sample | 40 | – |
| Total | 46 | – |
| Home observation study | 23 | 21* |

*Includes the wives of controls for the outcome study for men.

nothing of her childhood, or because a topic was insufficiently probed. However, larger fluctuations occur where analyses include some key variables for which information was not available. This was particularly the case with data from Social Services records and for the teachers' or houseparents' questionnaires because of the sampling on sibs. The general approach has been to maximise the use of known data. For example, data on subjects who refused the interviewer are included in certain descriptive tables when these are known. The various sources of information and available data are summarised in Table 5.1.

In the analyses that follow, variations in table Ns of not more than one case either way are not noted. Wider variations are given in the table headings. It will be noted that the Ns for the controls in the observational study refers to the inclusion of the wives of control men. These men were part of a parallel study of the boys who were in the two children's homes at the same time as the girls discussed in this volume. The controls for the boys' study were chosen in the same way as the female comparison sample. The interviews for the boys are not described here because data collection was still in progress at the time the study of the girls was completed.

# 6 The prospective study: The childhoods of the two samples

## The children's homes

### General characteristics

Both of the children's homes were purpose-built institutions designed on group cottage lines and administered by the Children's Department of the local authority in their area. The children in the homes had been placed for long-term care by all of the Inner London boroughs. At the time of the original study in 1964 the first home had 340 children and the second 377. Each occupied its own distinctive site surrounded by a substantial fence. The first home was a single estate of detached houses along both sides of a tree-lined avenue situated just outside the Greater London area and isolated from the surrounding neighbourhood. The second home was similarly set out but occupied a larger site within a south London suburb, with one of its two avenues giving onto a suburban street. The first home has subsequently been demolished. The second has recently been closed. When visited at the start of this study, the general impression was of an open and physically pleasant environment.

Both homes were well provided with facilities (our description is taken from King et al., 1971). There were nursery and primary schools, swimming baths and shops in both establishments. In addition, one had its own church and the other a community centre. The self-contained nature of the two institutions was often commented on during our interviews. Many subjects felt that although the homes provided containment and comfort for the younger children, the lack of experience in handling the outside world had been a serious problem as they became teenagers and went to secondary schools outside.

The living units in both homes were known to the staff and children as 'cottages', with each cottage being identified by the name of a tree or plant. The first home had 22 cottages in use at any one time, variously designed to hold a maximum of 15–20 children. The general pattern was of the kitchen, living areas, staff sitting-room, bathroom and lavatory on the ground floor, and bedrooms upstairs. Just over half the children slept in bedrooms containing five beds whilst more than one fifth had their own room or shared with just one other child. In the second home 30 of the 36 cottages were semi-detached and the remainder detached. All were designed to hold up to twelve children and had substantially similar accommodation. No children were in bedrooms with more than four beds, and a fifth were in single or twin rooms. Nearly all cottages had extra toilet facilities for children playing outside. In 1964, 89 per cent of children in the first home were in cottages containing 15 or more children, whilst in the second home 92 per cent of children were in cottages containing 10 to 14.

Whilst none of the cottages in either home was luxuriously furnished, all were able to provide a reasonable standard of comfort. There were, for example, enough easy chairs for people to sit down if they wanted to, and most rooms had carpets or rugs on the floor. Some cottages would have benefited from redecoration, but without exception they had a clean and 'lived-in' appearance. Most of the cottages in both homes had been successful in avoiding an institutional atmosphere by varing the patterns of curtains, bedspreads, wallpapers and so on from room to room. All of the children had some private space in which to keep their possessions — some had drawers, others lockers — although no housemother in either home felt that these facilities were entirely adequate. The second home was particularly lacking in hanging space for clothes to which the children could have direct access. All cottages had a television, although these were not provided by the local authority; usually, staff and children contributed to the rental.

### Staffing

The staffing of the two homes was very similar. Between them they employed the equivalent of 255 full-time staff to care for 717 children — an overall staff:child ratio of about 1:3. In both homes each cottage was in the charge of a housemother permanently assigned to that unit: 32 per cent of housemothers at the first home, and 17 per cent at the second were married women whose husbands lived with them in the units. Occasionally, the husbands were employed by the institutions as housefathers, and in such cases the married couple shared responsibility for their household. There were five such living units in the first home and one in the second. More usually the husband pursued a full-time occupation elsewhere and would help out in the cottage during the evenings even though not a full-time member of the staff. More than 80 per cent of housemothers in both establishments had worked in the same unit for a year or longer at the time of the original study and many of them had five or more years experience in the same cottage, where they had watched the children grow up.

In the first home there were two additional grades of child-care staff attached to the cottages — deputy housemothers and assistant housemothers. Deputies carried somewhat more responsibility and had a slightly higher salary than assistants. The grade of deputy housemother did not exist in the second home, where all junior staff were referred to as assistant housemothers. At the time in question, there were *no* male junior staff in either home, although there had been some deputy housefathers in the first home prior to the 1964 study, and a few assistant housefathers were appointed subsequently.

Junior staff were allocated permanently to cottages, with the policy of both establishments being to keep the staff in the same unit, unless severe problems arose in relationships between staff and children. Even so, 56 per cent of deputies and 84 per cent of the assistants in the first home had worked in the same unit for less than one year. In the second home, 55 per cent of the junior staff had worked in the same unit for a similar period. In both cases the figures reflect the high turnover of junior staff in the two homes, rather than transfers between units, since less than a quarter of the junior staff in each home had worked on two or more units during their stay. The consequence of these staff changes was that nearly all children experienced several changes of caregivers, and some had had a very large number of parental figures. Unfortunately, the records did not document staff changes in a manner that allows quantification of these changes for each child. The mean ratio of assigned cottage staff to children was 1:5 in each home, and the staff were considerably stretched to provide tolerably acceptable staff ratios, despite the fact that they were not employed on a shift basis and worked long hours.

Virtually all the full-time child-care staff in the homes were themselves resident in the cottages. Allowing for days off duty the best staffing pattern that could develop was as follows: a cottage with two permanent members of staff would have both of them on duty during the day and evening for three days of each week only, with four days when one member had to cope alone. A unit with three staff had two of them on duty for six days and all three on duty for the seventh. What was striking about the staffing of the units was that in neither home were there personnel spare to cope with staff illness and holidays. At such times the units carried on with whoever remained. This may be the reason that the turnover of junior staff was high.

Much of the responsibility for deciding the daily routine of the living units lay with the housemothers. Meals were cooked by the cottage staff in the household kitchen and could be taken at the convenience of adults and children in the cottages. With certain limits, care or credit allowances were available to purchase clothes or toys for the children, either from the local stores or the shops within the homes. Houseparents were usually able to take the children with them to make the purchases. In both homes each housemother was given a weekly housekeeping allowance from which she was able to buy food and household goods for the unit. Most housemothers had regular orders with the local milkman, baker, grocer and greengrocer who delivered goods to the cottages.

There was very little specialisation in roles between the staff. Although housemothers took responsibility for buying goods and for administration, they could also be found cooking, cleaning and tidying, and washing and caring for the children.

*Daily life*

In most cottages the children were wakened between 6.45 and 7.30 a.m. They washed and dressed themselves and then came down to breakfast, the youngest being helped by the adults. The cottages generally required the children to help in preparing meals, setting the table or washing up. At least one member of staff ate with the children at meals. In some cottages staff had separate crockery, but this was comparatively rare. In many cottages breakfast was a straggling affair, with some children having finished and left before others started. This pattern held for other meals as well.

Only the very youngest remained in the cottages during school hours. Over half in both homes went to the primary schools that were run by the local authority within the grounds. The older children went to secondary schools outside, and many travelled long distances by public transport. The policy concerning secondary schooling was deliberately to spread the children amongst many schools, so that not more than 13 children from the first home and 23 from the second went to the same school. This was to prevent concentrations of deprived children in local schools. Only a very small proportion attended special schooling of any kind.

All of the children had their own clothes in adequate, if not plentiful, supply. Most had some choice of what they wore, usually by going with the housemother to make purchases or, if older, buying things themselves with their allowances. Virtually all of them had their own toys and most had their own books. Although the cottages were short of storage space, nearly all of the children had some personal space in which to keep their possessions. The children could use the gardens and the grounds more or less as they wished. Most had the run of their cottage, although some housemothers were more restrictive. In most cottages children spent time in the staff quarters; they could bring paintings home from school and hang them on the walls of their bedrooms, and all children received pocket money which was given out by the housemothers. They were encouraged to save and the housemothers would then help them with purchases. Despite this they often made comments at interview about how little knowledge and experience they had in dealing with this aspect of everyday life when they finally left care. The children were permitted to go to other cottages to play and to have tea and could, in return, bring their friends back to their cottages. Birthdays were special occasions on which they received cards, a small present and a birthday tea. There was a full range of clubs and activities in the evenings and weekends and these were generally well remembered when the subjects looked back on their childhoods.

In order to quantify these impressions of the children's lives, King *et al.* (1971) developed a child management scale which assessed the degree to which the child-care practices were institution- or child-oriented. In principle, child-oriented practices were seen to have four characteristics: (1) that they were flexible, being adapted to take into account individual differences amongst the children or the different circumstances of their lives; (2) that the organisation of activity was such that the children were allowed to choose whether to participate or to do so at their own pace, rather than being regimented; (3) that the child's world was personalised so that they had their own possessions and an opportunity for privacy; and (4) that child–staff relationships were characterised by minimum social distance, the sharing of living space, and frequent unstructured interactions took place in informal situations (e.g. the staff and children ate or watched television together). In all these counts the two homes were assessed as having a high level of child-oriented practices, although there was a statistically significant difference between the two homes with less personalised practices being more common in the first.

In summary, the two homes in which the subjects spent the greater part of their institutional experiences were considered to be adequately provided, child-centred and non-institutionalised. There was reasonable continuity of senior cottage staff, many of whom spent years caring for their children, but a high turnover of junior assistants. The staffing ratios made it difficult for the house staff to provide continuous and personal attention for the children, but it is clear that the quality of care provision was generally good. It would, however, be misleading to conclude that the children had generally stable parenting so far as their housemothers were concerned. It was not possible to quantify changes of houseparent because the records of the children's stays were incomplete and because the homes' own records were not available. Nevertheless, it is clear from the children's own accounts that changes of houseparent were common. This was so not only because houseparents left the homes or retired, but also because the children themselves were moved between cottages. This occurred sometimes because of clashes between the child and the houseparent, sometimes because policy decreed that certain cottages should provide for children of a particular age range only, and sometimes because re-admission to the homes following an unsuccessful placement elsewhere necessitated the child being admitted to another cottage.

In a few cases, the houseparent–child relationship was very long-standing — even resulting in the houseparent fostering the child on leaving the Residential Child Care Service. However, this kind of continuity was exceptional. When considered alongside the frequent changes of more junior staff, the children's 'parenting' experiences in care can best be described as containing multiple changes of care-giver but with some more stable figures. The contribution of such stable figures to adult outcomes are discussed in Chapter 10.

**Admission to care**

*Reasons for admission*

The fact that these two homes functioned as long-stay institutions is a strong indication that a substantial proportion of the children were admitted because of major failures in parenting and not simply through temporary family hardships. This can be documented more formally by considering the circumstances surrounding the children's admission to care as indicated by social services records. The child-care files for 107 children from the total originally selected for study (including boys) were available. Although missing files tended to be concentrated in two boroughs, there is no reason to suppose that their admission policies were radically different from the other Inner London areas, or that the files were missing for any systematic reasons. These losses appear primarily to have occurred following the 1974 reorganisation of Child Care Services when the Greater London Council — through whom the placements had originally been made — transferred the notes to the new boroughs.

In coding reasons for admission to care all the contemporaneous evidence in the file was taken into account rather than simply relying on the reasons stated on the reception into care forms. This was because an assessment was wanted of the family environments in which the children spent their early years and the extent to which these reflect parenting problems. As is generally the case, the RIC forms usually cited the most pressing or outstanding reason for admission. Further, a substantial number of the placements in these two long-stay homes were transfers from care-nurseries or other shorter-stay establishments, so the reasons for admission to the two homes had to be sought earlier in the child's care history.

Table 6.1 presents the characteristics of the children's parents and families prior to their admission. It is apparent that serious problems in parental functioning preceded the children's reception into care. Nearly one third of total admissions were on fit person orders and 88 per cent of the children had been in other residential care provisions before their long-term admission to the two homes. A proportion of these were assessment or nursery placements prior to transfer, but a substantial number of children had had a number of shorter care admissions previously. The data from those care notes that were available indicate very high rates of parental difficulties. The majority of families had one or both parents with psychiatric problems or a criminal history, their marriages were marked by discord and instability and their parenting was often neglectful or abusive. Parental deviance or disorder or severe parenting problems were mentioned for all but 7 per cent of children.

Table 6.1   Family characteristics prior to the children's admission:
             Official records

|                                             | %<br>(n=107) |
|---------------------------------------------|:------------:|
| Paternal psychiatric disorder               | 21           |
| Paternal criminality                        | 29           |
| Paternal criminality and/or disorder        | 42           |
| Maternal psychiatric disorder               | 35           |
| Maternal criminality                        | 21           |
| Maternal criminality and/or disorder        | 48           |
| Deviance or disorder in either parent       | 70           |
| Marital discord and/or separations          | 73           |
| Poor circumstances and/or poverty           | 76           |
| Child neglect/abuse or abandonment          | 56           |

(From King *et al*. data.)

|                                             | %<br>(n=249) |
|---------------------------------------------|:------------:|
| Two or more placements prior to admission   | 88           |
| Fit person orders                           | 29           |

*Age at admission and the pattern of early experiences*

Two-thirds (68 per cent) of the total sample of girls in the two homes who were in the follow-up age group were first admitted to care under the age of five. Of those interviewed, about half were also in *long-term* care by this age. Approximately one-fifth were long-stay admissions by the age of two and a further 29 per cent were so by the age of five (Table 6.2).

The early experiences of those who were over two before their admission to long-term care can be further subdivided according to the degree of disruption or disturbance in the parenting they received. Disrupted or disturbed parenting was rated if the child had previously been received into care for at least one month, or if there was evidence of abuse, neglect or serious parental marital discord. All sources of information were used for this purpose, including the King *et al*. original data, the Social Services case notes and the interviews. Separations due to short-term parental mental or physical ill-health but not involving admissions and care were not counted as disrupted parenting, nor were parental marital separations in the absence of clear evidence of associated persistent discord or poor parenting. The rating is therefore an assessment of the quality and stability of the parenting the children experienced. It will be appreciated that the stability of the non-disrupted' families is primarily in comparison with the

*Table 6.2    Age at admission to care and pattern of early experience*

| | |
|---|---|
| *Age at first admission to care* | % |
| Under 2 years | 39 |
| 2—4.11 years | 29 |
| 5—10.11 years | 32 |

(Data on the total 'white' sample from King *et al*. records: n=103)

| | |
|---|---|
| *Age at admission to long-term care* | % |
| Under 2 years | 22 |
| 2—4.11 years | 29 |
| 5—10.11 years | 49 |

(Data on the sample selected and interviewed: n=80)

| | |
|---|---|
| *Pattern of admission to long-term care* | % |
| Admitted under the age of two | 22 |
| Admitted age 2—4.11 years | |
|    From non-disrupted parenting | 13 |
|    From disrupted parenting | 16 |
| Admitted age 5—10.11 years | |
|    From non-disrupted parenting | 14 |
|    From disrupted parenting | 35 |

(Data on sample selected and interviewed)

remainder of the families who had children admitted. The fact that the parenting of all of them finally suffered long-term early breakdown indicates that the early childhood environments were in no cases entirely satisfactory.

As Table 6.2 shows, the majority of girls entering care over the age of two had had such disrupted parenting experiences, with the largest single category for the two homes being those entering on or after the age of five following such experiences. The importance of these early experiences for subsequent life-history and functioning will be considered in detail later.

**Children's memories of life in the homes**
The findings from the King *et al*. study outlined earlier showed that both of the homes were run on child-centred lines with considerable effort made to provide a comfortable and non-institutional environment for the children. The family-like atmosphere of the majority of cottages should have been enhanced from the children's point of view by the fact that the great majority had sibs in care with them, generally within the same cottage. Of those in the interview sample, only 8 per cent had no sibs in care with them.

Table 6.3    Recall of relationships when in the homes

| | Age 5—10.11 years | Age 11—15.11 years |
|---|---|---|
| *Relationships with sibs* | n=72 | n=58 |
| | % | % |
| Good | 21 | 29 |
| Neutral | 43 | 50 |
| Mixed | 10 | 5 |
| Poor | 26 | 16 |
| *Relationships with peers* | n=81 | n=66 |
| | % | % |
| Good | 6 | 30 |
| Neutral | 58 | 53 |
| Mixed | 4 | 8 |
| Poor | 32 | 9 |
| *Relationships with staff* | n=81 | n=67 |
| | % | % |
| Good | 15 | 25 |
| Neutral | 35 | 30 |
| Mixed | 16 | 16 |
| Poor | 34 | 28 |

The ns for the older age period fall because of discharges from the home.

The subjects' recall of their relationships in the homes are much more negative and less harmonious than these appeared to King *et al.* when the girls were children or adolescents (Table 6.3). Very few subjects recalled their relationships with unrelated peers or with staff in the early years as generally positive. Even relationships with sibs were not predominantly so. In general, peer relationships were seen as neutral or negative, with a small 'mixed' group who had clearly positive *and* clearly negative relationships. Relationships with staff tended to be even more negatively evaluated. Half the subjects recalled these as poor with some or the majority of staff as compared with 31 per cent who had some or predominantly positive relationships. Few remembered important attachments or saw the houseparents as being like real parents to them. Many of the subjects recalled their relationships when in the children's homes in a rather undifferentiated way in which neither adults nor other children were remembered as individuals. It was *not* that they generally experienced the regime as harsh, punitive or excessively restrictive (in that, most agreed with King *et al.*, 1971), but rather that their life lacked personal meaning or affection.

Relationships with staff in the early teens showed a similar pattern although more subjects report them as predominantly positive. There was a clear tendency for negative relationships with peers to become neutral or positive as the children got older although it was still only a minority of teenagers who had generally positive relationships with other children in care.

## Parental visiting

Data on parental visiting was seldom recorded in the Social Services notes and it is therefore necessary to rely on the subjects' own memories in assessing the frequency, quality and significance of parental contacts. However, agreement between sibs was very high on the frequency of visits by parents and we may therefore have some confidence in their reports (see Appendix D). There are some problems in quantifying contacts adequately because of the variable nature of much parental behaviour. It was not uncommon, for example, for a parent to visit monthly or more for a year or so following admission but for these visits to become less and less frequent as time went by. Equally, spasmodic parental visiting or weekends spent at home by the child might change to a regular pattern in the year prior to discharge. The children were divided into three groups according to the contact pattern. At the one extreme were those children who saw their parents fewer than four times a year over the whole of their in-care experience. On the other, there were those children who maintained at least monthly contacts. All those with contact patterns between these two extremes were placed in an intermediate category. This was the case even if the *sum* of their contacts produces a more than monthly average. The pattern for the regular contact group therefore involved regularity as well as frequency of visits by or to parents. In addition, the quality of the relationships with parents was assessed from the subjects' accounts. The parental contact patterns are given in Figure 6.1.

Only a third of girls had regular contact with one or both parents during their time in care up to the end of primary schooling. A further fifth had only sporadic contact, and the remainder had no parental contact of any consequence. Relationships with parents during these visits were generally remembered positively but without strong feelings of attachment. Thus none of the sporadically visited girls remembered these contacts as being clearly important to them and only 15 per cent of girls who were in regular contact did so.

Parental visiting bore an important relationship to the chances of the child's later return home and the quality of relationships she then experienced. It is apparent (Figure 6.2) that those children where one or both parents maintained regular contacts were much more likely to return home and that subsequent family relationships were more likely to be satisfactory. Conversely, although the numbers are small, a return home for those children for whom relationships with parents had been effectively severed was always associated with persistent discord between the child and the parents or within the family more generally.

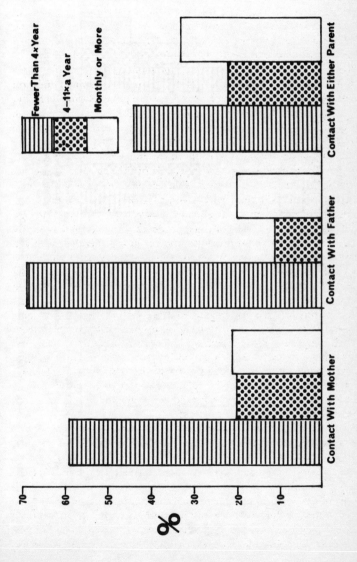

*Figure 6.1  Contacts with parents when in care*

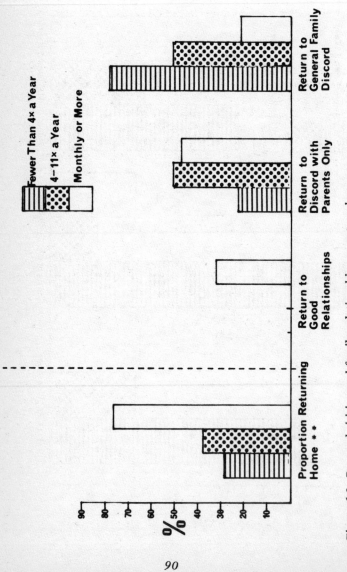

Figure 6.2 *Parental visiting and family relationships on return home*

## The childhoods of the comparison group

The comparison subjects were taken from a group who spent their childhoods in an Inner London area similar to those in which the parents of the in-care children also lived. However, unlike the control subjects in the retrospective study, the majority of the prospective sample lived in somewhat less deprived neighbourhoods. They were further distinguished from that sample in that admission to care during childhood was, by definition, a reason for exclusion. It should be expected therefore that their childhoods would be somewhat less disadvantaged than the retrospective study comparison group.

### Family circumstances

Despite these considerations there was a substantial amount of adversity of one sort or another in the childhoods of the comparison sample. Twenty-nine per cent spent their early years in dwellings shared with other households and, in all, nearly two-fifths were brought up in housing of poor quality (that is, lacking basic amenities such as bathroom, running hot water or inside toilet, being seriously overcrowded or suffering major structural defects). The social class distribution showed a predominance of skilled manual families but with 13 per cent of subjects coming from semi- or unskilled backgrounds. Nearly one-third of girls came from sibships of four or more.

*Table 6.4   The childhoods of the comparison sample*

|  | % |
|---|---|
| *Predominant type of housing* | |
| Family house | 44 |
| Purpose-built flat | 27 |
| Shared house | 29 |
| *Housing quality* | |
| Good | 5 |
| Satisfactory | 56 |
| Poor | 39 |
| *Social class* | |
| Professional/managerial | 5 |
| Clerical/skilled manual | 82 |
| Semi-/unskilled | 13 |
| *Sib group size* | |
| Only child | 12 |
| Family of two or three | 56 |
| Family of four or more | 31 |

*Family relationships and parental deviance*
High rates of family deviance and discord were also reported. Twenty per cent of subjects recalled their mothers as having psychiatric problems evidenced by overt distress resulting in visits to the family doctor, by hospital contacts or by drinking problems. Seven per cent of girls recalled such problems in their fathers, together with similar rates of criminality. In addition, 5 per cent recalled hard or harsh discipline exerted by their mothers and fathers. (The definitions for all these ratings are as in the retrospective study.) However, all of the comparison sample remained with their parents until after their eighteenth birthday.

No direct comparison with the retrospective study control group is possible because of the differences in sampling criteria. It will be recalled that in the first study an index of childhood family adversity was used that involved two or more adverse experiences including: hard or harsh discipline, parental marital discord or separations, parental psychiatric disorder and criminality and reception into care. By definition this last item does not occur in the prospective study comparison group. On this index, 26 per cent of the retrospective study contrast group had adverse childhoods. This compares with only 7 per cent for the control group in the prospective study. This confirms that the prospective study control group was somewhat less disadvantaged in childhood. This is not unexpected because of the wider geographical area from which this group was drawn.

**Summary**
This chapter has detailed the differences in childhood experiences for the ex-care and comparison samples. The data confirm that the ex-care sample came from a group of families with parents who were suffering a wide range of psychiatric handicap and deviance. The frequent and early admissions of the children to care show that these admissions were due to failure in parenting, however caused, rather than by problem behaviours in the children themselves.

The children's experiences in care were generally remembered in a negative or neutral way, especially with regard to relationships with staff. The data from King *et al.*'s original study of the homes show that these two institutions were generally well run, child-centred and caring. Despite this the subjects' memories of their time in care suggest that the nature of their institutional experience often deprived their lives of personal meaning or affection.

The control sample were from a group of predominantly stable, skilled, working-class families, but with a substantial minority having experienced maternal psychiatric problems, poor living conditions and a large family. They were similar to other general population groups from the same area of inner London (Rutter *et al.*, 1975b).

# 7 The prospective study: Outcome in adult life. Current circumstances and adjustment

In this chapter the findings concerning the adult adjustment of the ex-care and comparison subjects will be considered (Quinton *et al.*, 1984; Rutter and Quinton, 1984). The assessment of parenting behaviour and the parenting characteristics of the two samples will be presented separately in Chapters 8 and 9. Here the concern is with current living and work circumstances, and with more general aspects of current social functioning.

## Current circumstances

By the time of the follow-up, three-fifths of the ex-care women had had children compared with just over one third of the comparison sample (60 per cent v. 36 per cent). Four of the ex-care group were no longer parenting any of their children (for details see Chapter 9). Similar proportions of both samples were currently cohabiting (67 per cent v. 74 per cent) but a significantly higher proportion of the co-habiting ex-care group was unmarried (31 per cent v. 10 per cent).

The comparison sample were more likely to be living in single-family houses (37 per cent v. 54 per cent) and to be owner-occupiers (20 per cent v. 37 per cent) although these differences between the two groups on the type and tenure of housing were not statistically significant. A more accurate picture of their current living conditions can be obtained by considering their current housing problems and housing resources, using the index of housing problems used in the retrospective study. 'Poor' housing was rated if the women lacked or shared a bathroom, kitchen or lavatory, if a child shared a bed with sibs or a bedroom with its parents, or if the house had major structural defects. Ex-care women were almost twice as likely to have such problems (22 per cent v. 12 per cent) although only a minority were this badly housed and the difference fell short of statistical significance. When the definition was widened to include those with overcrowding or without a telephone or washing machine over two-fifths of the ex-care sample had such problems compared with about one-quarter of the comparison sample (44 per cent v. 24 per cent) again a difference below the 5 per cent level of significance. This lack of resources is reflected in the social class distribution of the ex-care group where over half (53 per cent) were either in semi- or unskilled manual families or were single people on social security, compared with 14 per cent in the comparison sample.

There were significant differences between the two groups in educational attainment, but not in the frequency of further qualifications. Fewer ex-care women had achieved 'O' level or CSE examination successes (7 per cent v. 35 per cent) and only 11 per cent had gone on to further training, in nearly all cases either in secretarial work or hairdressing. The comparison women were twice as likely to have further qualifications but the choice of occupations was the same, apart from one university degree. The importance of educational factors in adult psychosocial outcome is discussed in Chapter 10.

## Psychosocial adjustment

Individual measures of psychosocial adjustment showed marked differences between the two samples (Figure 7.1). Nearly one-third of the ex-care group had currently handicapping psychiatric disorders, compared with only 5 per cent of the comparison sample. The great majority of disorders in the ex-care group consisted of longstanding personality problems, whereas this was not true for any of the illnesses of the control women. The psychiatric assessments were based on well-tested and reliable interview methods. A rating of personality disorder was made if the subject described a longstanding history of problems in functioning going back to the early teens and which adversely affect interpersonal relationships or work history to a marked degree. However, such a diagnosis does *not* imply that the behaviours and problems rated were considered to be a permanent feature of the individual's functioning, impervious to change in the face of improved circumstances or relationships, but only that the individual had longstanding problems in functioning in many areas of life.

There were problems in making a rating of personality disorder for the ex-care sample since they had so frequently *experienced* unsatisfactory relationships in their teenage years. It was thus difficult to assess the contribution of their own functioning to such problems. For this reason, particular care was taken to make a rating of personality disorder only if there was clear evidence that the pattern of problems had persisted from the early teenage years over several relationships and in a number of different contexts. Case descriptions of subjects included in this group are given later in this chapter.

The differences between the samples in psychiatric problems were paralleled in other aspects of their lives. The *ex*-care women were five times as likely to have had broken cohabitations and, if currently cohabiting, over four times as likely to be experiencing discord in their current relationships. In all, over two-fifths were rated as having substantial and persisting problems in relationships with men as against only 2 per cent of the control subjects.

On the other hand, it should be emphasised that these problems

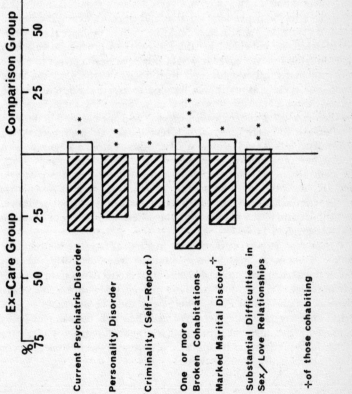

Figure 7.1  Current psychosocial adjustment

95

apply to only a minority of the *ex*-care women. Although they were more likely to have psychiatric or interpersonal problems than the comparison group, over two-thirds were free of major difficulties of this sort.

### Overall psychosocial outcome

The separate aspects of current circumstances and psychosocial adjustment described above provide a useful comparison between the samples on a number of dimensions. On the other hand, these variables differ greatly in the extent to which they indicate problems in individual functioning. Some, such as personality disorder, are by definition measures of pervasive difficulties. Others, such as broken marriages or cohabitations, may reflect bad luck, previously poorer functioning or problems in the partner. Others, such as bad housing or fewer resources, give no clues on their own as to the person's current adjustment.

Because a variety of difficulties in work or relationships may occur in the absence of psychiatric or personality problems a more inclusive overall rating of psychosocial functioning was needed. For such a rating some combination of the outcome variables was required. Since this was to be a major dependent variable and since no external criterion existed, no statistical approaches could be used to evaluate the correlations between the individual variables in order to produce a weighting of individual items. Moreover it would not have been correct to create a series of statistical weights and then to apply these to the same sample. For these reasons it was decided to create *a priori* an overall psychosocial outcome measure and then to derive the subjects' scores from their ratings on the individual items. The principle used in deriving the index was to ensure that the subjects at one extreme represented a problem-free group and those at the other extreme a group with pervasive current problems. In between were two further groups – one with a history of difficulties but no known problems in the past two years, and the other with some current problems such as psychiatric disorder, criminality or marital difficulties, but of insufficient pervasiveness for inclusion in the poor group. The criterion for the four outcome groups are given in Table 7.1.

As would be expected, there were marked differences between the samples on the overall psychosocial outcome measures: 30 per cent of the ex-care women but none of the control group had a poor psychosocial outcome. On the other hand, 40 per cent of ex-care women were currently without difficulties. There was thus considerable heterogeneity in outcome, with the differences between the samples being explained by the differences on good and poor outcomes. The groups did not differ significantly on the proportions with some current problems or a history of problems only.

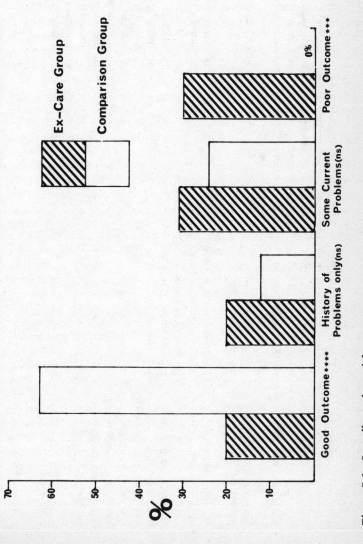

*Figure 7.2  Overall psychosocial outcome*

*Table 7.1  Criteria for overall psychosocial outcome classification*

| 1. Good outcome | 2. Past problems only | 3. Some current problems | 4. Poor functioning |
|---|---|---|---|
| No broken cohabitations. | No current psychiatric, criminal, drink, drug or work problems in the past two years but previous history of one or more. | Some current problems, i.e. any items in group 4 currently not sufficiently to rate in that group. | Current *handicapping* personality disorder and/or two or more problems in sex/love relationships. |
| No marital discord. | | | *and/or* four or more of the following: |
| No psychiatric history or current problems. | | | (a) discordant marriage. |
| No criminal history or current criminality. | Past problems in sex/love relationships must have given way to stable relationships, otherwise rate (3). | | (b) broken cohabitations. |
| | | | (c) two or more problems in social relationships (see 1). |
| No problems in social relationships, i.e. has confiding relationships, is trusting of others, has regular contacts with friends (weekly on average). | | | (d) living in hostel, hospital, or sheltered accommodation. |
| | | | (e) current psychiatric, drink or drug problems. |
| | | | (f) two or more adverse work items (see 1). |
| | | | (g) current criminality or criminal history. |

No work problems,
i.e. none of:

(a) six or more jobs in
past four years.

(b) ever fired since age 18.

(c) walked out of three or
more jobs since 18.

(d) persistent friction
with workmates.

* *Sex/love items*

(1) Two or more terminated cohabitations.
(2) Persistent discord in two or more cohabitations.
(3) Violence in two or more relationships.
(4) Two or more deviant cohabitees.
(5) Persistent problems in making or sustaining
love relationships.

99

## Drinking problems

It is important to consider the contribution of alcoholism or drinking problems to the poorer outcomes for the ex-care women. Overall 22 per cent of this group compared with 2 per cent of the comparison women had a history of drinking difficulties. A criterion-based assessment of alcoholism was not made but all of these instances involved a period of a year or longer when the women had bouts of heavy drinking that caused them difficulties or concern — for example, eight or more drinks every night, drinking associated with aggression or loss of work, or drinking associated with regular abuse of other substances. In 56 per cent of these cases the problems had clearly been present within the past two years, and in 39 per cent they formed part of the woman's current difficulties. As would be expected, a history of drinking problems strongly related to current psychosocial functioning. Thus 45 per cent of those ex-care women with personality disorders had had drinking difficulties as against 5 per cent of those without personality problems. However, 62 per cent of those with poor overall psychosocial functioning did *not* report any drinking problems. Thus there was a clear excess of poor outcomes amongst the ex-care women even when drinking problems were taken into account. On the other hand, drinking problems were very strongly related to parenting difficulties and to the pattern of parenting breakdown. Their contribution to these outcomes is discussed in Chapter 9.

## Case examples of outcome groups

A clearer understanding of the meaning of these differences in outcome can be gained through case examples of the outcome groups. Since the differences between the samples were most marked with respect to poor outcome, several examples of this rating are given. All examples were chosen randomly from amongst those in each group. Names and other identifying information have been changed for reasons of confidentiality.

## Good outcome group

*Carol — ex-care*  Carol, her husband and three children lived in a rented cottage in the country. They had met when she was 16 and married when he was studying for a degree. She showed no psychiatric symptoms and had a score of just 1 on the malaise inventory (abnormal functioning being shown by a score of 7 or more). She was an attractive woman in both her physical appearance and personality, and a very capable manager in the home. The marriage was very happy. The couple rarely quarrelled and more minor irritability and arguments were settled by discussion. Carol talked very warmly of her husband. They shared common friends and leisure activities. The interviewer summed her up as a happy well-adjusted mother and wife.

*Pat — ex-care*   Pat had been married seven years and lived with her husband and two pre-school age children on a new private housing estate in a small town in the north of England. Her husband was a scaffolder. She was a neat, quiet and friendly person. She had met her husband when she was living in a hostel following discharge from care and when he was a seaman. They lived together for a while before their marriage. Pat had no psychiatric problems and no worries except the usual ones over bills or the children's health. There was some irritability between them, but this was of very short duration. They had had no major rows since the early years of their marriage. The couple had less time together now because she was working part-time in a local factory. She considered their marriage to be 'fairly ordinary, a bit dull I suppose', but it was rated as happy and supportive. Pat had good confiding relationships with her husband and friends, and the couple had two other couples with whom they exchanged regular visits. The interviewer summed her up as a remarkably well-adjusted person (given her childhood) with realistic views of the future and of what she might expect from life.

*Caroline — comparison subject*   Caroline, her husband and two young children lived in a new two-bedroomed low-rise council flat in Inner London. Her husband was a sales engineer and Caroline had not had outside work since her youngest child was born. Caroline was a calm person with a generally sunny disposition who very much enjoyed her marriage and her family. The only argument with her husband that she could recall occurred a year previously over a television programme. Roles within the family were divided along traditional lines and she was quite happy with this. Although the couple had few leisure activities, they chatted together frequently and the marriage was warm and caring.

*Mary — ex-care*   Mary was interviewed at the home of her former housemother who had subsequently become her foster-parent when she retired from the children's home. At the time of interview Mary was on leave from the air force. She was a single woman working in a skilled technical grade and living in barracks. She had joined the air force almost immediately upon leaving care, because she thought she would like the outdoor life. She felt that her experience in the forces had been very important to her and had helped her to learn both that she had to get on with people and that she had to learn to stick by regulations and agreements. She very much enjoyed her present life which provided her both with a career and a social circle. She had a longstanding special friend in whom she felt she could confide, and whom she had got to know since joining the forces. She also had a regular crowd with whom she went around. This crowd was very important because it was a source of companionship, as well as a group amongst whom she could relax. She often went to pubs and discos with them, as well as going on boat trips and participating in other activities. Some of her friends had taken drugs regularly, but Mary herself had never done so. She had, however, in her teenage years been charged five times for drinking under age. Her social circle had included members of the opposite sex since she was about 17. She has never lived with a man, but her relationships with them seemed quite satisfactory and normal for her age. She did not show any psychiatric symptoms and scored very low on the malaise invento₁y — a self-rating questionnaire that indicates the probability of the presence of psychiatric disorder (Rutter *et al.*, 1970).

Mary impressed the interviewer as a very normal, well-adjusted intelligent young woman. She appeared to be someone who operated well within a structured environment and who therefore had had no major difficulties either in the children's home or subsequently in the air force. She made friends easily, and has lots of acquaintances with whom she was able to share interests. At the time of interview she had no desire to marry or settle down and aimed to enjoy her freedom for a little longer.

### Intermediate outcome group: History of difficulties but no problems in the last two years

No detailed examples of this group are provided since in current circumstances and functioning they were similar to the good outcome group. For example, one ex-care woman had a brief depressive episode following a temporary marital separation; another had had a more serious marital breakdown after which she had left her children with her first spouse for six months because she could not cope emotionally. She was now happily living with a new spouse in new accommodation and caring for her children well with no current problems. One young mother in the comparison sample had had psychiatric treatment for school refusal in her secondary school years, but was now happily married and running her own small business. A further example is of an ex-care woman living with her second husband in a poor prefabricated house. She has three children and was expecting another, the first by her second marriage. The first marriage had foundered on her husband's criminality and violence, which precipitated temporary psychiatric problems. She had had no significant psychiatric symptoms in the previous three years, since meeting her present husband. She felt her life had completely changed. Her only problem now seemed to be appreciating that she was quite so happy.

### Intermediate outcome group: Some current problems

*Janet — ex-care*  Janet was described as a bright, witty and sharp young woman. She lived with her husband in a 'Coronation Street'-like area in a West Midlands town. Her husband was a carpenter. They had one child aged four. Janet had changed a great deal in the past few years. As a teenager she had been heavily involved in shoplifting and drugs and was known as a leader of a gang that was involved in a lot of fighting. She took drug overdoses on several occasions. All of this behaviour had diminished since the birth of her son and there were few signs of psychiatric problems at the time of interview. However, she was still prone to aggression and this affected her marriage and her parenting. She felt that her husband was a plodder and not helpful around the house, but she was resigned to her lot. She recently had a bad patch of irritability and misery when she thought she was pregnant. She was annoyed that her husband left her on her own so often and she had started having frequent rows with him. Their social life has become increasingly separate and she confided more in her friends than in him. Janet felt she had changed him as much as she was going to be able to. She was placed in this outcome group predominantly because of her current marital difficulties. Note that her problems were insufficient for a rating of personality disorder despite her very deviant teenage history.

*Jennifer — comparison subject* Jennifer, her husband and six-month old baby lived in their own house in the Medway towns. She was described as attractive but quiet and reserved and socially isolated. Her husband was a butcher for a local chain store. Her isolation and lack of assertiveness were features of her teenage years at which time she had no peer group and did not keep up with her friends. Her husband, who was ten years older than she was, had been her only boyfriend. Over the three months prior to the interview she had been tearful, felt that life was not worth living, and had passing suicidal thoughts. She was irritable with her husband and son several times a week. Jennifer had no regular friends and no confidants apart from her husband. She admitted to problems in mixing socially. Overall she was mildly depressed but not sufficiently so for a rating of handicapping psychiatric problems. Apart from her irritability, her marriage was happy but humdrum with no shared interests or activities. Jennifer was placed in the intermediate outcome group on the grounds of her social isolation and her current mild depressive symptoms.

*Debra — ex-care* Debra was in care from about the age of 2 to 18½ years. On her discharge from care she moved to Oxford with a man whom she had met in her final residential placement. They had lived in a council house there and he worked for the Social Services Department. They were subsequently transferred back to London when he took a job in an Assessment Centre and they lived together for the next four years. She had rather a chequered employment history, often leaving jobs after a few months because she got fed up with them.

However, when she had found employment that she enjoyed — for example, doing clerical work for the local council — she had stuck with it for a year and a half. At follow-up she was working for a charitable institution and enjoying the work. In her teenage years she had no stable and regular friends. In the end her relationship with her co-habitee broke up, and at the time of the interview she was living on her own.

Psychiatrically she had no clear disorder, but there were a number of adverse features. She had no definite friends although she claimed a fair amount of superficial contact. She was now going out with a man much older than herself whom she distrusted. She felt he lied to her and was not frank about their future. She had no confidants, except amongst her sibs, and even they seem to feel that she was somewhat unsociable. She claimed that she could talk to friends at work, but preferred to keep most things to herself. He major problem at the moment, although she would not admit as such, was heavy drinking. She used to drink every night — both beer and spirits — and the interviewer noted that she could not wait to get out to the pub at the end of the interview.

It seemed that Debra had been very upset at the break in her relationship with her cohabitee and had not recovered from it well. On the positive side, she still enjoyed getting involved with projects involving helping other people. She was very cooperative at interview, but somewhat detached in her style of response.

The assessment of Debra was that she still had a number of significant problems relating to her in-care experiences. She did not, however, have sufficient difficulties to put her into the poor outcome group. It seemed that she was at a point at which either a little ill-luck or a little good luck could push her rather more firmly towards poor or good psychosocial functioning.

It is apparent from the first two examples within this section that the 'some problems' outcome group was comprised of generally satisfactorily functioning young people who had some features in their current lives that precluded them from inclusion in the strictly defined good group. The third example defines the lower limit of the category. On the whole, a substantial gap exists between this group and the following examples of women with a poor outcome.

## Poor outcome group

*Lorna — ex-care*  Lorna was interviewed in a Battered Wives Refuge in Reading having left her husband because of his repeated violence and bizarre behaviour. Her first child was by a man with whom she had never cohabited and her youngest two were by her husband. All three children had just returned from foster care. Lorna had worked in a laundry following her discharge from care at the age of 18. She had lived in some dozen hostels in London before moving to the present area when she was 22. Her eldest son was fostered during this time. She started to live with her husband 'because it was somewhere to live permanently and I wanted Jason back'. Since then she had left her husband three times but always returned. She had had 12 jobs in the past six years none of which had been satisfactory or happy experiences. In the previous few months she had had psychiatric problems for which she had received tablets from her doctor. She had panic attacks and cold sweats daily. These still occurred about once a week. On the other hand, she was not a great worrier. She did not cry and was not suicidal. Lorna was rated as having current psychiatric difficulties, probably related to her recent marital circumstances, but not as having a personality disorder. She felt able to confide in people in the refuge but had no regular confidants. Her general sociability and attitude to friendships were positive.

*Eileen — ex-care*   Eileen had one son of four and a young child of 17 months. She lived in a run-down block of flats in south London. She had been separated from her husband for two years. The flat showed signs of extreme poverty with polystyrene tiles falling off the ceiling and the purple paintwork that often seems to afflict the houses of the poor. During the interview her social worker arrived to help her organise a visit to the launderette. Eileen was in her dressing-gown throughout two interviews. During her teens she had had two unsuccessful foster placements, was placed in a hostel and then in bed and breakfast lodgings and, subsequently moved on to squatting. It was that time that she first became pregnant. Her teenage work history was erratic and she was fined once for bad timekeeping. She had not worked since having the children (having been fired again when she was pregnant). She always found it hard to hold jobs because she got fed up with them quickly. She had been sacked 3 or 4 times. In her teens she was in a deviant gang of regular drug-takers who terrorised old women. When she finally began cohabiting there was no reason for it; it was just 'all the rage at the time'.

Eileen rated herself well above the deviancy cut-off on the malaise inventory. During her second pregnancy she had regularly turned to drink, so that in the mornings she was drunk and neglected the baby. At that time she had psychiatric treatment. Eileen relied heavily on her social worker for help. She had a friend in the flats but was generally suspicious of people and found it hard to pick the right friends. Although, at the time of interview, she said she had no current worries or anxieties and was not depressed, clearly she relied heavily on others to enable her to cope with daily life. Eileen was rated as having a personality disorder.

*Angie — ex-care*   It took a great deal of time to catch up with Angie, and when finally traced it was through the help of her cooperative social worker. She was at that time living in a flat in north London with her two-week old baby and the putative father of the child. They had moved back into this flat as squatters, having been evicted from it by the council for non-payment of rent some months before. Angie had another child who was permanently in care. Her current state was a very sorry one. She was heavily involved in drug abuse, taking, on her own account, large amounts of valium and also what she called 'fit' pills (i.e. presumably for epilepsy). Her speech during interview was often rather slurred and her ability to keep on one train of thought or topic for any length of time was impaired. When the interviewer arrived for the first interview she was packing her cases with the intention of leaving. Her cohabitee with whom she had been living for about 15 months had given her a 'working over' the night before, and she had a black eye and broken lip. She claimed that this was occasioned by her going out for a little drink with some friends; her spouse's account was that he got angry because she was drunk and was not looking after the baby. This brought about a fight between her spouse and her spouse's brother who was at the time living with them. She was setting off, she claimed, because her spouse was threatening to take the baby with him and to return to Ireland.

Angie had already been showing very disturbed behaviour when she returned from care to live with her mother at about the age of 14. Her brothers tried to keep her in order by hitting her, but they themselves were often under the influence of drugs and they fairly soon turned her onto this track also. Her teenage peers were nearly all deviant boys and there is a strong suggestion that Angie engaged in promiscuous sexual relationships with them. This behaviour was one reason for her brothers beating her up. Her first pregnancy was at the age of 16, but she miscarried. She married another man shortly after this, but really never lived with him because he was in prison for most of the time. During her teens she was involved in much street violence. She claimed to have had several pregnancies before finally giving birth to her first child at 19. Her history from then on was a succession of bed and breakfast and squatting accommodation. This involved several separate cohabiting relationships. Angie had certainly been accused, both by her family and by officialdom, of prostitution and this seemed likely to be the case. During the year prior to interview she had been in the local hospital for overdoses on several occasions, although it was not clear how many of these were deliberate and how many just the result of her drug-taking activities. Angie was considered to have current major personality problems and this automatically put her in the poor outcome group. She was socially isolated, apart from a large circle of occasional drinking and drug-taking acquaintances. She said she had friends, but in the next breath would describe them as people with big mouths to whom she would not tell any secrets. She was suspicious also of her family. She had received some baby clothes from the lady upstairs but did not know this lady's name. Angie had one friend for whom she babysat regularly and it seemed highly likely that this was to allow that friend to engage in prostitution also.

The interviewer's comment was that Angie was clearly one of the most disturbed and unsuccessful outcomes of all the ex-care women, both in terms of her current psychiatric state, her general functioning, her social relationships and her parenting. Because of her heavy involvement in drug-taking and her association with a similarly deviant and disturbed crowd, her chance of making any significant improvement in the future seemed very low, and it was felt that her current new baby would be in care within a reasonably short time.

These examples of outcome grouping illustrate the range of variation in outcome, especially in the ex-care subjects. They also provide some descriptions of the behaviours classified as personality disorders. More generally the case histories emphasise the current and context-related nature of judgements concerning outcome. Thus Lorna, although having clear problems that placed her in the poor outcome group, appeared to be the victim of a series of unhappy circumstances. It was difficult to assess her own contribution to these problems, but pervasive personality features did not seem to be implicated. These outcome groupings clearly represent one point in time assessments, even where enduring features such as personality disorders are concerned. They represent the 'outcome' at the age at which the subjects were seen, not a judgement of the permanent effects of their earlier experiences.

## Official criminality

The final set of outcome data to be presented in this chapter concerns official criminality as recorded by the Criminal Records Office and supplied by the Home Office. These data have been left until last because they are available on the complete samples of women, not just on those interviewed. In a few cases the returns indicated whether the subjects had a record but not the date or nature of their offences. These data are included in the tables where appropriate. The data also allowed a division of criminal activity into juvenile and adult crime. Records were available for all ex-care and comparison women.

These data confirm the markedly higher rates of criminality reported by the ex-care subjects themselves (Table 7.2). Over one quarter of the women had criminal records; in roughly equal proportions this involved juvenile crime only, adult crime and crime in both age periods. Only one control woman had had any involvement with the courts, and that at the age of 19.

The great majority of offences for women involved stealing of one sort or another. The next largest group of offences involved disorderly behaviour, causing damage or drunkenness, followed by assaults (often on the police).

Table 7.2    *Official criminality*

|  | Ex-care group (N=93) | Comparison group (N=51) |
|---|---|---|
|  | % | % |
| Has a criminal record | 27 | 2 *** |
| *Of those with a record* | (N=25) | (N=1) |
| Juvenile crime only | 36 | 0 |
| Adult crime only | 36 | 100 |
| Both | 28 | 0 |
| One court appearance only | 48 | 0 |
| More than one appearance | 52 | 100 |
| *Types of offence* (number of offences) |  |  |
| Assault | 11 | 0 |
| Robbery | 2 | 0 |
| Burglary | 1 | 0 |
| Auto crime | 0 | 0 |
| All other theft or dishonesty | 74 | 2 |
| Sexual offences | 10 | 0 |
| Disorder/criminal damage/drunkenness | 23 | 0 |
| Offensive weapon | 7 | 0 |
| Drug offences | 5 | 0 |
| Other offences | 7 | 1 |
| *Total* | 140 | 3 |

**Summary**
This chapter has shown the significantly poorer outcome for the ex-care women both as regards their current social functioning and their current environmental and family circumstances. However, the data also showed the considerable heterogeneity in outcome with the *majority* of ex-care subjects now functioning satisfactorily.

# 8 The assessment of parenting by direct home observation

## LINDA DOWDNEY, DAVID SKUSE, DAVID QUINTON AND MICHAEL RUTTER

In the prospective study the interview measurement of parenting was supplemented by direct home observations of mother–child interactions. Observational assessments were used for both methodological and theoretical reasons. Methodologically, it was desirable to have a check on the quality and validity of the interview reports for, although interviews have considerable advantages in economy and coverage, there are limits to the data that can reliably be collected by them. These limits derive from the fact that parental reports are necessarily affected by the parents' perceptions of the child and by their ability to report interactions accurately, especially where this concerns details of the sequencing of events. Biases may also arise when, as in this case, the interviewers cannot be kept blind to the childhood experiences of the mothers.

But there were additional reasons for using the two approaches beyond a check on biases. When these studies began there was no evidence showing whether effects of severe early adversities might appear in gross distortions of parenting or only in more subtle aspects of behaviour. There was therefore, a need to have both a broad assessment of parenting as it normally occurred from day to day, and also a detailed evaluation of mother–child interactions when the mother was freed from competing daily stresses or parenting demands. Interview measures were appropriate for the first of these assessments and direct home observations for the second.

The decision to observe in the children's own homes was made because behaviour is influenced by the social and physical setting in which it takes place. For example, mother–child interactions in the laboratory differ significantly from those in the home (Moustakis *et al.*, 1956). In this study it was important to obtain as naturalistic a series of observations as possible. Secondly, it was found during piloting that cooperation was significantly better when the investigator was prepared to go to the family than when the family had to travel to a laboratory.

### Selection of the observed sample
The decision to include an observational assessment had consequences for the choice of the age group of children on whom to assess parenting. Direct home observations become more problematic the older children become. For this reason we could not take the age range used

in the retrospective investigation. There were, moreover, good reasons for moving to a younger age group for the observational study, apart from ease of measurement. The age group of 2–3½ was chosen: first, because this was the modal age of children born to mothers in the sample; secondly, it covers a phase of development where children normally become more oppositional and negative, thus presenting control issues to all parents; thirdly, since early social communication was an important focus of interest, it was necessary to choose an age group in which the development of speech was rapid and when the input from the parent was particularly important; and finally, two year olds are remarkably unselfconscious in the presence of an observer (Dunn and Kendrick, 1982). Parents find it hard to resist the powerful influence of a child of this age who persists with normal routine and behaviour despite there being a stranger in the house. It therefore seemed unlikely that routine patterns of interaction between parents and children in this age group would be seriously biased by the presence of an observer.

## Observational measures: Dimensions of parenting

The retrospective study showed that differences in parenting between the mothers with children in care and the comparison sample were particularly marked in areas relating to the child's emotional security. Therefore, the observational scheme focused particularly on this aspect of parenting, rather than on parental behaviour that might foster cognitive development. The features of parenting measured included parental responsivity, disciplinary control, responses to distress, and the quality and affective tone of social communication. The measures of *maternal responsiveness* covered the mother's responses to child behaviours such as requests for help, signs of distress and difficult or disruptive acts; whether she was able to anticipate problematic behaviour; able quickly to allay distress or anxieties and able to deal with her child's approaches in a flexible and imaginative way. The ways in which parents attempt to *control* their toddlers' behaviour are important in developing the child's sense of autonomy and in increasing his self-control. The style and effectiveness of control is also important because inefficient parental handling can have implications for the parent's relationship with the child more generally. For example, this can arise through the development of cycles of coercive behaviour which may make it more likely that disruption will continue (Patterson, 1982). Alternatively, with very young children parents' backing away from children's difficult behaviour may perpetuate the difficulties (Maccoby and Jacklin, 1974). The ways in which mothers handle *distress* is another indicator of parenting capacities because the effective handling of a distressed child calls upon the emotional resources of the parent. She needs to be able not only to respond to distress in a calm and soothing way but also, through promoting a rapid diminution of the child's behaviour, to reduce the probability of her own irritation.

It is apparent that the quality of parenting with respect to responsitivity, control and reactions to distress must be assessed not just through what the parent does with or to the child, but also through what she and the child say to each other during cooperative or confrontational interactions. Attention was therefore paid to the quality of *social communication*, with particular emphasis on the extent to which mothers used conversational interchanges to extend the child's understanding at a conceptual and at a concrete level, and also to show pleasure, interest and approval in the child's activities. The measurement of *expressed affect* was necessary first because it is clear that the meaning of utterances frequently depends on the accompanying tone of voice, and secondly because the mother–child relationship becomes apparent not just in what is said but in how it is expressed.

## Procedure

When the interviewing part of the study was completed, the interviewer asked the mother whether she would help some colleagues in a study of the behaviour of normal toddlers at home. If the mother agreed she was visited by one of the observational team who explained the study in more detail, stressing that she would not be able to talk to the mother or child during the observation sessions. They fixed a time when the mother could be at home on her own with the selected child and, if appropriate, the observer arranged payment for the minding of other children. These arrangements were necessary because the presence of others complicates the recording of the mother–child interactions and may make the measures between mothers non-comparable. During the observational sessions mothers were asked to go on with their everyday activities in the usual way and not to do anything, such as playing with the child, that they would not normally be doing at that time. Observations were made for a period of two hours on each of two separate days.

The intention in conducting direct home observations was to obtain as representative a sample of day-to-day mother–child interaction as possible and therefore mothers were not given identical tasks to do with the children. However, a degree of standardisation was desirable to provide some directly comparable measures between the mothers. A period of joint-play at the end of each session was used for this purpose. Play provides the opportunity to look at maternal sensitivity, responsivity and warmth in a non-stressful situation, and allows an assessment of the way a mother uses the opportunity for positive interaction with her child. On the first occasion the child was given a toy cash register to play with, half an hour before the end of the session. The mother was not asked to help the child but her response was noted. The toy was such that the mother's help was necessary to allow the child to use all the toy's possibilities. On the second occasion the child was given as a present a simple picture story book without words a quarter of an hour before the end of the session. On this occasion the mother was asked to look at the book with her child. The story was easy to understand and mothers could take the opportunity either to give a perfunctory rendition of it or to elaborate the simple fiction in imaginative ways. This play session had the advantage of finishing the observational study on a positive note. The overall structure of the observational study is given in Figure 8.1. The methodology of the sequential and time-sampling periods is outlined in the next section. A more detailed description can be found in Dowdney *et al.* (1984) and Mrazek *et al.* (1983).

### Principles of the recording scheme

It has been argued that one advantage of direct observations is that they avoid the problem inherent in other methodologies of making assumptions concerning the meaning of behaviour (Blurton-Jones, 1972). In practice, however, the recording of human activity necessarily involves some level of abstraction and some judgement as to meaning or intention. For example, the conclusion that a mother is 'affectionate' to her child is based on behaviours that are taken to indicate this characteristic. On the other hand, observations make it possible to tie these more abstract categories to specific and distinguishable events. Thus, a concept such as 'warmth' can be defined in terms of particular observable parental behaviours. For example, a mother might kiss her child or stroke her hair, and these acts will be classified as affectionate behaviour and recorded as 'mother affectionate touch'. This linking of particular behaviours to more overarching dimensions of parenting is necessary in order to reduce a mass of information to manageable proportions and to provide measures of theoretical relevance to the issues under investigation (Lytton, 1971).

### Types of measure

In recording mother–child interactions we were concerned not only with the *frequency* with which particular kinds of interaction occurred but also in certain instances – such as disciplinary episodes – with the *sequence* of alternating behaviours by the parent and child. Frequency measures are necessary to show how often particular events such as a child's approach to its mother or a disobedient act occur. But on their own such counts are of limited interest. More revealing are the sequences of interaction that follow upon such happenings. Here we are concerned not simply with what parents and children do but what kind of action is followed by what reaction, how long the sequences go on and how they terminate. This is particularly important in understanding the style and effectiveness of disciplinary control, the nature of the mother's response to distress and the sensitivity with which she deals with her child's approaches.

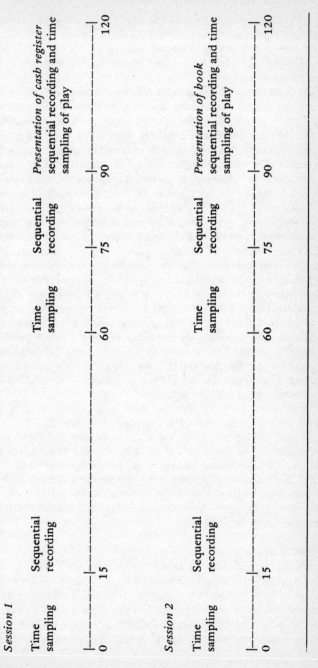

*Figure 8.1 The structure of the observation sessions*

*Sequential recording* Much research into the sequential nature of parent–child interactions records the behaviour of the dyad over a given period of time and analyses the temporal relationships between the behaviours using sophisticated statistical procedures. One difficulty with this method is the problem of picking out from the ongoing stream of behaviour those sequences of especial significance to the issues under investigation.

An alternative approach was developed for this study. We decided in advance that we were particularly interested in three different kinds of sequence: (a) episodes involving discipline or control; (b) situations where the child showed distress; and (c) times when the child attempted to gain the mother's attention or to start an interaction. For each of the sequences there was a specification of the initiating or 'key' event, following which the observer recorded the alternating mother–child behaviours. For example, in the area of control, sequential recording began if the child showed opposition to or non-compliance with a maternal instruction. Pre-specified outcomes determined the termination of sequential recording. In the case of control episodes, recording continued until either the child complied or the mother ceased to attempt to exert her authority. In responsivity sequences recording was terminated if the child was successful in engaging the mother's attention. This was defined as having occurred if by the sixth element in the sequence the pair was involved in joint conversation or play. *Every* sequence following a key event was recorded and time-interval sampling abandoned whilst the sequence was being noted. Single or multi-element maternal and child behaviours were recorded in a turn-taking fashion without concern for the precise duration of each behavioural event. The duration of each sequence was determined later from the audiotape of the interaction.

In the great majority of cases the codes used to summarise mother and child behaviours avoided using categories that described the interaction itself. For example, if the child hit the mother and she smacked him in return the mother's behaviour was recorded as a hit, not as a 'retaliation'. However, some 'interactional' categories were used where these did not involve judgement as to the person's intention. These codes were used predominantly for joint activities such as play or conversation: principally because sequential subdivision of these episodes is virtually impossible.

### Social communication

A continuous record was made of the nature and duration of all periods of joint play, joint activities (such as housework) and of conversations. For non-verbal interactions this record was made during the observation using predetermined categories. In addition a detailed analysis of verbal interactions was made from a transcript of the middle hour of each observational session. The method of coding was oriented towards the social nature of communications with categories ranging from dismissive or unhelpful remarks ('that's not a dog'), through minimal acknowledgements ('oh', 'yes', 'mmm') and so on up to elaborating comments. *Elaborations* encompassed remarks that widened the scope of conversation by introducing new ideas or information such as colour, or number, or the relative properties of objects ('that's hotter than that, isn't it?'). Included in this category were comments that linked the child's current activity to some feature of the outside world.

*Reliability and validity*
The inter-rater reliability of all the measures used was tested and found to be high with respect both to the individual elements and to the sequential codings (Dowdney *et al.*, 1984). However, ultimately the issue of validity is more important than that of reliability. In particular, it is necessary to ask whether the behaviour observed during the observational sessions is representative or characteristic of the pattern of mother–child interaction at other times; how far the measures provide an adequate differentiation of the families; and the extent to which they relate to or predict other aspects of family functioning.

The first issue is whether the observation sessions tapped the parental behaviours that are relevant to measures of the quality of parenting. This was approached by comparing an overall outcome measure from the interview data (see Chapter 9) with an overall judgement made by the observers (Table 8.1).

Table 8.1  Agreement between global ratings of parenting by interviewers and observers

|  |  | Observers' ratings | | |
|---|---|---|---|---|
|  |  | Good | Intermediate | Poor |
|  | Good | 9 | 4 | 1 |
| *Interviewers'* | Intermediate | 1 | 15 | 2 |
| *ratings* | Poor | 1 | 3 | 8 |

$$\chi^2 = 30.99 \quad 4\text{df} \quad p < 0.001$$

Two points emerge from this comparison. First, mothers varied greatly in their style of interaction and, in most cases, observers had no difficulty in making an overall rating of parenting. Secondly, there was a generally high level of agreement between the two measures. We may conclude that four hours of home observation *does* tap important dimensions of parenting. Of course, perfect agreement between these two methods of assessment is not to be expected. In the first place the interview is based on a much wider sample of parental behaviour including many features — such as relationships with sibs, or problems with bed-time — that could not have occurred during the observational period. Secondly, the interview assessed parenting under the ordinary conditions of family life, whereas the observations were designed to assess parenting under circumstances relatively free of competing pressures. Nevertheless, it is important for the assessment of validity that there should be substantial overlap between them.

The next issue is whether the observers' overall 'gut' judgements were reflected in the quantitative molecular measures of mother–child interactions. Further analysis showed this to be the case (Dowdney *et al.*, 1985a). The overall judgements of poor parenting were strongly associated with much more child distress, with much more oppositional behaviour, and with more smacking and threatening behaviour by the mother. It is, of course, important to ask whether these differences simply show that some children are more difficult to parent than others, rather than reflect the quality of parenting. That this is not the case is clear from the more detailed analysis of the parenting assessments in the next chapter. At this point we may conclude that the observational measures of parenting were both reliable and effective for the purposes for which they were designed.

# 9 Parenting outcome and parenting behaviour

LINDA DOWDNEY, DAVID SKUSE,
DAVID QUINTON AND MICHAEL RUTTER

The parenting history and the current parenting behaviour of the two prospective samples as assessed by both the interview and the observational measures can now be presented in detail. As discussed in the previous chapter, these two evaluations served different purposes. The interview data were concerned with both the history of the women's pregnancy and parenting experiences and with an account of their current parenting behaviour taking into consideration a wide variety of contexts. The observational data were concerned with a detailed direct assessment of the mother's parenting behaviour when she was parenting just one child, without other pressures or distractions. In both cases it is important to note that the phrase 'parenting outcome' refers to parenting history and behaviour at only one point in time. It in no way carries the implication that any difficulties that are reported or observed are a permanent feature of the mother's behaviour.

The first question that needs to be asked is whether the patterns of associations with childhood adversity seen in the retrospective data were confirmed by the prospective study. Did parenting breakdown occur and was it confined to the ex-care group? Did these young mothers show more problems in the current parenting of their children? Were moderate parenting problems a common feature of the experiences of many young mothers, regardless of childhood background? Beyond this, however, the prospective study allowed an examination of a number of key questions that could not be answered by the retrospective study. In particular, what was the *strength* of any associations across the generations? That is, how many young women who had markedly deficient early parenting experiences turned out to have parenting problems themselves? Were there particular observable patterns in the details of their current parenting that distinguished them from mothers with a normal family upbringing? And finally, if continuities did occur, what are the processes mediating them. Did they arise from the persistence of social disadvantage, or were they explained by the impacts of early adversities on personality development?

## Parenting history

It is clear that there were marked differences in the parenting histories of the two groups (Table 9.1). Nearly twice as many of the ex-care women had become pregnant and given birth to a surviving child by the time of the follow-up interview. Moreover, whereas only 5 per cent of the control group had first become pregnant before the age of 19, two-fifths of the ex-care sample had done so. It is clear also that the previously institutionalised women who now had children were less likely to be parenting in a stable marital relationship; only 61 per cent were living with the biological father of all their children compared with all those in the comparison group, and 22 per cent of the ex-care group were without a current husband.

*Table 9.1  Pregnancy and parenting histories*

|  | Ex-care group | Comparison group |  |
| --- | --- | --- | --- |
|  | % | % |  |
| Ever pregnant | 72 | 43 | ** |
| Pregnant by age 19 | 42 | 5 | *** |
| Has a surviving child | 60 | 36 | * |
| *Of those with children* | n=49 | n=15 |  |
| Without spouse | 22 | 0 | * |
| Any child ever fostered or in institutional care | 18 | 0 |  |
| Any temporary or permanent parenting breakdown | 35 | 0 | * |
| Living with the father of all the children | 61 | 100 | * |

**Parenting breakdown**

It is evident from Table 9.1 that a number of the women who had been raised in the children's homes had experienced serious breakdowns in parenting. Moreover, such breakdowns were confined to the institutionalised group. Nearly one in five had had children taken into care for fostering or placement in a children's home, and there had been one case of infanticide. For one reason or another, 12 per cent of the ex-care mothers had children whom they no longer looked after and with no apparent likelihood of their being returned. Altogether, just over a third had experienced some form of transient or permanent parenting breakdown. That is, there was a time when they had given up the care of one or more of their children to official bodies, relatives or friends for a period of six months or longer. In the great majority of these cases the women had left their children to the care of others because they could not cope with the demands of life at the time, rather than because the children had been compulsorily removed as a result of abuse or neglect. The details of these parenting breakdowns are given in Table 9.2. Among the nine women who had a child taken into care, five subsequently had children for whom parenting had not broken down.

Taken together, these data repeat the findings of the retrospective study that serious parenting breakdown usually occurs against a background of markedly inadequate parenting experiences in childhood. These breakdowns were also systematically associated with other features of the women's life-histories. For example, all those with children taken permanently into care or adopted were first pregnant before the age of 19. This was true also for the three cases where the children were now living with their father. In contrast, only half of those with temporary breakdowns had early pregnancies, a rate similar to that for those mothers without breakdowns in parenting (50 per cent v. 52 per cent). The rates of marital separation and discord amongst those with breakdowns was also very high — 82 per cent had had such problems compared with 41 per cent of those ex-care women without separated children.

As with the retrospective study, these parenting breakdowns were associated with current difficulties in handling the children who were at home. Five of the six women who had suffered permanent breakdowns in the parenting of their first child and who now had children at home were rated as currently poor on an overall assessment of current parenting (this rating is explained in the next section). The current parenting of those who had suffered temporary breakdowns only were more varied. Five of these women had children within the assessment age group. Two of these mothers were now rated as parenting well but three showed 'poor' parenting. These findings suggest that the outcome picture is not a static one. Parenting breakdowns did not necessarily imply enduring deficits, although at this stage the picture for this subgroup of mothers was not encouraging.

However, these figures on parenting breakdowns are not very revealing on the current parenting behaviour of the two samples. To examine this in more detail we need to turn to the assessments of current parenting from the interviews and observations. These were examined in two ways. First, the molecular measures of parenting behaviour in the two groups were compared in four broad groupings: social communication and emotional expressiveness; joint play; disciplinary control; and sensitivity to the child's cues, approaches and distress. The comparison of the two groups of mothers on these areas of parenting is the main focus of this chapter. Secondly, the interview assessments were used to divide the mothers into three broad outcome groups according to the quality of their parenting. Such overall groupings are necessary for the investigation of the processes of

Table 9.2  Ex-care mothers with temporary or permanent parenting breakdown

| Family | Age | Sex | Nature of breakdown | Currently with | Current parenting rating |
|---|---|---|---|---|---|
| 1 | 10 years | Boy | In care | Long-term fostering | Not parenting |
|  | 8 years | Boy | In care | Long-term fostering |  |
| 2 | 4 years | Girl | In care | Long-term fostering | Not parenting |
|  | 6 weeks | Girl | None | With mother | Too young to assess |
| 3 | 7 years | Girl | In care | Adopted | Poor |
|  | 2 years | Girl | Fostered | With mother |  |
|  | 2 weeks | Girl | None | With mother |  |
| 4 | 2 years | Boy | Fostered | Awaiting adoption | Poor |
|  | 5 years | Boy | In care | With mother |  |
|  | 3 years | Girl | In care | With mother |  |
| 5 | 11 years | Girl | In care | Adopted | Some problems |
|  | 10 years | Boy | In care | Adopted |  |
|  | 8 years | Girl | None | With mother |  |
|  | 3 years | Girl | None | With mother |  |
|  | 14 months | Girl | None | With mother |  |
|  | 2 months | Boy | None | With mother |  |
| 6 | – | Girl | Infanticide | – |  |
| 7 | 8 years | Boy | Foster-care | Short-term fostering | Poor |
|  | 5 years | Boy | Foster-care | With mother |  |
|  | 15 months | Boy | Foster-care | With mother |  |

| | | | | | |
|---|---|---|---|---|---|
| 8 | 4 years | Boy | None | With mother | Poor |
| | 2 years | Girl | Foster-care | With mother | |
| | 1 year | Girl | None | With mother | |
| 9 | 5 years | Boy | Short-term care | With mother | Poor |
| | 17 months | Boy | None | With mother | |
| 10 | 4 years | Girl | Marital breakdown | With father | Not parenting |
| 11 | 9 years | Boy | Marital breakdown | With father | Not parenting |
| | 8 years | Girl | Marital breakdown | With father | |
| | 5 years | Boy | Marital breakdown | With father | |
| | 4 years | Girl | Marital breakdown | With father | |
| 12 | 7 years | Boy | Marital breakdown | With father | |
| | 10 months | Girl | None | With mother | Child too young to rate |
| 13 | 10 years | Girl | Marital breakdown | With mother | Good |
| | 9 years | Girl | Marital breakdown | With mother | |
| | 4 years | Girl | Marital discord | With mother | |
| | 1 year | Girl | None | With mother | |
| 14 | 2 years | Girl | Failure to cope | With mother | Poor |
| | 7 months | Girl | Failure to cope | With mother | |
| 15 | 9 years | Girl | Failure to cope | With mother | Poor |
| 16 | 7 years | Girl | Failure to cope | With mother | Good |
| | 3 years | Boy | None | With mother | |
| 17 | 2 years | Boy | Marital breakdown | With mother | Poor |

All separations due to marital discord lasted six months or longer.

Breakdowns categorised as 'failure to cope' involved the child being looked after by other adults but not being in care or fostered. The majority of those formally admitted to care also involved failure to cope.

inter-generational linkage discussed in the remaining chapters. The way in which these groupings were devised will be discussed first, before the details of parenting behaviour are presented.

### Overall measures of parenting from interview

The overall measures of parenting were constructed in the same way as the rating of overall psychosocial disadvantage described in Chapter 7. That is, criteria for the division of the sample into 'good', 'intermediate' and 'poor' parenting outcomes were established *a priori*. The principle used in deriving the index was to ensure that the subjects in the 'good' parenting category were a problem-free group. Similarly, the subjects in the 'poor' group had clear-cut difficulties. Those in the 'intermediate' category were neither problem-free nor had marked problems. Two outcome measures were defined in this way: current parenting and overall parenting outcome. The criteria for these two outcome ratings, showing the ways in which they are derived from the four broad groupings of molecular measures, are given in Table 9.3.

The current rating was based on the interview measures of the present quality of parenting only, thus a mother could be rated as parenting well at the time of follow-up even if she had a history of parenting breakdown. The overall parenting outcome measure took both the current assessment and the previous history into account. In this case, all those still separated from any child for one reason or another were placed in the poor category. If, however, these separations were a thing of the past and the mother was now parenting satisfactorily (i.e. in the 'good' or 'intermediate' groups on the current assessment) a rating of 'intermediate' overall outcome was made. It should be apparent that these two outcome groupings served different purposes. The first was simply an assessment of the mother's current performance as a parent. The second used a broader definition of outcome, and was concerned with the occurrence of marked parenting difficulties throughout the mother's history as a parent so far. In this case the women in the 'good' outcome group had never had any parenting difficulties of any consequence whilst those in the 'poor' category continued to have major unresolved problems. The first rating is more appropriate for the investigation of issues concerning the impact of current circumstances on parenting outcomes. The second is better for examining issues of inter-generational continuity.

### Outcome on the overall interview measures

The data on parenting breakdown present a somewhat gloomy picture even though it is apparent that two-thirds of the ex-care mothers had suffered no serious failures in parenting and less than one fifth had had children received into care. A different perspective on the range of outcomes is provided by the summary outcome ratings (Figures 9.1 and 9.2). Because so few of the comparison sample had children aged two

*Table 9.3  Criteria for the overall classification of parenting outcome*

*Current parenting*

| Good | Some problems | Poor |
|---|---|---|
| High or moderately high in sensitivity. | In neither the *good* nor the *poor* outcome group, e.g. a warm but aggressive parent or a parent intermediate in sensitivity with moderately firm but somewhat inconsistent control. | Low on sensitivity and/or low on expressed warmth PLUS at least two of: indulgent, very aggressive, ineffective or inconsistent control. |
| High or moderately high expressed warmth. | | |
| No or infrequent shouting or smacking. Control moderately to firmly effective, consistent and predictable. | | |

*Overall parenting outcome*

| Good | Some problems | Poor |
|---|---|---|
| In *good* current parenting group. | In *some problems* group on current parenting. | In *poor* group on current parenting. |
| Plus | Plus | Plus |
| No separations from any child of longer than four weeks. | Those in the good group on current parenting who have a history of separations where all children are now with the mother. | All those currently separated from a child, e.g. children in care or living with relatives. |

years or over the comparison data in this analysis include the spouses of the male comparison subjects (N=14) as well as the comparison subjects who had children in the age range (N=13). There were no significant differences in the backgrounds or parenting of these two groups of women.

Over two-fifths of the ex-care mothers had a current rating of poor parenting compared with one in ten of the comparison group — a four-fold difference. On the other hand, nearly one third (31 per cent) of the institution-reared group showed good parenting, a rating made on just less than half of the comparison sample. The groups did not differ significantly on either good or intermediate parenting currently. The difference between them is accounted for by the higher proportion of ex-care women with clear-cut difficulties. This contrast is more marked when the overall parenting outcome measure is considered. Here, because of the inclusion of parenting history in the comparison, the proportion of ex-care women with a good outcome is reduced. In this case the twofold difference between the two groups on 'good' parenting outcome is also statistically significant.

*The contribution of drinking problems to parenting difficulties*
The higher rate of alcohol abuse in the ex-care women was reported in Chapter 7. A history of drinking problems did not increase the probability that a woman would be a parent at follow-up when 63 per cent of those without such difficulties had had children compared with 55 per cent of those with them. However, difficulties with drink were strongly related to parenting problems. Amongst those currently parenting none of those parenting well had a history of alcohol abuse compared with 8 per cent of those with some parenting problems and 24 per cent of those rated as parenting poorly. Moreover 67 per cent of mothers with children currently being looked after by others had a history of drinking problems. Parenting breakdowns were less common but still frequent amongst the mothers without drinking difficulties and occurred in 28 per cent of cases. However, the pattern of break-down and its outcome was very different. Of the six mothers with drinking problems and separations from their children four seemed to have suffered permanent breakdowns in parenting. In two cases children had been taken from the mothers by the authorities and in two cases they had been given over to the care of their fathers. The two remaining mothers in this group currently had their children with them but were under close social work supervision and it seemed likely that further admissions would occur. Amongst the eleven mothers with parenting breakdowns but no alcohol abuse five now had all their children with them, one expected the last of her three children to join her from foster-care when she was rehoused from a refuge, and one was engaged in a court case to obtain custody of her child from the father. Two other cases in this group involved adoptions in the

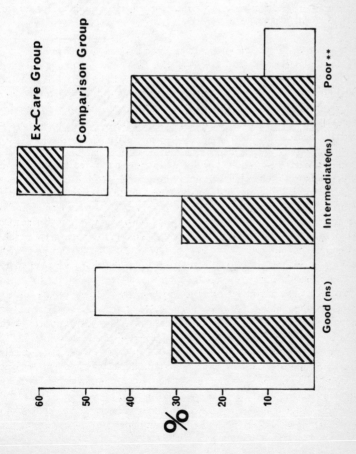

Figure 9.1  Current parenting outcome

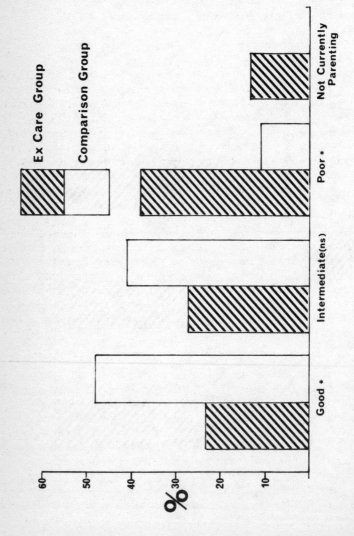

Figure 9.2  Overall parenting outcome

mothers' teens, and there was one permanent breakdown and one infanticide. It is apparent that where drinking problems occurred they were heavily implicated in parenting difficulties. However the high rate of parenting problems occurring in the absence of alcohol abuse suggest that this is but one of many factors contributing to a poor parenting outcome.

### Cases examples of current parenting
The individual meaning of the overall interview measures of parenting is best illustrated by specific examples. These were chosen from within each group through the use of a table of random numbers. All personal details have been changed to ensure confidentiality.

*Good parenting*

*Sylvia — ex-care*  Sylvia, aged 24, lived with her second husband in a poor quality council house. She had three children by her first marriage and was expecting another child at the time of follow-up. The children were Mary aged 8, Christine aged 5 and, Tracy (the target child) aged 4. Sylvia was first pregnant when she was 16 and, although engaged to the child's father, she elected to go into a mother and baby home rather than to set up home with him. She did not see him again until Mary was three months old, because meanwhile he had been in prison. They subsequently married but he left her when she became pregnant with Tracy and at that point she decided to divorce him because of his criminality and his unreliable behaviour.

Tracy was born without complications following a normal pregnancy. She was, however, a child who suffered from chest trouble and sore throats and had recently had three stitches in her head after running into a swing. She was described as a boisterous and active child but easy to manage and helpful round the house. She had never been separated from her mother and did not go to playschool because her mother believed that the children should be at home together with her. Sylvia felt that Tracy had plenty of company from other children in the area.

The family woke up at about 6 a.m. and the two older girls set out the breakfast. Mother did not have breakfast herself but stayed with the children whilst they had theirs. When Mary, Christine and her husband had gone off to school, mother would wash and dress Tracy, letting her try to do these things on her own but helping where necessary. Tracy then helped mother in the house or went shopping with her. At about noon Tracy had a rest and then they had lunch. Afternoons were often spent visiting other mothers who had children of Tracy's age until it was time to meet the older two from school. Her sisters then occupied her whilst Sylvia prepared the evening meal. They had this together as a family when father returned from work.

All three children went to bed between 6.45 and 7.00 p.m. when one or other parent went through a tucking-in routine.

Tracy was no trouble with regard either to eating or sleeping. She has no food fads and was not difficult at bed-time. There was very little distress reported. The only time that she cried was when she hurt herself or when she was told off. Control incidents were also infrequent. About once a week Tracy used rude words of which her mother disapproved. Sylvia's response was to speak to her sternly but not to smack her or shout at her. This technique was said to be effective. Sylvia reported that on rare occasions she might also have to send Tracy to her room, but she could only recall two instances in the child's life when this occurred and so this technique was not recorded in the response sequence. About once a fortnight Tracy would have a bout of temper. Sylvia's first response was to reason with her and if this was unsuccessful to raise her voice, and if this failed, to ignore her. Occasionally smacking or sending Tracy to her room terminated the episodes but such events were too rare to rate. Sylvia said that Tracy was a good child and that there were no battles between them. When these more minor disputes occurred they were usually resolved by an apology from Tracy which Sylvia acknowledged and accepted.

Tracy played well with her sibs but there were daily squabbles over toys or the television. Mother waited to see if these resolved themselves, and if not she would raise her voice and threaten the participants. She very seldom had to intervene physically in such disagreements or to remove the disputed plaything. Tracy was not a child with anxieties or fears. Rather she appeared happy and secure. If she was hurt her mother comforted her, cleaned the graze or rubbed the hurt better and tried to make light of it.

Tracy was getting to a stage when she like to play on her own. Nevertheless, she and her mother played and did things together everyday. Mother was always available and joined in whenever Tracy demanded it. Sylvia let her help dry the dishes and do the hoovering. In the afternoon when the older two came home, Sylvia would often sit with the three of them and draw, or play spelling games. She and Tracy watched 'Play School' together every morning. Sylvia said, 'I like playing with her, she's funny.' She felt she had no favourites amongst her daughters but that in personality the middle one was most appealing.

In sum, Tracy was seen as a good and undemanding child. This assumption was supported by her behaviour during two long interviews. Sylvia's relationship with her was warm and unfussy and she had a good appreciation of the personality differences between her daughters. Her control methods were firm and effective with very little smacking or aggression.

*Gillian — ex-care*   Gillian was aged 28. She lived with her (first) husband in a flat conversion which they were buying. Her husband was a mechanic. She herself worked all day as a secretary during which time her only daughter Petra was at a babyminder. Gillian did not like working whilst her daughter was small (she was not yet three) but the financial circumstances made it necessary. The pregnancy was unplanned but, apart from financial worries, she was very happy about it. She was described as a pretty, pleasant and confident woman who had come through a very difficult childhood with strengths rather than deficits.

Gillian described Petra as a happy, loving child but very headstrong and strongwilled. This characteristic led to a number of day-to-day battles between them. For example, Petra was always playing with the television or playing with water in the sink when her mother was trying to do jobs. Gillian's available time for housework was at a premium because she worked all day, and she appreciated that these battles were due to circumstances. She could not allow Petra to do the things that she would be able to tolerate if she were at home all day. For example, when her daughter got up to the sink Gillian asked her to get down; Petra refused. This interchange occurred about six times with rising irritation. In the end Gillian would have to put her down physically or smack her bottom. Smacks over this occurred two times per week on average. Control incidents also arose daily because Petra got food off the shelves or out of the 'fridge and played with it on the floor. Gillian's general approach was to ignore the behaviour initially and then to do something when she felt it had gone far enough. The control sequence proceeded with increasing defiance and usually terminated in a smack. Petra cried for a minute or two. Gillian always made it up with her if she felt she had been mean, and gave her daughter a cuddle. If this did not occur Petra would come and cuddle her.

No other children come to the flat to play with Petra but sometimes at the weekends she played with cousins of the same age. When this occurred the play was uneventful. However, such occasions occurred too infrequently for parenting to be assessed with respect to the management of peer relationships. When control issues arose Gillian was rated as winning 70 per cent of the battles. The relationship was always re-established, usually initiated by her daughter. Petra was a very confident, outgoing child and there were no intervention sequences for fears and worries.

Daily routine was very stable. Gillian would get up between 6 and 6.30 a.m. Petra woke in her own time at about 7.00 a.m. She was always happy in the morning and they usually had a cuddle. Her mother encouraged her to have some breakfast before they all set off for work or school. They had their evening meal together as a family whenever possible. Petra had no feeding problems.

Petra went to bed regularly at 8.30 during the week. The routine was to have a bath, brush her teeth and have a drink. Her mother put her to bed and, before going to sleep, Petra would often lie and talk to Gillian about her day. There was a special hand-kissing ritual which rounded off bed-times.

Petra had a huge selection of toys. Gillian played with her daily even though time was limited. They played pretend-making tea, or 'Petra's got a bird in her hand', and similar games. They did puzzles together every evening and Petra was read a story daily. When Gillian was doing housework her daughter was always with her and helped dust or wipe things.

Despite the daily minor control episodes, Gillian's mildly aggressive style and only moderate effectiveness, the relationship was happy and secure with a great deal of open affection and interaction.

## Intermediate parenting

*Alison — comparison group*  Alison and her husband, a photographic technician, lived in their own house with their son Peter, aged two. Alison did not go out to work and spent much of her spare time decorating the house. She was described as a friendly and welcoming person, but a rather timid young mother.

Peter was a planned baby but Alison was rather anxious during the pregnancy, having had a previous recent miscarriage. She had had a five-hour labour and forceps delivery. Her initial reaction to this was that she did not want more children. When interviewed, she had no clear plans but did not expect to become pregnant again.

Alison was usually up when Peter awoke. This could be at any time between 7.30 and 9.00 a.m. He came down on his own to get his toys and said 'Hello' to his mother. They had breakfast together but a mid-day meal was much more variable, depending on what they had been doing. Peter usually ate on his own in the evenings because there had been difficulties with food fads and father had objected to his behaviour. Apart from this change in timing, Alison had no clear policy over Peter's faddiness and gave him what he wanted with no insistence that he eat it. Recently, she had begun to talk to him and distract him before the evening meal in the hope that he would eat what he had been given. This had been partially successful.

Peter's bed-times were haphazard. He had a sleep in the afternoon and was then often awake until 11.00 p.m. He slept in his parent's bed. Alison was now trying to break him of this afternoon nap and instead would lie with him on his own bed in the evening until he fell asleep. He usually awoke after 2–3 hours and she would lie with him again. She was unaware that at that age he would understand if she tried to talk to him about bed-times and sleeping patterns.

Peter was a child who wailed and whined if he was not able to get his own way or if he was tired. This happened daily for one reason or another and got his mother down. If he was tired she tried to distract him and calm him down (4–5 times per week), but control episodes over naughtiness were not resolved this way. For example, most days he switched the television on and off and, when told not to do so he would smack his mother or lash out and defy her. She tried to talk to him first but this seldom worked and she ended up shouting at him. About a third of the time such episodes would end with a smack but then Peter would wail until he was allowed to do what he wanted. Mother thought he won these battles 90 per cent of the time. Reconciliations did not occur unless she had smacked him hard and felt guilty. She then made it up with him. Normally these negative episodes were 'just forgotten'. Alison was worried about her aggression to him and said that once or twice a month she ended up shaking him, dumping him on the sofa and walking away until she had calmed down. After this she would cuddle him. Peter was not an anxious child and had no separation problems. However he led a sheltered and quiet life and seldom played with other children. Alison's attitude to him when he was hurt, unless it seemed serious, was to tell him to get up and not make a fuss.

Alison cuddled Peter a lot and much of their interaction was warm, but she felt she was too busy to play much even though she had no outside work. She would do something with him 2 or 3 times a week, either building with bricks, or drawing or looking at pictures. When doing housework she tried to get him to play in the garden or watch the television rather than involving him in what she was doing. This occupied 2–3 hours of every day. Usually he played on his own within sight of his mother. He tried to involve her in his games but she was not very active in her response.

In sum, Alison was rated as a warm mother but one who had a limited idea of what she might expect from a two year old. Because she was socially isolated she could make no comparisons with what other mothers did. In personality she was a gentle person, but control episodes usually ended up with her shouting, and not infrequently smacking. These were not seen as major problems, but Alison had sufficient current difficulties to prevent her being rated as showing good current parenting.

## Poor parenting

*Valerie — ex-care*  Valerie had three children: Jason aged 5, Brian aged 3 and Sarah aged 18 months. Jason was born when Valerie was 18; he was the child of a former boyfriend with whom she never lived. The younger two were the children of her present husband. The family lived in the upper flat in a conversion owned by the Council. Valerie's husband was a van driver. He had been in his present job for six months, having been unemployed for the six months before that.

The pregnancy and birth with Jason were difficult with the boy being jaundiced and spending two weeks in an incubator. With Brian (the target child) things were different. She was pleased about the pregnancy because he was her husband's first, but afterwards she wanted no more children and asked for a sterilisation. This was performed following the birth of the next child, Sarah.

Brian had been a very difficult boy, particularly over the previous eighteen months. He had suffered from 4 to 5 throat infections and had also been having speech therapy. By the time of interview his speech was much improved. He had always been a very demanding child and much more difficult than the other two. 'He wants his own way all the time,' Valerie said. 'If he can't get his own way he'll sulk, and if that doesn't work, he'll throw and kick things. He's quite naughty. If another child has got something he wants, he'll create hell until he gets it. I have to handle him differently from the others, or he'll cry and answer back and swear at you. I have to have a firm hand or he gets away with everything.'

When he was 10 months old Brian had convulsions following a viral attack. These did not recur, but he learnt to make himself pass out to gain attention. When he first started nursery school (in the year prior to the interview) he did not want his mother to leave and would cry, swear, hold his breath and go blue, passing out for a few seconds. Valerie seemed unaware that Brian's behaviour might be associated with anxiety. She described his actions as 'unreasonable attention-seeking' and said she just shut herself off from it. This went on for several months. This also happened if he was naughty and she smacked him. At first it bothered her and she would fuss over him. 'Now,' she said, 'I know differently, I take no notice, I just watch him.' When he was 12 months Brian was placed on the At-Risk Register because he bit through the television wire and was burned. Not long before the follow-up both boys had been rushed to hospital as a result of swallowing the contents of a bottle of aspirin. When Jason had come to her that morning and said he felt sick she said, 'Go and be sick and get back into bed,' until she realised something was wrong.

Daily routine was variable. The boys woke each other 1½ hours before mother got up. Jason played in his room but Brian roamed the house squirting toothpaste in the bathroom, collecting food from the kitchen and generally causing havoc. When Valerie got up she gave the boys breakfast in the kitchen but fed Sarah in another room. Meals were regular and there were no feeding problems. There was only one family meal in the week.

Bed-times were erratic. Brian often fell asleep on the sofa at 6.00 p.m. and mother undressed him and put him to bed, but twice in the previous week he had been up until 11.30 p.m. because they had all gone out. In the summer the boys were often up until 9.30 p.m. There were no sleeping problems once the boys went to bed.

Brian cried a great deal in response to frustration (more than daily).

If his frustrations seemed justified Valerie reasoned with him, but because he often cried for 'no good reason' she smacked him a lot. 'It gets on my nerves when he cries,' she said. He had temper tantrums daily when he could not get his way and then he threw the furniture around. When he did this she smacked him hard on the bottom. 'That usually works,' she said. 'He goes on crying but then it's for a reason.' Sometimes he would come and say sorry (but not usually), then she would let him have what he was previously denied. 'So that he'll realise tantrums don't work.' Valerie felt a good deal of this was made worse because of her poor relationship with her husband and because between them they did not handle Brian consistently.

The boys fought daily, usually provoked by Brian who would kick Jason 'for no reason'. Jason hit back and Brian came to her crying. She told them not to do it but they started again within 10 minutes. In general, she ignored their behaviour or shouted at them, but occasionally she would put Brian in his room. He always came back down in five minutes.

Brian did not play with constructive toys or do writing or colouring. He preferred things you could throw around. She played very little with him, and when busy made the boys play in the front room.

Valerie was described as a chatty and open person, but somewhat prone to depression and an unsatisfactory manager. The children were the focus of her life and she clearly cared for them but was fondest of her daughter. Her parenting of the boys had a number of clear problems which placed her in the poor outcome group.

*Ann — ex-care*   Ann, aged 23, lived with her unemployed husband and three boys Mark aged 6, Victor aged 4 and Wayne aged 2, in a council house in the north-west of England. The family were very poor. The curtains of the living room were kept drawn right through the interview although this was conducted during the day. The house had central heating but this was too expensive for them to use and it was not turned on. They used the gas fire in the living room but did not heat the bedrooms. Wayne, the target child, shared a bedroom with his parents. The family lived on Social Security.

Ann had had a previous pregnancy by another boyfriend in her mid-teens but this did not go to term. Her husband was the father of all three boys. She became pregnant with Wayne whilst taking the contraceptive pill and did not want more children. She threatened to give the child to her sister if he were a boy. Her husband was not interested in this pregnancy, since at the time he was in and out of prison and the marriage was going through a bad patch. Wayne was born six weeks early and was in special care for 6–7 weeks after a long labour and caesarian delivery.

Ann said Wayne was both loving and aggressive, but easier than the other two, partly because she felt more confident as a mother. When she had her first baby she was taking drugs (LSD and Mandrax) and had little clue about being a parent.

Her husband got up at 6.45 a.m. but she remained in bed. Wayne woke then and played in his cot until his mother got up at 8.00 a.m. Breakfast (Shredded Wheat) was prepared by the eldest boy who got bowls ready for his brothers. The boys ate when and where they could. There was no routine. The family did not have separate dining space even in the kitchen. The family ate together in the evenings at about 5.00 p.m. but in addition the boys usually also had cereals when they got home from school. At weekends the family got up at 10.30 a.m. The boys got breakfast. There was no special weekend meal. The boys usually ate sweets on Sundays until their meal in the evening at 6.00 p.m.

Wayne was messy with his food and often threw it around. Often, also, he refused it. Mother then tried to persuade him and sang to him to distract him. If this did not work she got exasperated and tipped it over his head. During the day he ate a lot of biscuits and sweets. At bedtime he usually fell asleep on the sofa, but sometimes when he was tired he would take himself off to bed or go with his brothers. He undressed himself and settled down to sleep on his own straight away.

Wayne cried over something more than daily. When this was through tiredness mother would first ignore him in the hope that the crying would stop and would then put him to bed. He cried 'for no good reason' about twice a week. She first ignored him, then tried to pacify him with a biscuit and then tried to distract him. There were daily temper tantrums. These occurred when he was frustrated and could not get his own way. Wayne would wail and stamp for a long while (maybe 20 minutes) and mother would ignore him and finally talk to him or comfort him. There were daily naughty behaviours such as throwing the ornaments around or tearing wallpaper. Ann's interventions were inconsistent. Sometimes she laughed at him. On other occasions she ignored him, then instructed him not to do what he was doing. On about half of these occasions she would smack him. Such disputes were usually reconciled through a move either by the child or the parent. Ann smacked Wayne 3 to 4 times a week. Her parenting was not considered to be particularly aggressive.

Wayne fought with his brothers over toys every day. These fights involved hair-pulling and similar behaviours. Ann always tried to ignore this in the hope it would stop. About 80 per cent of the time she ended up shouting at them and separating them.

Wayne was afraid of the dark and had the light on when he went to bed. If he was hurt she comforted him, but if he was upset for what she called 'sentimental reasons' — for example, separation anxieties — she usually ignored him and might even laugh. Physical affection between mother and son was frequently demonstrated. Ann liked playing with him and did something with him daily. For example, he had an easel and chalk and she encouraged him to draw. At night time she often (4–5 times a week) played bricks with him or sang to him. They watched 'Play School' together. He usually helped her with housework, doing pretend dusting.

In summary, Ann was rated as moderately warm and affectionate but low on sensitivity. Her main technique for handling something she did not understand was to ignore it. Her control style was generally indulgent and she often laughed at Wayne's disruptive behaviours. There was, however, considerable inconsistency in this in that it depended upon her mood whether she shouted or smacked him or found the incident amusing. She herself felt that most problems were left unresolved.

### Overall measures of parenting from direct observation

Observational studies produce very large amounts of data. In order to get an overall picture of the magnitude of the differences between the samples before looking in detail at the individual measures, some summary ranking on parenting behaviour is useful. This was accomplished first by pooling the data from the ex-care and control groups and then ranking their scores on seven different features of mother-child interaction. These comprised: the mother's handling of control and distress; the emotional tone of her speech to her child; the quality of their interaction during play; and features of the mother's sensitivity and responsivity. The ranking was then used to compare the groups on how many women were showing problems on one or more of these areas. Unlike the summary interview measures, the observational ranking was based entirely on a woman's score in relation to other mothers and did not involve any judgemental ratings on the part of an investigator. Difficulties in an area were defined in terms of being in the most extreme 25 per cent on a particular dimension. A 25 per cent cut-off rather than a more extreme 5 or 10 per cent was used because the percentile was based not on the general population, but on the pooled sample that included mothers likely to show problems in parenting. The direction of the 25 per cent was chosen on common-sense grounds; thus it included the least frequent positive affect, the highest frequency of child distress and of control episodes, the highest number of child initiations, the greatest proportion of initiations ignored, and the lowest frequency of joint play. The summary score was provided by the number of dimensions on which the mother ranked in the most extreme 25 per cent.

A comparison of the two groups on this overall score indicated that over one third (35 per cent) of ex-care women were experiencing difficulty in at least four areas; this was not so for any mother in the control group. In contrast over two-thirds (71 per cent) of the control group mothers were in the best 25 per cent on at least one of these

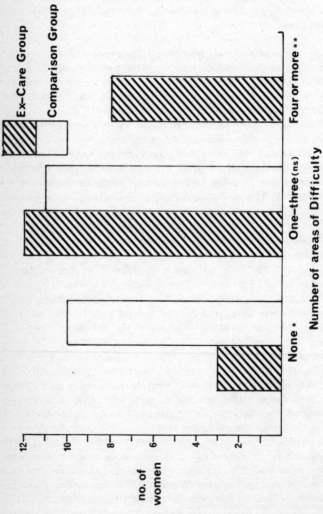

Figure 9.3 Overall observation measure of parenting

measures, but this was the case for only one in nine of the ex-care sample.

It is clear that the observational data — gathered by researchers who were blind to the childhood background of the women — showed a picture broadly similar to the interview data in that the difference between the groups was greatest in the proportions who had widespread parenting difficulties. The parenting problems appeared somewhat less severe on the observational measures, probably because many of the mothers with the most severe parenting difficulties were excluded because they had no child at home on whom parenting could be assessed. This is likely since amongst the nine women who currently had children who were not living with them only three had children at home in the observational age group and of these three one was not observed because the daytime care of the child was predominantly conducted by others outside the home. Two of these three mothers were rated at interview as showing poor current parenting and the other as having some problems.

## Specific dimensions of parenting
The overall interview and observational measures of parenting provide an indication of the rate of parenting problems in the two groups, but they do not demonstrate the specific types of difficulties experienced. In order to examine that issue we need to turn to the more detailed measures on the specific dimensions of parenting outlined earlier: social communication and emotional expressiveness; joint play; disciplinary control; and sensitivity to the child's cues, approaches and distress.

### Interview findings

*Emotional tone* Mothers were rated on the warmth with which they talked about their child during the interview. The proportions of the ex-care and control groups who described their children warmly did not differ (55 per cent v. 56 per cent) but there was a substantial, but statistically non-significant, difference on the proportions with low expression of positive feelings (24 per cent v. 7 per cent).

*Play* The frequency of parental involvement in play varied greatly according to the age of the child. Since nearly all the control group children were below school age, and in order to provide a direct parallel to the observational study, this analysis was restricted to those mothers with children in the age range 2–3½ years. Overall, the mothers in the two groups played with their children to the same extent, but there were some differences in the types of play activities in which they engaged. In particular, the ex-care mothers were somewhat less likely to be involved in play requiring creative involvement for the child, such as make-believe games or drawing, and somewhat more likely to engage in rough-and-tumble play. However, these differences fell short of statistical significance.

*Table 9.4    Interview measures of affection and play*

|  | Ex-care group | Comparison group |
|---|---|---|
|  | % | % |
| *Expressed warmth* | | |
| Low | 24 | 7 |
| Moderate | 21 | 37 |
| High | 55 | 56 |
| $\chi^2 = 3.99$   2df   ns | | |
| *Daily play with child\** | | |
| *Creative play* | | |
| 'Let's pretend' games | 24 | 38 |
| Constructional play | 28 | 43 |
| Drawing, reading, writing | 56 | 67 |
| None of the above | 40 | 19 |
| *Passive or physical activities* | | |
| Watching television | 28 | 33 |
| Rough-and-tumble play | 36 | 19 |
| Help with housework | 56 | 48 |
| No statistically significant differences | | |

\* Comparison based on 2–3½-year-old children only.

*Disciplinary style*   Inconsistency in discipline was frequent in both groups. An aggressive style of control (with frequent recourse to smacking, irritable shouting, and the like) was also relatively frequent. The ex-care mothers were somewhat more likely to use an aggressive style as the preponderant disciplinary method, but the difference was not statistically significant. This contrast between the groups was reflected also in the frequency of smacking. Twice as many of the ex-care mothers smacked the children daily (40 per cent v. 19 per cent), but again the difference fell short of statistical significance. Most of the mothers in both groups showed at least moderately effective disciplinary control (effective, that is to say, in that the disciplinary act resulted in the intended change in the child's behaviour). However, clearly ineffective control was substantially and significantly more frequent in the ex-care group (26 per cent v. 4 per cent).

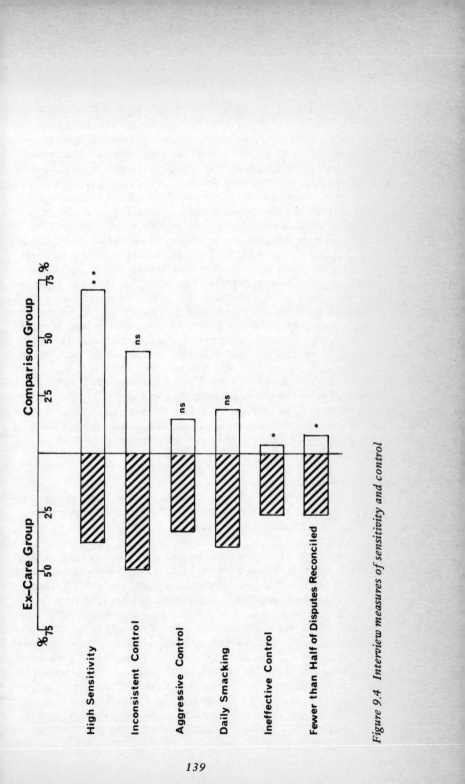

Figure 9.4 Interview measures of sensitivity and control

*Maternal sensitivity* Much the biggest difference between the groups concerned the mothers' 'sensitivity' in the handling of distress or disputes — a rating based on the interviewers' judgement of the mothers' overall handling of their children. Insensitivity was rated when mothers seemed unable to perceive reasons for their children's distress ('He's always crying for no reason'), or when they moved excessively rapidly into control without first trying to evaluate or sort out what was happening, or when they described the child's fears or anxieties as 'naughty' behaviour. 'Sensitivity' on the other hand, meant that the mothers showed some appreciation (in overt behavioural terms) of why their children behaved in the way they did, that they made differential responses according to the specifics of the child's behaviour, and that they showed a flexible and adaptive approach to child-rearing with an appropriate variation according to what was going on, to the child's response and to whether the parental action was effective. Forty-two per cent of currently parenting ex-care mothers were rated as low on sensitivity compared to only 7 per cent of the comparison group — a highly significant difference. This relative lack of appreciation of the children's perspectives was also evident in the failure to bring about reconciliation following disciplinary episodes. In the control group, 85 per cent of the women reported that at least 8 out of 10 episodes resulted in some kind of harmony, with attempts to 'make up' or restore the relationship; this was so for only half (54 per cent) of the ex-care women. At the other extreme, a quarter of the ex-care mothers and their children failed to achieve reconciliation in over half of their disputes, compared with less than one in ten of the control families (26 per cent v. 8 per cent).

## Observational findings

We can now consider the individual observational measures of parenting and parent–child interaction. A more detailed statistical presentation of these data is given elsewhere (Dowdney *et al.*, 1985).

*Emotional tone* In both the ex-care and the control group there was immense variation in the frequency with which positive emotion was expressed (as reflected in a warm tone of voice, encouraging remarks, words of approval, or physical actions such as affectionate touches or cuddles). The difference between the groups was not significant. However, there was a tendency for positive remarks to be marginally less common in the ex-care group. Although negative remarks (comprising a critical or hostile tone of voice, disapproving or threatening comments, and physically aggressive behaviour such as smacking or shaking) also showed great individual variation, the rate was over 70 per cent higher in the ex-care group, a significant difference.

Examination of the social contexts within which maternal emotion was expressed showed that the negative feelings were not restricted to

*Table 9.5   Observation measures of maternal affect*

|  | Ex-care group | | Comparison group | | |
|---|---|---|---|---|---|
|  | Mean | SD | Mean | SD | |
| Positive affect | 221.26 | (111.94) | 271.76 | (138.80) | ns |
| Negative affect | 35.52 | (26.72) | 20.56 | (16.99) | * |
|   Within confrontations | 16.83 | (14.09) | 10.37 | (9.36) | ns |
|   In other interactions | 18.70 | (14.12) | 10.21 | (8.28) | * |

The mean figures are the number of 10 second intervals over the four hours of observation in which the behaviour occurred.

disciplinary episodes. Indeed in both groups, just over half the negative emotion was expressed during interactions such as playing or talking together rather than in the context of some form of confrontation (i.e. a control or distress episode). The between-groups differences for the separate emotion-within-context measures showed that the higher rate of negative maternal emotion in the ex-care group applied across all contexts, although the difference was most marked outside confrontations.

*Child's approaches to mother*   A count was kept of the child's attempts by verbal or physical means to gain the mother's attention or to engage her in some activity. A 'new' approach was scored if there had been at least a 20 second gap since the last attempt. There was a striking difference between the groups on this measure with a substantially higher rate of initiations in the ex-care group where the children made on average 38 approaches to their mothers over the four hours of observation compared with 25 approaches by the comparison children, a difference significant at the one per cent level. The possible reasons for this difference are discussed below. The most common type of initiation concerned the children's attempts to share with the mother their interest or excitement in some play activity; such approaches made up just over a third of initiations in both groups. Other approaches included non-specific verbalisations — approximately one quarter of initiations in both samples, requests (16 per cent in both groups), and questions (15 per cent and 9 per cent respectively).

*Approaches by the mother*   Unlike the difference between the groups in the rate of child initiations, the rate of maternal approaches was closely similar (in 37 v. 31 10 second intervals per hour). Moreover, neither the topic of the maternal initiations (i.e. whether to express interest in the children's play, to exercise control, or to engage in caretaking activities, etc.); nor the form of the initiation (i.e. whether a question, instruction or an explanation) differentiated the groups. In both samples some two-fifths of the maternal initiations failed to lead to any established form of interaction, the exchange terminating within three verbal interchanges. The most likely outcome for interactions persisting beyond three elements was a conversation (28 per cent of outcomes) but one in six (15 per cent) resulted in joint play. The children in the ex-care group were slightly (but not significantly) less likely to become engaged in play through their mother's initiations (12 per cent v. 19 per cent), and ex-care group mothers were also marginally more likely to precipitate children's distress or confrontation following their approaches (12 per cent v. 8 per cent).

*Play and other joint interaction* The observational findings agreed with the interview data in showing no difference between the groups in the overall amount of play and conversation between parents and their children. There was a very wide variation between mother–child pairs on the amount of social interaction during the four hours of observation, ranging from just over 1½ hours to nearly the whole observational period. Broadly speaking, four main types of interaction were seen: (1) joint play (the most frequent type); (2) talking together; (3) some joint action such as polishing the furniture; and (4) caretaking activities, such as dressing or washing the child. Within both groups mothers varied greatly on the form of their interactions with children but there were no significant between group differences.

*Communication* The content and quality of mother–child dialogue was coded from transcriptions of the audiotapes of the middle hour of each observational session. During the sessions notes were kept of non-verbal behaviour or happenings that gave meaning to the verbal statements in order to aid later interpretation of the dialogue. The transcribed data were coded into eight categories: social communication; simple acknowledgements; praise; facilitating comments; open questions; relevant responses; non-facilitating comments and other statements.

In both groups praise (for example, comments such as 'well done' or 'that's a good girl') was sparingly used, with only four such comments per hour on average. In contrast, the use of minimal acknowledgements (one word responses such as 'oh', 'mm' or 'right') was common, but the ex-care mothers were nearly twice as likely to give no response at all to their children's communications (8.5 v. 4.4 per hour). This finding raises the possibility that the higher rate of child initiations in this group may have been the result of lower parental responsiveness and therefore a need for the child to make more overtures in order to gain the mother's attention.

Facilitating comments constituted much the largest single category.

Table 9.6    *Maternal communications*

|  | Ex-care group Mean | SD | Comparison group Mean | SD |  |
|---|---|---|---|---|---|
| Minimal acknowledge | 47.38 | (25.06) | 46.06 | (26.99) | ns |
| Ignore | 17.16 | (12.20) | 8.86 | (9.14) | ** |
| Praise | 8.14 | (7.84) | 8.25 | (7.52) | ns |
| Facilitating comments | 123.85 | (49.21) | 142.08 | (41.69) | ns |
| Non-facilitating comments | 25.75 | (15.52) | 21.42 | (17.85) | ns |
| Description or naming | 41.59 | (29.65) | 43.73 | (29.17) | ns |
| Elaborating comments | 39.13 | (19.23) | 62.66 | (27.09) | ** |
| Other | 258.44 | (70.38) | 283.16 | (94.02) | ns |

The figures given are the mean rate per hour of maternal statements from the transcriptions of the middle hour of each observation period.

Included in this group were suggestions to help joint activities, such as an instruction to bring a stool to the sink to help with washing up; suggestions of new activities; the giving of verbal help and practical assistance, such as showing the child where to put a jigsaw puzzle piece; open questions or comments; responses complying with the child's suggestions or requests; and responses relevant to the child's make-believe play. The ex-care mothers were slightly less likely to facilitate activities in this way but the difference fell well short of statistical significance (62 v. 71 per hour).

Non-facilitating comments (a group of statements that included simple negations of the child's verbalisations without further comment or explanation, e.g. 'That's not a dog'; as well as postponing statements such as 'I'll help you later') were infrequent. Descriptive or naming utterances without further explanation or elaboration were more common, but once again the two groups did not differ.

The same lack of difference applied to miscellaneous statements with a less clearly defined social communication purpose such as: closed questions; requests for clarification; repetition of what the child had said; 'don't know' responses; and simple confirmations.

The largest difference between the groups concerned maternal comments that provided elaboration by widening the scope of conversation. This might be done by adding new information ('Look at those horses going up the road; they're going to have new shoes at the blacksmith's'); by the teaching of abstract ideas or relative relationships ('That's hotter than that, isn't it?'); by the introduction of pretend activities; by the extension of a pre-existing make-believe game, or by linking a current activity to some other aspect of the child's experience outside the immediate situation. Such elaborating comments occurred at a rate of just over 30 per hour in the control group but just under 20 in the ex-care group. Elaborating statements of this type probably play an important role in the provision of information that aids children's cognitive performance; equally, their reciprocal quality may facilitate the development of children's conversational skills. However, also, they have socio-emotional effects in that they serve as a way for mothers to show an active interest in their children's activities and because they give a content and context to the mother–child relationship.

*Disciplinary control*   In order to understand the qualities of parenting, it is necessary to look in more detail at the unfolding of the sequences of mother–child interaction when the child does something of which the mother disapproves or when he or she is upset or distressed. When either control or distress episodes occurred the mother and child interactions were recorded as a continuous sequence of alternating child/parent behaviour.

Control episodes (i.e. sequences or interactions initiated by the child being aggressive, destructive, oppositional or non-compliant) were 50 per cent more frequent in the ex-care group (19 v. 13 per four hours) – a difference significant at the 5 per cent level – although the overall period of time spent in such episodes was much the same in both (in 66 v. 55 10 second intervals in four hours). The difference between the groups lay in the higher rate of very short control episodes lasting two 10 second intervals or less in the ex-care sample. This is consistent with the interview data which suggested that these mothers were more likely to be ineffective in their discipline. Distress episodes during which the child whined or cried were also somewhat more common in the ex-care group but occurred on some occasions in all but seven of the families.

The ways in which mothers in both groups handled control issues showed a wide variety of styles (Table 9.7). Some women displayed patience and good humour, whereas others adopted a more confrontational approach, threatening or shouting at their children. However, the majority employed a mixture of styles – on some occasions being forceful and overtly disapproving, but at other times using persuasion and reasoning in an attempt to achieve compliance. Perhaps the significantly higher proportion of the ex-care women's 'managerial' responses (meaning distractions, explanations, persuasions and suggestions) arises from the fact that this group had more brief episodes of control. Patterson's (1982) model of coercive interchanges suggests that relatively low-key maternal managerial responses would in some circumstances act as negative reinforcers, making more likely further coercive (i.e. oppositional or non-compliant) behaviour. Thus the short-term goal of control resolution is achieved at the cost of an increased likelihood of further child coercion. Ex-care women tended to employ a wider mixture of styles in disciplinary episodes; 87 per cent using all modes of responding compared with 65 per cent of the control group.

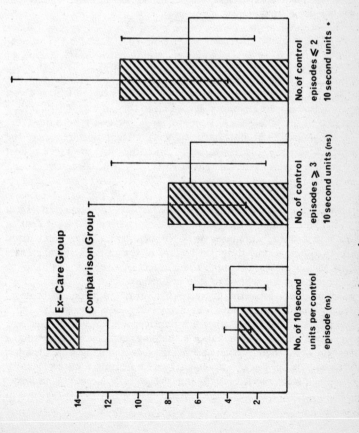

Figure 9.5 *Duration of control sequences*

*Table 9.7   Maternal responses within control episodes*

| | Ex-care group | | Comparison group | | |
|---|---|---|---|---|---|
| | Mean* | SD | Mean | SD | |
| Managerial | 14.56 | (7.60) | 10.45 | (8.40) | * |
| Instruction | 33.09 | (12.72) | 36.60 | (11.37) | ns |
| Imperative | 7.26 | (6.22) | 7.00 | (5.93) | ns |
| Passive | 15.35 | (13.42) | 16.20 | (16.74) | ns |
| Aggressive | 11.74 | (7.93) | 10.75 | (8.54) | ns |
| Other | 19.22 | (8.19) | 19.95 | (15.05) | ns |

\* These means are calculated from the percentage of responses falling in each category.

*Managerial* responses include suggest or distract: *imperatives* include prohibitions or restraint: *passive* responses include ignoring or leaving the room: and *aggressive* responses include threats, smacks, rough handling and sarcastic remarks, but exclude negative intonation alone.

*Distress episodes*   Although distress episodes were somewhat more common in the ex-care group (8 v. 6 in four hours), this was not because of a greater tendency of control episodes to result in distress. Distress episodes were examined according to the context in which they occurred. On the whole these were similar in the two groups but there was a substantial, but not statistically significant, difference on the amount of 'coercive' distress through which the child protested against some prohibition or maternal refusal to comply with a request (5 v. 3 episodes in four hours). In nearly all (93 per cent) cases this arose through maternal non-compliance, but in a small proportion of cases it followed the mother curtailing some activity or taking an object away from the child. This type of distress occurred in 74 per cent of the ex-care families compared with 48 per cent of the comparison group. In other words, the main feature of the distress of the ex-care group was that it arose through some aspect of the mother's handling of behaviour that she wished to stop or prevent.

Maternal responses to distress that arose outside of control sequences were grouped into four main categories: negative, positive, passive and minimal (plus 'other'). A response was considered 'positive' if it involved maternal compliance or helping, explaining, suggesting or distraction or if there was an approving or encouraging tone of voice, and verbal or physical expressions of warmth (such as making comforting statements or cuddling the child). 'Negative' responses included comments or injunctions made in an angry or hostile tone of voice; the verbal or physical expression of negative emotion (such as threatening the child or smacking him); high-level imperatives; and non-compliance to the child's demands. A 'passive' response was scored if a mother ignored or left her child in a distressed condition. The category of 'minimal' response was used for instances in which the mother responded with just an acknowledgement or non-specific comment.

The two groups of mothers tended to deal with their children's distress in a broadly comparable fashion, with positive responses being by far the most frequent reaction. 'Negative' responses were somewhat more frequent in the ex-care group but not significantly so. This parallels the general finding that in all contexts the ex-care women tended to be more negative. When mothers were evaluated individually (in contrast to average values for the group as a whole) it was apparent that half (50 per cent) of the ex-care women displayed negative affect in response to their children's emotional upset, in contrast to one in six (15.8 per cent) of the comparison group women — a difference that approached statistical significance.

## Discussion

The implications of the results presented in this chapter can be considered first in the context of the broad sweep of parenting histories, and secondly with respect to the detailed and specific observations on the quality of mothering.

A central question of this study was whether particular types of parenting inadequacies would be found in women who were raised in children's homes. As we have mentioned, for a minority the parent–child relationship itself could not be sustained. Just over a third (35 per cent) had experienced temporary or permanent separation from a child or, in a few cases, from all their children. There had been one case of infanticide. This result might suggest that an institutional upbringing is significantly likely to result in extreme parenting deficits of a serious and lasting kind. However, an examination of the case histories showed that this was likely to be true of only a handful of cases. The majority of parenting breakdowns had occurred several years before the women were interviewed, with first-born children, and at times of great psycho-social stress and adversity. The findings discussed in this chapter refer to a period some years after the young women had come out of care, when their parenting could be assessed in more favourable social circumstances. The observations, for instance, usually took place by arrangement, with just one child at a time, when the mother did not have other competing demands. On the other hand, the interview and observational data agreed well and gave rise to a closely similar picture: such agreement suggests that the behaviours seen at observation were representative of average domestic interaction.

Both assessments of parenting provide evidence of great heterogeneity in outcome. The findings suggest that, with but few exceptions, women who had been raised in institutions retained a normal capacity to feel and express a wide range of emotions in their personal relationships. The great majority of ex-care women were both affectionate to their children and actively involved with them, although a significant minority were low in expressed warmth. Moreover, the evidence did not suggest that most lacked parenting skills, nor indicate that they were rejecting or neglectful. On the other hand, they were in some important respects different from the comparison group women. They were much more likely to lack sensitivity in the handling of their children; they were more prone to irritable and aggressive responses; their discipline was less likely to be effective; and they tended not to play with their children in activities that developed the children's creativity, initiative and independence. The overall picture suggests that ex-care women were concerned and caring parents. However, as a group they were less skilful in picking up their children's cues, and less likely to respond to their children's behaviour in ways that circumvented difficulties.

The difference in their parenting is perhaps best illustrated by a consideration of their handling of control issues. Their problems in this area did not stem from any particular management style. The difference lay in their greater tendency to intervene briefly and in a negative way, when responding to minor oppositional behaviours. Moreover, it was not just when dealing with a misbehaving child that they were more negative; expressions of criticism, threats, a harsh tone of voice and so on were more common across all contexts. Interestingly, this difference was most marked outside confrontations (the difference within confrontations falling just short of statistical significance). Thus the fact that ex-care women tended to be more negative towards their children was not just because they were involved in more confrontations; the findings seem to reflect a difference in affective style rather than simply a less effective way of exerting discipline. It seemed that the brief control episodes were more expressions of unfocused maternal irritation than systematic attempts by the mother to change some particular aspect of her child's behaviour. Patterson (1982) has commented on the tendency for mothers of aggressive children to 'natter', and 'nag' their children frequently over nothing in particular. Whether or not the pattern we observed in the ex-care group reflects this quality requires further exploration. These data emphasise the complexity of the issue of disciplinary efficiency. The ex-care mothers' descriptions of how they manage their children's behaviour showed that a relatively high proportion of them were inefficient in exerting discipline. The observational data confirmed this picture. The best indicator of successful discipline, of course, is a child who does not engage in disruptive behaviour. Optimum control strategies aim to prevent unacceptable behaviour rather than to bring it to a halt once it has occurred. To what extent such success is best achieved by immediate responses to oppositional behaviour itself or by management outside disciplinary episodes is yet to be studied. However, the findings from our study allow a preliminary analysis of this issue.

There is certainly more to discipline than how misbehaviour is managed. Occasions for discipline may be averted by the prior statement of rules, prompts, cautions and lessons. Discipline involves anticipatory as well as reactive elements (see Radke-Yarrow and Kuczynski, 1983), and the emotional context of interactions also has implications for disciplinary efficiency (Patterson, 1982). The frequency with which parent–child confrontations arise is likely to be influenced by the parents' skills in responding to the children's needs and in helping them acquire effective approaches to problem-solving. The ex-care mothers' style of interaction may have been less than optimal in this connection: they tended not to use elaborating comments; they expressed negative affect both within and outside confrontation; and they tended to make frequent brief unfocused disciplinary interventions. The associated tendency to ignore, or not to respond to, their children's overtures and their relative lack of sensitivity to their children's needs may have important disciplinary implications. Perhaps parents need to acquire a disciplinary 'currency'. That is to say, if children are to be expected to comply with parental wishes, it may be necessary that parents first show that they are willing to respond positively to their children's demands. In that respect, the ex-care mothers' tendency to ignore or rebuff their children's approaches may have had adverse consequences through promoting negative interactions between parent and child. The fact that these mothers talked, played and initiated interactions with their children as much as the control group mothers might not compensate for this. Rather, the finding that the interactions were less likely to have arisen as a response to the child's demands may be more significant. This relative lack of maternal response may explain the finding that the children of ex-care women made far more spontaneous approaches to their mothers. Perhaps the children needed to persist in attempts to engage their mothers' attention, just because the mothers lacked sensitivity in picking up more ordinary cues.

## Summary

We may conclude that as a group the ex-care mothers were showing more parenting problems than the comparison sample. All the serious parenting breakdowns occurred in their group, and they also showed more subtle difficulties in the ways they currently parented. However, the data also showed that many problems occurred early in their parenting careers; that skills developed with experience; and that serious problems only occurred amongst a minority of ex-care mothers.

We need now to turn to the question of how these continuities and discontinuities might have arisen.

# 10 Adult functioning and its antecedents

The first issue we need to address in examining the nature of the inter-generational links in parenting problems in the ex-care sample is whether the continuities that exist apply particularly to *parenting*, or whether they reflect the persistence of a range of overlapping psychosocial problems of which parenting is just a part, as they did in the retrospective study. Therefore we need to ask first, what the overlap between parenting and other psychosocial problems is; and secondly, whether these current problems were related to earlier behavioural or emotional difficulties. However, we need also to explore the alternative hypothesis: that is, whether the inter-generational continuities and discontinuities are more associated with different patterns of *experience* in the women's lives than with their own functioning.

## The overlap of outcomes in adult life
The association between the overall ratings of parenting and psychosocial functioning is given in Figure 10.1. Four main conclusions may be drawn from these data. First, there was *no* association between the two measures in the comparison group. This implies that parenting difficulties, especially of a moderate kind, need not necessarily be a consequence of overall psychosocial impairment. Secondly, the two measures overlapped to a very considerable extent in the ex-care group. As a consequence there were very few ex-care women with poor current parenting but good psychosocial functioning on other outcome measures (3/42), and scarcely any with good parenting but a poor psychosocial outcome (2/42). Thirdly, the main difference between the groups applied to the proportions with both or neither sets of difficulties. There was little evidence of parenting links across the two generations when parenting difficulties *occurring in isolation* were considered. Indeed, intermediate levels of parenting problems shown by women with generally good psychosocial functioning were more a feature of the comparison group (30 per cent v. 12 per cent in the ex-care women). This finding suggests the inference for the fourth conclusion: namely, that the explanation for isolated parenting difficulties of a mild to moderate degree may well be differerent from that for severe and generalised psychosocial problems that include parenting difficulties as one of many areas of concern. These findings

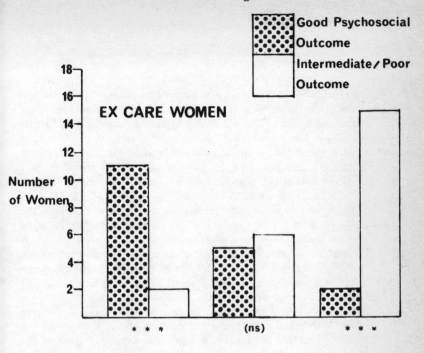

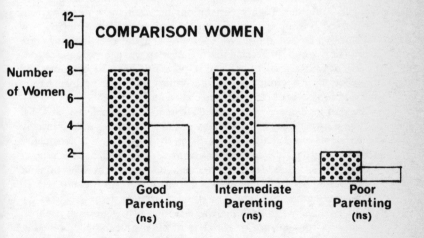

*Figure 10.1   Association between parenting and psychosocial adjustment*

are consistent with those from the retrospective study where moderate levels of current parenting problems unassociated with early adversities occurred largely in the comparison group (see also Egeland *et al.*, 1984).

### Correlations between individual psychosocial measures

The overall outcome measures were created from a combination of individual ratings. The question of overlap can therefore be further examined by looking at the associations between these. Kendall's rank-order correlation is an appropriate statistic for describing how such ordered variables tend to go together. This statistic gives a standardised coefficient based on the amount of agreement between two sets of rankings. These coefficients vary between +1.0 (indicating that the highest rank on one variable is always associated with the highest rank on the other) and −1.0 (indicating that the highest score on one variable is always associated with the lowest on another). A coefficient of 0.0, therefore, means that there is no association between the variables. The first row in each table gives the correlation between the individual items and the overall social functioning rating. The last column gives the correlation of these items with parenting.

The tables confirm the pattern of association between the overall measures, with social functioning and parenting being strongly related in the ex-care sample but not in the comparison group. In general, the correlations between items within the latter sample were very low except for those between generally poor social relationships and specific problems in relationships with the opposite sex, and with psychiatric disorder. Higher correlations between these items were to be expected because the criteria for the ratings overlap. Similarly, the correlations between the individual items and the overall rating were lower in this group, indicating that the overlap was generally much less. This is consistent with the fact that poor psychosocial outcomes did not occur in this group, and that a variety of single problems were involved in the overall rating of 'some current difficulties'.

Correlations between the individual items and overall psychosocial functioning were higher in the ex-care sample indicating a substantially greater association. This follows from the high rate of personality disorders, a rating that depends on the presence of deficits in a number of areas. Nevertheless, several other features are worthy of comment. First, the number of cohabitations a woman had had was not related to the other outcome items. That is, the pattern of more frequent cohabitations amongst this sample was a feature of the group as a whole, not simply a consequence or correlate of other psychosocial problems. Secondly, official criminality was not strongly related either to psychiatric problems or to more general difficulties in relationships suggesting that criminal activities (which were common in this group)

Table 10.1  *Rank-order correlations between individual outcome measures*

*Ex-care women*

|  | 1 | 2 | 3 | 4 | 5 | 6 | 7 | 8 | 9 |
|---|---|---|---|---|---|---|---|---|---|
| Social functioning | — | .67 | .53 | .23 | .33 | .56 | .47 | .18 | .53 |
| Psychiatric disorder |  | — | .70 | .10 | .24 | .52 | .23 | .13 | .49 |
| Personality disorder |  |  | — | .10 | .32 | .46 | .12 | .14 | .38 |
| Official criminality |  |  |  | — | .19 | .24 | .19 | .12 | .25 |
| Poor social relations |  |  |  |  | — | .30 | .14 | -.04 | .15 |
| Sex/love problems |  |  |  |  |  | — | .39 | .23 | .09 |
| Quality of marriage |  |  |  |  |  |  | — | .09 | .47 |
| No. of cohabitations |  |  |  |  |  |  |  | — |  |
| Current parenting |  |  |  |  |  |  |  |  | — |

*Comparison women*

|  | 1 | 2 | 3 | 4 | 5 | 6 | 7 | 8 | 9 |
|---|---|---|---|---|---|---|---|---|---|
| Social functioning | — | .33 | * | -.11 | .49 | .23 | .25 | .20 | -.11 |
| Psychiatric disorder |  | — | * | -.04 | .31 | -.04 | .17 | .10 | * |
| Personality disorder |  |  | — | * | * | * | * | * | * |
| Official criminality |  |  |  | — | -.05 | -.02 | -.06 | -.07 | * |
| Poor social relations |  |  |  |  | — | .48 | .15 | -.04 | .17 |
| Sex/love problems |  |  |  |  |  | — | * | -.28 | .09 |
| Quality of marriage |  |  |  |  |  |  | — | .15 | .37 |
| No. of cohabitations |  |  |  |  |  |  |  | — |  |
| Current parenting |  |  |  |  |  |  |  |  | — |

* Coefficient cannot be computed.

were not, taken in isolation, good indicators of overall psychosocial functioning.

## Continuities in individual functioning

The next issue is whether there was evidence for continuities in individual functioning. That is, were the difficulties that the ex-care women showed in adult life associated with a history of psychosocial problems going back to their childhood? The Rutter A and B scales — the house-parent and teacher questionnaires measuring emotional and behavioural problems in middle childhood — were used to examine this.

All studies of children in long-stay institutions have shown a high prevalence of emotional and behavioural problems (e.g. Pringle and Bossio, 1960; Wolkind, 1974). Our findings provide no exception to this picture: six times as many of the ex-care girls (35 per cent v. 6 per cent) showed disturbed behaviour at school, a highly significant difference. This disturbance took the form of both emotional and conduct problems, although the latter were more common. The ex-care children also showed high rates of disturbance on the questionnaires completed by house-parents where 26 per cent of children had deviant scores. No comparison data were available on these questionnaires. In all, over half of the ex-care group (53 per cent) were rated as disturbed on one or both of the measures.

Figures 10.2 and 10.3 show the extent to which such problems were precursors of later psychosocial difficulties. Of the women with emotional or behavioural problems when young, 71 per cent showed poor parenting compared with 37 per cent of those without such problems, a statistically significant difference. On its own, delinquency before the age of 18 was not significantly related to parenting outcome, but an index involving one or both of these indicators of earlier disturbances was. (The slightly lower percentage of women with poor parenting on the latter rating compared with the questionnaire scores on their own is an artefact of the combination of missing data from the two measures. This is because cases in which one rating was non-deviant and the other item missing had to be omitted from the analysis.)

In contrast, poor social functioning was not related to the combined questionnaire/delinquency index at a statistically significant level although there appeared to be a trend in the same direction. This was also the case for the two childhood measures considered singly. However, significant associations were found between earlier behaviour and both poor social functioning and personality disorder when the analysis was confined to those girls showing conduct disorder or mixed emotional/conduct problems on either or both questionnaires. Here, half the girls with such difficulties showed poor social functioning in adulthood compared with 22 per cent of those without such problems. The figures for personality disorders were comparable (45 per cent v.

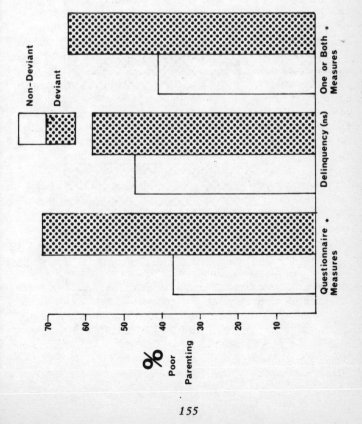

Figure 10.2  Emotional/behavioural disturbance in childhood and parenting

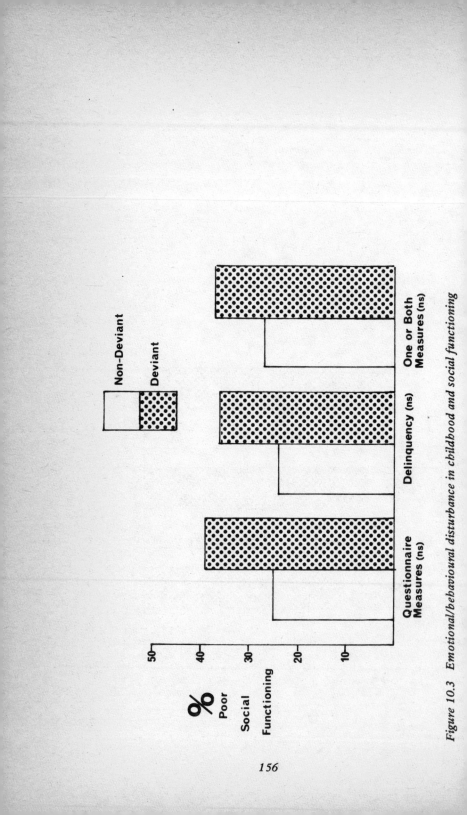

Figure 10.3  Emotional/behavioural disturbance in childhood and social functioning

22 per cent). We can therefore conclude that there were significant continuities between the girls' earlier behaviour and their functioning in adult life.

However, it cannot necessarily be concluded from these data that parenting was more strongly related to earlier emotional/behavioural disturbances than social functioning was because the 'poor outcome' ratings on both measures may not be equivalent and because the social functioning rating takes in a wider variety of behaviours and experiences into account. This may mask a relationship between early emotional problems and later difficulties through the contribution of the better functioning of others — spouses, for example — to particular ratings such as marriage. On the other hand, the possibility of a stronger relationship with parenting must remain open. Parenting, although offering rewards, may be a more stringent test of current coping skills and the ability to sustain relationships. This possibility is supported by the data which show that, whilst current marital relationships were not associated with childhood deviance, lower sensitivity, lower warmth and aggressiveness in parenting all were, although the differences reached statistical significance only for an aggressive style of discipline (see Figure 10.4).

It is apparent, however, that the ex-care/comparison group differences on parenting were *not* wholly explicable in terms of emotional/behavioural functioning before maturity. Even amongst those without such problems when young, the outcome for the ex-care women was substantially worse than that for the comparison sample, only 10 per cent of whom showed poor parenting. This indicates that the parenting difficulties of the institution-reared women were by no means entirely a function of emotional/behavioural disturbance that was already apparent in childhood. There are a number of possible explanations for this excess of parenting problems even amongst the ex-care women not showing problems in early adolescence. First, it may simply be that more sophisticated measures are needed to detect continuities in functioning in this 'non-deviant' group. Secondly, it may be that the impact of early experiences in part relates to behaviours specific to parenting and therefore that these would not be expected to show in measures of earlier functioning. But thirdly, the explanation may be that the linkages between institutional rearing and poorer parenting in the absence of behavioural problems in childhood reflect continuities in the context of parenting rather than in some intrinsic process involving individual development. This possibility is considered in detail in Chapter 11. But first, the question of the contribution of earlier deviance to drinking problems will be outlined and the issue of the experiential antecedents of adult problems discussed.

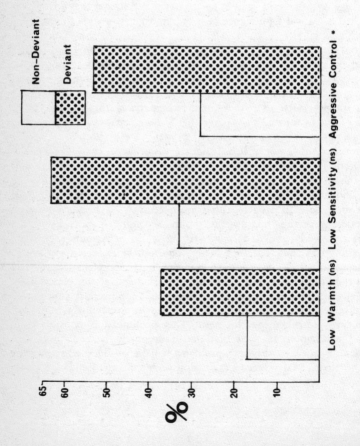

Figure 10.4 Deviance on questionnaires and parenting behaviour

### Earlier adjustment and drinking problems

The contribution of drinking problems to parenting difficulties was discussed in the last chapter, and it is important to know whether these problems were associated with earlier signs of emotional or behavioural difficulties. The answer is that they were — 35 per cent of the young women showing deviance on the teachers' questionnaires had a history of drinking problems compared with 18 per cent of those not showing problems earlier, a significant difference. The contrast was even more marked for those showing drinking problems currently where those scoring high on the teachers' questionnaire were four times as likely to have problems with alcohol (17 per cent v. 4 per cent).

The overall findings for the association between alcohol abuse and criminality were similar to those for the B scale, with 40 per cent of those with criminal records having drinking difficulties compared with 16 per cent of those without. However, criminality was more strongly related to drinking problems in the teenage years only than to current abuse. Thus 62 per cent of those with only teenage drinking problems showed criminal behaviour compared with 30 per cent of those with current drinking difficulties. The numbers are too few to determine whether this is a meaningful difference, but it may be that there are two distinct groups with a history of alcohol abuse: those whose drinking problems were mainly a consequence of the social environments in which they were placed on leaving care, and those who show a more persistent history of alcoholism less associated with purely environmental factors.

### Experiential antecedents of adult functioning

*Age at admission to care and pre-admission experiences*
The childhood experiences of the ex-care women involved both overt discord and disruption at home prior to long-term admission to care, and the more harmonious but discontinuous multiple caretaking of the institutional environment. Previous studies have shown that admissions to long-term care before the age of two have discernible sequelae much later in childhood (Tizard and Hodges, 1978; Hodges and Tizard, submitted) and it is necessary to determine whether this was also the case for functioning in adult life.

Figure 10.5 gives the relationships between the age at long-term admission, prior parenting experiences, and the adult social functioning measures. The findings show that those admitted under the age of two had a high rate of difficulties in adult life, with 39 per cent of women having *marked* current problems. It is clear, however, that those admitted later, following disrupted parenting experiences, were *equally* likely to have poor outcomes as adults. This is in marked contrast to those admitted after two from less disrupted parenting circumstances. This pattern was also evident for parenting outcomes: 56 per cent of

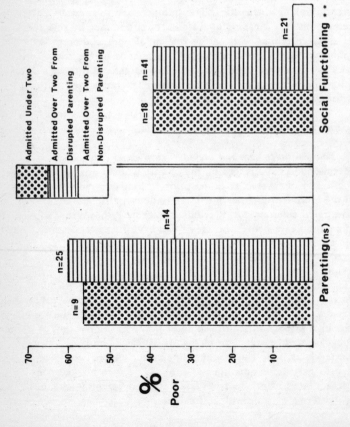

Figure 10.5  Age at admission to care, prior parenting and outcome

those admitted under two showed poor overall parenting — a rate comparable to the 60 per cent for those admitted after age two years who had experienced disrupted or disturbed parenting, but substantially higher than the 29 per cent for those admitted after two years of age from non-disrupted homes. Chapter 11 examines the extent to which these differences were related to variations in later life-history, and the extent to which they reflected direct effects on functioning.

*Quality of experiences in care*
The associations between in-care experiences before the age of 12 and later psychosocial functioning and parenting are given in Table 10.2. The quality of relationships with the staff in the homes were strongly related to both outcome measures. Those reporting mixed or poor relationships were more likely to have currently poor functioning, and those reporting only good relationships to have fewer parenting or other problems, although not all the differences reached statistical significance. Similar patterns were apparent for relationships with other children. These associations of outcome measures with relationships when in-care remained substantially the same for the period of the children's secondary schooling.

*Contacts with parents*
The association between the frequency of parental contact when in care and the outcome measures is given in Figure 10.6. It is clear that the group with regular parental contact had much lower rates of problems both in parenting and in social functioning later. These findings support the general conclusion from this analysis that features of the subjects' experiences when in care are strongly related to outcome in adult life, especially to parenting. The nature of this relationship will be discussed in Chapter 11.

*Secondary schooling*
Life in the children's homes up to the end of primary schooling (which was conducted within the homes' own schools) provided a similar environment for all children. The situation was very different when they reached secondary school age. At this point they were dispersed amongst a wide number of schools to prevent the concentration of disadvantaged children in any one of them. They thus had to cope with a new experience, to travel often a considerable distance (a thing to which they were unaccustomed) and to make friends with a new set of peers, even if some of these were also from the homes. Schooling outside provided the children with a new, non-institutionalised environment and the policy of dispersal provided a great variety of new experiences to the girls as a group. However, the power for good of these new experiences has to be set against the stress of a change for which the girls were often unprepared practically or emotionally.

Table 10.2   *Relationships in care under age 12 and outcome*

| | | Relationships with staff | | | Relationships with peers | | |
|---|---|---|---|---|---|---|---|
| | | Positive | Neutral | Poor | Positive | Neutral | Poor |
| | | % | % | % | % | % | % |
| *Social functioning* | Good | 42 | 29 | 10 | 20 | 32 | 3 |
| | History only | 16 | 25 | 15 | 40 | 13 | 24 |
| | Some problems | 42 | 25 | 32 | 40 | 21 | 45 |
| | Poor | 0 | 21 | 44 | 0 | 34 | 28 |
| | | (*) | | | (ns) | | |
| | | % | % | % | % | % | % |
| *Overall parenting* | Good | 44 | 29 | 21 | 50 | 36 | 11 |
| | Intermediate | 33 | 29 | 17 | 25 | 20 | 28 |
| | Poor | 22 | 43 | 63 | 25 | 44 | 61 |
| | | (ns) | | | (ns) | | |

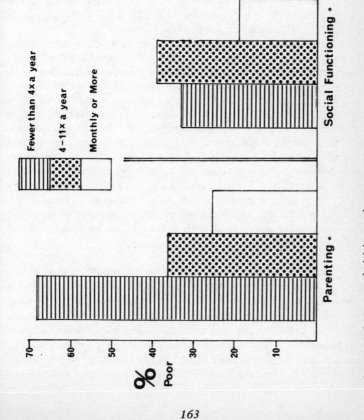

Figure 10.6  Parental visiting and outcome

Therefore, we need to examine the quality of their reactions to secondary schooling and the associations between these and their functioning when they reached adulthood.

*Positive and negative experiences*   The women were asked to describe in detail their secondary school experiences, behaviour and achievements, and were rated both on objective measures such as persistent truancy, examination successes and membership of a stable peer group, and on their recollections of the pleasure or unhappiness derived from their schooling. In addition, ratings were made of positive evaluations of various aspects of school life including academic learning, craftwork, sport or positions of responsibility. These measures were based on accounts of the pleasure and the sense of personal achievement they obtained and not on external estimates of 'success' such as examinations or reports. Summary ratings of schooling were then made. *Negative experiences* were coded if the subject reported two or more of: persistent truancy, no peer group in school, or marked unhappiness with school work or with peer relationships. *Positive experiences* were coded if there were two or more of: CSE or 'O' level successes, a clearly positive evaluation of school work or of relationships, or a positive recall of three or more areas of school life including sport, responsibility, arts and crafts and academic lessons.

The ex-care women were significantly more likely to be rated overall as having had negative school experiences (48 per cent v. 22 per cent); to have been markedly unhappy with school work (54 per cent v. 22 per cent); to have been persistent truants from before their final year in school (42 per cent v. 24 per cent); and to have been unhappy in their relationships with peers (30 per cent v. 15 per cent) (these last two differences were just short of significance). The two groups were much more similar with respect to positive experiences. There were no differences on the overall rating (37 per cent v. 32 per cent) or on clearly positive evaluations of school work (9 per cent v. 12 per cent) or peer relationships (11 per cent v. 15 per cent). More striking here is the *lack* of positive impact of school on children from ordinary inner city families. The one sizeable and significant difference between the groups was in the proportions with some CSE or 'O' level successes (7 per cent v. 35 per cent).

*School experiences and outcome*   The relationship between overall school experiences and outcome is given in Figure 10.7. The presence or absence of positive experiences was not related to adult functioning in the comparison group. The picture was different amongst the ex-care sample. For them, 39 per cent without positive experiences had poor social functioning compared with only 8 per cent of those with positive schooling. This pattern applied also to parenting, where 59 per cent of those without positive experiences were in the poor parenting group as

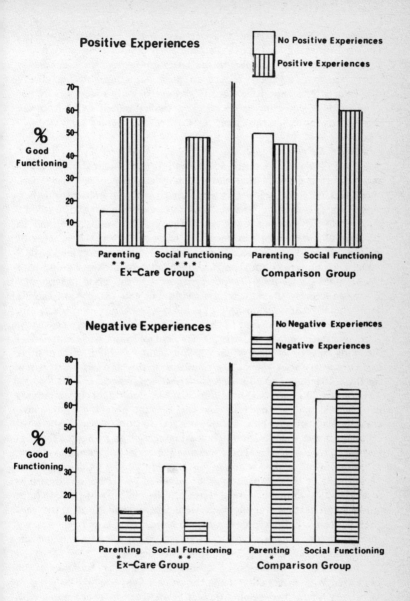

*Figure 10.7  School experiences and outcome*

against 21 per cent of those who reported their schooling positively. As might be expected, parallel findings were found for the presence of negative experiences. Here also the associations were strong in the expected direction for the ex-care sample but did not relate to outcome at all in the controls. Indeed, in the latter group negative relationships at school were inversely related to poor parenting showing clearly that poor school experiences in the absence of early adversities are not a precursor of parenting problems. This finding parallels that from the retrospective study on the significance of teenage problems.

*Education and further training*
Since very few of the ex-care women had formal examination successes at school it is unlikely that the associations between positive experiences and outcome are largely explained by IQ differences. Furthermore, the association between positive experiences and outcome remains for this group even when the comparison is confined to experiences *not* involving examination successes, where 42 per cent of those with good experiences show good functioning compared with 9 per cent of those without them, although amongst the small group with examination passes four (71 per cent) were in the 'good functioning' group. Moreover, there is no association in the comparison sample between outcome and positive experiences, with or without examination successes: 65 per cent of those without positive experiences show good outcome compared with 50 per cent of those with experiences including academic success and 80 per cent of those with positive experiences without them. The numbers in this analysis are too few for these differences to approach statistical significance.

However, formal qualifications may be important in improving life-chances, and we need to ask whether the generally more stable environments of the control subjects were associated with the girls' obtaining more qualifications on leaving school and whether this was associated with outcome. There were only marginal differences between the samples on further training: 89 per cent of the ex-care girls and 78 per cent of the comparison group acquired no further qualifications of any sort, a non-significant difference. The majority of those in both groups with further training took secretarial examinations (9 per cent v. 10 per cent) or did apprenticeships in hairdressing (1 per cent v. 7 per cent). One girl in each sample became a state registered nurse and one of the comparison group gained a university degree.

There was a statistically significant trend for training to be associated with better outcome in the ex-care sample where 44 per cent of those with further training showed good functioning compared with 18 per cent of those without any further qualifications. However, as with the school measures, this association was not significant in the comparison sample although a higher proportion of those with training were in the good social functioning group (78 per cent v. 59 per cent).

Futher training was much more strongly and significantly related to positive school experiences for the ex-care girls where only 5 per cent of those without positive experiences went on to take further qualifications compared with 24 per cent of those with them. This association did not appear at all in the comparison group where 20 per cent of those with positive experiences went on to further training as against 23 per cent of those without.

These differences between the two samples were substantially the same when both academic successes and further training were considered together. However, the inclusion of both variables tended to *reduce* the association between qualifications and outcome in the comparison sample where 58 per cent of those with qualifications showed good functioning compared with 68 per cent of those without. In both groups girls without any qualifications were more likely to have been pregnant by the time of follow-up (78 per cent v. 38 per cent in the ex-care group; and 52 per cent v. 33 per cent in the controls) although this reached significance only for the institutionalised sample. This was even more marked for pregnancy before the age of 19 (33 per cent v. 8 per cent in the ex-care sample; and 9 per cent v. 0 per cent in the controls).

Three conclusions may be drawn from these data. First, positive experiences at secondary school and subsequent career training have a clear effect on the life course and adjustment of the institutionalised group. Secondly, these experiences were not sufficient entirely to remove the effects of their childhood experiences since the proportion with positive experiences now functioning well was less than in the comparison group. Thirdly, the *lack* of positive experiences at this time had much more serious consequences for the ex-care girls than it did for those in the general population. This suggests that the institutionalised group may have been rendered more vulnerable to negative experiences than the controls. This vulnerability may involve both increased inability to cope effectively with stressful situations and a less supportive environment when these occur. Environmental factors may in addition prevent the adverse consequences of some stresses, for example by reducing the likelihood of early pregnancy or poor career decisions. These issues are discussed further in the next two chapters. First, we need to consider other features of the women's teenage life-histories.

### Positive relationships during the teenage years
Relationships with adults when in care have been considered earlier. The effects of positive relationships at this time can be extended to examine the effects of positive relationships during the teens more generally. Relationships were rated as 'positive' if the subject reported that for a substantial proportion of her teenage years, she maintained a stable relationship (or relationships) with one or more adults for whom she felt a definite attachment. The relationships need not

necessarily have been free of tension or arguments but there had to be clear evidence of positive feelings and of prolonged attachment to an adult who might be a parent, foster-parent, house-parent or any other grown-up (peer relationships and those with spouses were excluded from this rating). The presence of such clearly positive relationships made no appreciable difference to overall outcome: 46 per cent of women without good relationships in the teenage years showed poor parenting compared with 50 per cent of those with good relationships. The findings were similar for overall social functioning (36 per cent v. 24 per cent), neither difference being significant.

There is an apparent contradiction between these findings and those presented above concerning relationships when in the children's homes. This arises because that analysis was concerned with the outcomes from overall experiences and thus separated the subjects into those whose relationships with staff or peers were *only* good, or neutral or poor. The small group with both positive and negative relationships had outcomes similar to those in the poorly relating group and were therefore amalgamated with them. Here the effects on outcome of at least one stable and positive relationship (regardless of the presence of negative relationships) is examined and in this case there were no strong associations.

### Family relationships on return home
The findings with respect to family experience subsequent to discharge from residential care are summarised in Figure 10.8. In most cases this involved a return to one or both biological parents, but eight long-term fostering placements were also included. About half the girls returned to some kind of family environment, with the remainder staying in the institutions until they left to live independently. Although the numbers involved were quite low, a poor psychosocial outcome seemed less likely if the girl returned to a harmonious family setting or to one with no more than parent–adolescent disagreements. Of those going to a home with pervasive quarrelling and disharmony, half showed poor social functioning; a substantially worse outcome than for those remaining in care. But, once again this did not apply to the quality of parenting. Here the outcome was much the same whether or not the girls returned to a family and there was no consistent association with the characteristics of the home to which they returned. However, it should be noted that none of the three women who returned to non-discordant homes and had children at the follow-up showed poor parenting.

### Pregnancy history
In Chapter 9 a number of features of the history of pregnancy and childbirth were shown to differentiate the ex-care and comparison samples. The ex-care women were more likely to become pregnant

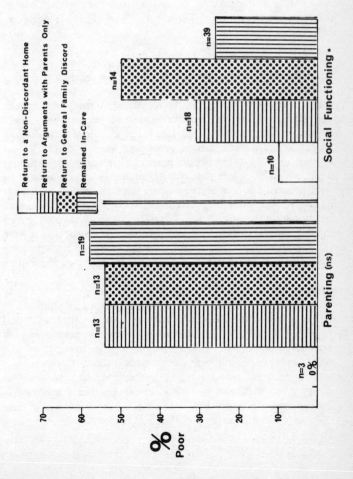

Figure 10.8 Later family relationships and outcome

before the age of 19 and it was more frequent for their first pregnancy to be unplanned and unwanted. In addition, the children selected for parenting assessment were somewhat but not significantly more likely to have spent time in a special care facility immediately following their birth (20 per cent v. 3 per cent). The frequency of birth complications (such as breech, forceps or caesarian deliveries) were similar in both groups (24 per cent v. 22 per cent).

It is important to determine whether these characteristics of their pregnancy and childbirth experiences relate to their overall parenting histories. As Table 10.3 shows, both the age at first pregnancy and whether the pregnancy was planned or wanted relate strongly to an overall poor parenting outcome in the ex-care sample. However, neither of these features related to parenting in the comparison group. This suggests that the impact of these pregnancy and childbirth experiences on later parenting is mediated by other features of the women's lives. The links between their earlier life-histories and their parenting are discussed in the next chapter.

## Summary

This chapter has discussed a number of the antecedents of parenting problems and poor social functioning for the ex-care and comparison samples. It was apparent that, as in the retrospective study, the current parenting difficulties of the institution-reared sample overlapped strongly with more general problems in psychosocial functioning. This was not so for the comparison group and we may conclude that the correlates of mild or moderate parenting problems are different from those of more severe difficulties. Measures of emotional or behavioural problems in the teenage years were associated with later parenting difficulties, but the relationships of these with overall social functioning were not strong. With respect to the links between emotional/behavioural disturbance and parenting, the associations were stronger for aggressiveness in control than for relational features such as expressed warmth or sensitivity, although there appeared to be some associations with these parenting characteristics also.

However, it was also apparent that the functioning of these young women in early adult life could not be wholly explained by continuities in emotional or behavioural problems relating to their earlier childhood experiences. A number of experiential factors were also associated with better outcomes. Moreover, the variations in the strength of the relationships between a number of antecedent factors and current functioning, and the differences in these associations between the two samples suggest that continuities with earlier emotional/behavioural problems may not be direct but mediated by other aspects of life-history. This question is examined in the next chapter.

*Table 10.3   Pregnancy history and poor overall parenting outcome*

|  | Ex-care group % Poor parenting | Comparison group % Poor parenting |
|---|---|---|
| *Age at first pregnancy* | | |
| Under 19 | 62 | 0 |
| 19 or over | 32 | 14 |
|  | (*) | (ns) |
| *Planning of first pregnancy* | | |
| Unplanned and unwanted | 85 | 0 |
| Unplanned but accepted | 43 | 14 |
| Planned pregnancy | 23 | 12 |
|  | (**) | (ns) |
| *Birth complications: index child* | | |
| None | 38 | 10 |
| Some (breech, forceps, caesarian etc.) | 70 | 17 |
|  | (ns) | (ns) |
| *Special post-natal care* | | |
| None | 44 | 12 |
| One or more days | 50 | 0 |
|  | (ns) | (ns) |

# 11   Processes of transmission

## Introduction

In the analysis of the retrospective study the characteristics and life-histories of the parents with children currently in care were detailed. These features included increased rates of parental deviance and disorder; serious childhood adversities; in-care experiences; strained family relationships in the teenage years; early pregnancies; and current material, marital and psychiatric difficulties. In the prospective study the early institutional experiences were, by definition, common to all the ex-care subjects and a high proportion also suffered family discord. Their later emotional/behavioural adjustment in early adolescence, their later marital and pregnancy histories and their current parenting frequently paralleled those of the mothers in the first study. Moreover, serious breakdowns in parenting, which were not uncommon, were entirely confined to this group. It was observations such as these that originally led to the idea of a cycle of transmitted deprivation perpetuated through family circumstances. On the other hand, the retrospective study showed that other factors were implicated in current parenting and in parenting breakdown; in particular, the characteristics of husbands and of marital circumstances, and features of housing and material conditions. Moreover, the presence of these current adversities was linked to early family hardships. What that study was unable to examine, as is the case with retrospective investigations, was the probability of a poor outcome given such early adversities, or the processes linking disadvantaged childhoods, adverse life-histories, current adverse circumstances and poorer parenting or social functioning in early adult life.

The first finding from the prospective study that should be emphasised is the considerable heterogeneity of outcomes. Only a minority, albeit a substantial minority, of mothers showed currently poor parenting or poor social functioning. Clearly, the marked childhood adversities, which they *all* suffered, were not being transmitted to the next generation in most cases. On the other hand, taking the ex-care and the comparison sample together, *all* those whose children did experience parenting breakdowns were drawn from families with marked early adversities. What, then, are the impacts of such childhoods and is it possible to identify the processes through which continuities or discontinuities occur?

Two general models for these processes were outlined in Chapter 1: the first concerned the perpetuation of disadvantages through the nature of the social structure and the second through the impact of adversities on personality development. There is a danger in discussions of these alternatives for one of the models to be advanced to the exclusion of the other, even though the general tendency to *discontinuity* in disadvantage does not support either strongly (Rutter and Madge, 1976). There can be little doubt that family circumstances and relationships affect children's development, and that discordant and disrupted family experiences can have markedly adverse consequences for children (Rutter and Giller, 1983; Quinton and Rutter, 1985). On the other hand, there can be little doubt that poverty and poor circumstances can markedly affect physical and mental health and the relationships of family members (Rutter and Madge, 1976; Brown and Madge, 1982). Social structural considerations are clearly necessary to explain how disadvantages are distributed within society and why, within certain disadvantaged sectors of the population, particular adversities show inter-generational continuities in some families but not in others. Conversely, family process models are sometimes unjustifiably used to explain away current social disadvantages as being a consequence of individual inadequacies.

In this chapter analyses are presented that consider both the impact of experiences on individual development and functioning and the impact of wider social variables as they operate at the family level. Here the two models for inter-generational continuities pose related but distinct questions. First, to what extent does the point from which the subjects start — that is, in long-term care and from disadvantaged homes — constrain their life-chances? Secondly, to what extent is the perpetuation of disadvantage or its converse a function of the impact of early experiences on personality development. That is, is there an increased probability that the behavioural sequelae to adverse experiences *lead* individuals into adverse circumstances? And finally, are the adverse effects of early hardships non-reversible by the time adulthood is reached?

At first glance, the data presented in Chapter 10 would seem to offer strong support for the view that continuities occur through experiential or genetic effects on personality development. Emotional/behavioural disturbance as rated on the houseparents and teacher questionnaires, was associated with poorer outcome on social functioning and parenting. The subjects' reports of relationships when in care pointed in the same direction — if it is assumed that their own behaviour contributed to these relationships. Further, there seemed to be little beneficial impact of longstanding positive relationships with adults during their teenage years. It is clear that children admitted to care constitute a group at high risk for deviant personality development and various psychosocial problems (Chapter 10). Such data have often led to the conclusion that early experiences have permanently damaging effects, and, where this damage is not yet apparent in behavioural or emotional problems, it is simply covert, present under the surface and waiting to be revealed. Such views are hard to reconcile with the well-documented fact that many — usually the majority — children do not succumb in the face of risk factors of a wide variety of kinds and severities (Rutter, 1979, 1985b). Nor are 'sleeper effects' a common phenomenon. More usually the long-term consequences of exposure to psychosocial risk show attenuation of sequelae with age and changing circumstances, or vulnerabilities apparent later under particularly stressful conditions only.

Interest in the question of resilience or invulnerability in the 1970s (Anthony, 1974; Garmezy, 1974) focused initially on factors in the child associated with resistance to stressors. It has remained an open question, however, whether the factors promoting resilience lie primarily in the children or their environment (Rutter, 1979, 1985b). The search for such factors does not just mean investigating positive influences that encourage optimal psychosocial development. Rather, the idea concerns influences, both positive and negative, that serve to affect resilience in children exposed to environmental hazards. In short, the focus is on factors that in some way *alter* the impact of risks — an interaction of some kind (Rutter, 1983; in press d) — and not just on beneficial influences. From this perspective, there is similarly no implication that effects permanently change the course of personality development; instead, the concern is to identify the variety of influences from both personal dispositions and environmental circumstances that serve to create continuities and discontinuities (Rutter, 1984b; in press c). This is the theoretical and analytic approach taken in this chapter.

## Genetic factors and disrupted parenting in early childhood

### Parental deviance and disorder

The ex-care group is clearly a group at risk for psychosocial problems. A major question to consider first is which factors in their background or experience constituted the risk, and in particular whether their poorer outcome was a function of their genetic endowment or their experiences in childhood. The study was not designed to differentiate between these two types of risk and obviously both were present. Nevertheless, some measure of possible hereditary influence can be obtained through attention to overt deviance in the parents of the ex-care women, since, as the children had been separated from their parents for much of their upbringing, such deviance may be used as an indirect measure of possible genetic factors. Contemporaneous Social Services records were available for 40 subjects. Parental deviance was rated as present if either of the girls' parents had had a criminal record in adult life, or had been treated for a psychiatric disorder, or alcoholism or being dependent on 'hard' drugs. Parental deviance was rated for two-thirds of the girls. The presence or absence of parental deviance was then assessed in relation to the various outcome variables.

Table 11.1    Parental deviance

|  | Absent (N=13) % | Present (N=27) % | Exact Probability (one-tailed) |
|---|---|---|---|
| Behavioural disorder (childhood) | 55 | 58 | ns |
| Juvenile delinquency | 23 | 15 | ns |
| Criminality (adult and child) | 23 | 30 | ns |
| Personality disorder (adult) | 8 | 41 | 0.03 |
| Poor psychosocial functioning | 23 | 41 | ns |
| Poor parenting | 43 | 42 | ns |

As shown in Table 11.1 parental deviance showed a significant association with adult personality disorder and a non-significant association with the other outcome variables. Because personality disorder was rated on the basis of the history of overall psychosocial functioning, the two ratings necessarily overlapped. However, they differed in that the former required persistently impaired functioning over many years, although not necessarily significant handicap at the point of follow-up. Conversely, the overall psychosocial outcome rating was based solely on current functioning without reference to persistence over time. As it happened, four of the 14 women with poor overall functioning did not show a personality disorder, and two of the 12 women with a personality disorder did not show current poor overall functioning at the follow-up assessment.

### Disrupted early parenting experiences
Comparable within-group analyses were undertaken with respect to whether or not the ex-care children experienced disrupted parenting during the first four years of life. Disrupted parenting was rated as having occurred if there had been short-term admissions into care, multiple separations through parental discord or disorder, persistent family discord, or admission into long-term institutional care before the age of two years. The findings (Figure 11.1) showed that the adult outcome, in terms of both personality disorder and overall psychosocial functioning, was substantially worse for those women who experienced disrupted parenting in infancy.

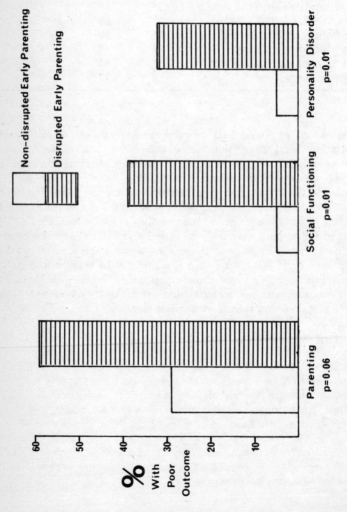

Figure 11.1 Disrupted parenting in infancy and outcome

Not surprisingly, disrupted parenting occurred more frequently in the subgroup of girls with deviant parents. Hence, the next question was which variable had the greater effect on outcome — parental deviance or disrupted parenting? Figure 11.2 presents the overall pattern of findings for the outcome measure of overall social functioning and for personality disorder. The numbers were too few to permit this analysis for parenting. A linear logistic analysis of these data is given in Appendix E. The data show that there was a highly significant main effect of disrupted parenting on social functioning but no main effect for parental deviance and no significant additional effect from their combination. Thus, in so far as these measures allowed a test of the matter, the findings indicate an important effect from early life-experiences that is not explicable in terms of biological parentage. The findings for personality disorder are more complicated in that there are significant main effects for both parental deviance and disrupted parenting, with a further significant effect for their combination, suggesting that both genetic and experiential factors are important in this case.

Ideally, it would have been desirable to consider separately the child's age at the time of admission to the children's home since the disrupted parenting that resulted from multiple caretaking in the institution was rather different in quality from that which stemmed from discord and disorder in the biological families. Earlier analysis showed that the outcome for children admitted to the institution in the first two years of life and who remained there throughout childhood was as bad as that for any other subgroup (see Figure 10.5). The numbers involved were rather few for the examination of the effects of the child's age of admission to long-term care after taking account of parental deviance and early disruption but this was attempted in a linear logistic analysis with respect to personality disorder, the outcome most strongly related to these early experiences (see Appendix E). This analysis repeats the findings from Figure 11.2 showing a significant main effect for both disrupted parenting and parental deviance, but not for age at admission. In that the inclusion of these two main effects provided a satisfactory fit to the data, it can be argued that age at admission is not an important variable once they are taken into account. However, both disruption and age at admission produced similar significant reductions in deviance when added to the model fitting parental deviance only, and it seems likely that these factors overlap. Since the best fit was provided by the inclusion of all three variables it is premature to conclude from these data that admission age is unimportant. Further comparisons of samples selected more specifically with respect to these variables is necessary to determine this point.

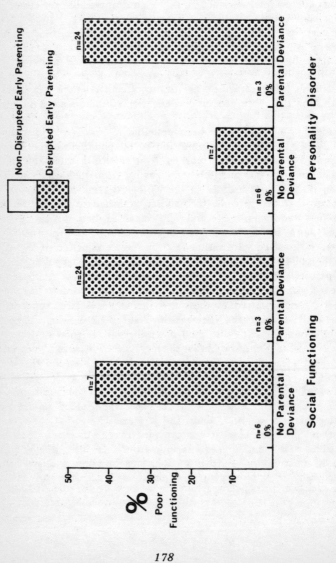

Figure 11.2 Parental deviance, disrupted parenting and outcome

*Circumstances at admission and pattern of discharge*

As already discussed, the children's experience of parenting during the infancy period showed a significant association with the women's social functioning in adult life. It might be thought that the finding implies that experiences during the early years have some sort of critical impact on personality development – perhaps as a result of influences on children's first acquisition of selective social attachments. However, the results summarised in Figure 11.3 indicate that that would be an unwarranted assumption. These data show that disrupted parenting in infancy was significantly associated with what happened when the young people left institutional care in late adolescence. Of the girls who did not experience disrupted parenting in infancy one third left the children's home to return to a non-discordant family environment. In sharp contrast this happened with a mere 5 per cent of those who had had disrupted parenting during their early years. More than half (61 per cent) of the girls admitted to the children's home when under the age of two years did not return to any type of family when they left the institution (not surprisingly, because few had a family to which they could return). In contrast, although this also applied to many of those who experienced disrupted parenting but were not admitted until after age two years (46 per cent), a number (24 per cent) also returned to a generally discordant family, usually the one from whence they had been taken many years before. These discharge patterns were *not* related to the girls' functioning as measured on the parent and teacher scales. It is apparent that the measure of disrupted parenting could not be considered solely in terms of what happened in infancy because what happened then served to influence the girls' circumstances on leaving the institution more than a dozen years later.

## Mediating and ameliorating factors

The analyses thus far have shown that disrupted parenting in the early years followed by institutional rearing in middle and later childhood significantly predisposed to poor psychosocial functioning in early adult life, of which poor parenting constituted one important facet. Nevertheless, many of the ex-care women did *not* show poor parenting and a substantial minority showed good parenting. It is necessary now to consider possible mediating and ameliorating factors that might explain that heterogeneity.

*Positive experiences at school*

It has been shown already (Chapter 10) that the girls' behaviour in middle childhood and early adolescence constituted an important link between infancy and adult functioning. The outcome was significantly worse for those girls already delinquent or showing disturbed behaviour at home or at school at that time. On the other hand, those who reported positive experiences at school showed markedly better

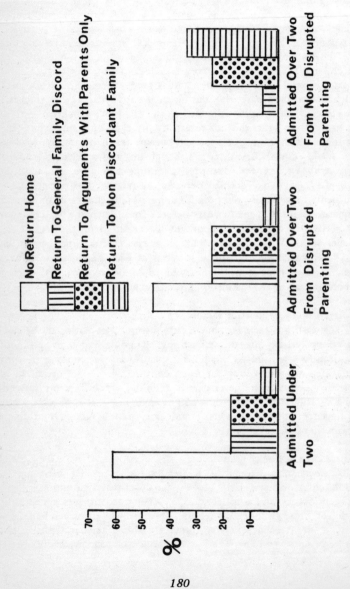

Figure 11.3 Disrupted parenting in infancy and family relationships on return home

functioning later, and it may be that such experiences exerted a protective or ameliorating influence. However, it is first important to consider whether these effects were simply artefacts of an association between poorer schooling experiences and behavioural deviance as indicated by the teachers' questionnaire.

Figure 11.4 shows that this is not the case. Although behavioural deviance was strongly related to the absence of positive school experiences (39 per cent v. 23 per cent), these experiences appeared to have a protective or an ameliorating effect when deviance was taken into account. However, since such positive school experiences were relatively infrequent in both deviant and non-deviant children (7 per cent v. 29 per cent), the overall beneficial contribution of schooling to more satisfactory adult outcomes was relatively small. Nor can it be concluded that such experiences necessarily had an effect on adult functioning irrespective of the circumstances in which the women later found themselves. As is considered in greater detail below, it is more likely that the effects of positive experiences in school arose through their impact on subsequent life-chances by virtue of their initiating or perpetuating chains of more positive or rewarding circumstances. Such chains can be illustrated by considering how the events leading to admission in childhood relate to the conditions upon discharge and the consequences of these for the girls.

*Family relationships on return home*
The family experiences of the girls on discharge from care and their relationship to overall outcome were discussed in Chapter 10. In most cases return home involved a return to one or both biological parents but eight long-term fostering placements were also included. About half the girls returned to some kind of family environment, with the remainder staying in the institutions until they left to live independently. Although the numbers involved were quite small, a poor psychosocial outcome seemed less likely if the girls returned to a harmonious family setting or one with no more than parent–adolescent disagreements. Of those going to a home with pervasive quarrelling and disharmony, half showed poor social functioning; a substantially worse outcome than that for those remaining in care. But this did not apply to the quality of parenting. The outcome was much the same whether or not the girls returned to their families and there was no consistent association with the characteristics of the home to which they returned. This was partly because those who returned to harmonious families were much less likely to be parents, or if parents only to have children below the age of two at the time of follow-up: that is, to have started their families later. None of the three who had children over two was in the poor parenting group, but this number was too small to affect the overall statistical significance of the effect of home life.

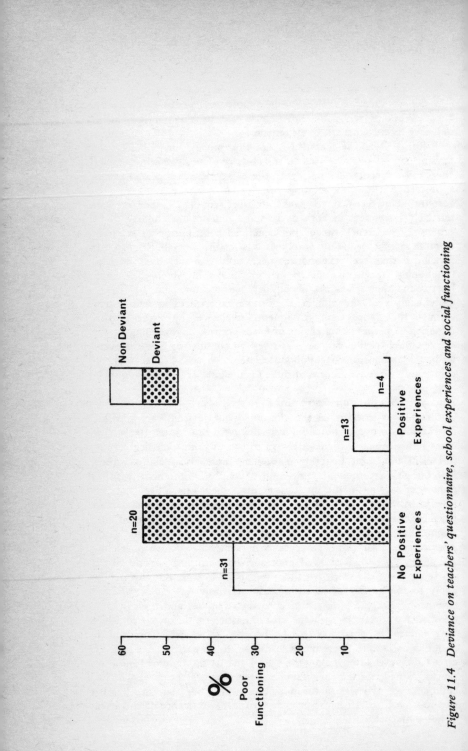

Figure 11.4 Deviance on teachers' questionnaire, school experiences and social functioning

The circumstances on return home also helped to determine what happened next. Those who returned to a discordant family environment were much more likely to become parents than those who returned to a harmonious family or those who remained in the institution until they achieved independence. Altogether, 93 per cent of the discordant family subgroup gave birth to a child (often as a teenager) compared with 51 per cent of those remaining in the institution and 30 per cent of those going to harmonious families, a rate similar to that in the control group. Of the 14 women returning to a discordant environment who had living children, five had had children adopted or in care and three had children living with the father. Also, the timing of the first pregnancy was associated with the quality of parenting as assessed at the time of follow-up. Three-fifths (61 per cent) of the women who became pregnant by the age of 19 years were rated as showing poor parenting compared with a third (35 per cent) of those who did not have their first baby until later. Return to a discordant home was also, as one might expect, linked with the likelihood of the girls' marrying for a negative reason (i.e. to escape from stressful circumstances, or because an unwanted marriage was forced by pregnancy). Of those returning to a discordant family over half married for a negative reason; compared with 20 per cent of those going to a harmonious home, and 46 per cent of those not returning to a family at all. These effects were also apparent for the probability of setting up home with a deviant spouse (that is, a man with a criminal record, psychiatric problems or a history of substance abuse). Sixty-one per cent of girls returning to a discordant home had first spouses with such problems, compared with 39 per cent of those who did not return to a family at all. Almost as striking, however, was the high probability that those returning to a harmonious home would have deviant first husbands. This was the case for 40 per cent of these women compared with only 13 per cent of the comparison group. In this case the pattern of rearing *itself* was a powerful influence on the choice of partner over and above the effect of the pattern of discharge. The effects of adverse experiences thus need to be seen in terms of chains of events and happenings, rather than the impact of any one single decisive stressor. Since the circumstances of family formation appear to be a critical link in those chains it is necessary to examine next the role of marital relationships in influencing later functioning.

### Marital support and the characteristics of spouses

As discussed in Chapter 1, the issue of continuities in behaviour and in the developmental process is crucially related to the issue of situational stability and the continuity of contexts. In order to examine the strength or permanence of some risk factor on personality development it is necessary to look for the points at which an individual's life situation alter most radically. In the transition to adulthood marriage is one of the most significant changes in a young person's psychosocial environment. ('Marriage' is here used to cover all cohabiting relationships with characteristic marital features such as sleeping and eating together, regardless of whether the couple are legally married or not.)

The first question to consider, therefore, is whether the woman's current marital situation and the characteristics of her spouse were associated with the outcome measures. A supportive spouse was rated if there was a harmonious marriage; if the woman talked warmly about her husband *and* if she confided in him. The data are given in Figure 11.5. A lack of support in the marital relationship was associated with high rates of poor current social functioning, the figures for unsupported women being similar to those for women without a current spouse. Closely similar findings were obtained when spouse deviance was considered instead of spouse support. Indeed, the statistical associations were greater when this more objective measure of spouse characteristics was used. A spouse was rated as deviant if he showed current psychiatric disorder, criminality, drink or drug problems, or longstanding difficulties in personal relationships. However, much more striking than the association between lack of support and outcome were the high rates of satisfactory social functioning for women with a currently supportive or non-deviant spouse. This was true for parenting also, where half the supported mothers were in the good outcome category — a rate similar to that in the comparison sample. However, the picture was different when support was absent. Here, amongst the controls over one quarter (29 per cent) of mothers were nevertheless parenting well, whereas this was not the case for any of the ex-care group. This suggests that factors associated with the backgrounds of these women made them less able to cope in the absence of marital support. The associations with deviance in the spouse are particularly noteworthy because the measures largely came from different informants (parenting and social functioning from the woman, and the spouse's psychosocial problems from the spouse himself). This association makes it less likely that the causal influences are due to the effects of the woman on her husband. This point is developed further below.

### Factors leading to the choice of spouse

*Assortative mating*  The findings suggest that the spouses' good qualities exerted a powerful ameliorating effect leading to better parenting and better functioning. There was a substantial overlap between whether the spouse had problems and whether he provided a supportive relationship but, with the sample size available, it was not possible to determine which feature made the difference. But before concluding that the spouses' support constituted an ameliorating feature it is necessary to ask whether the statistical association merely

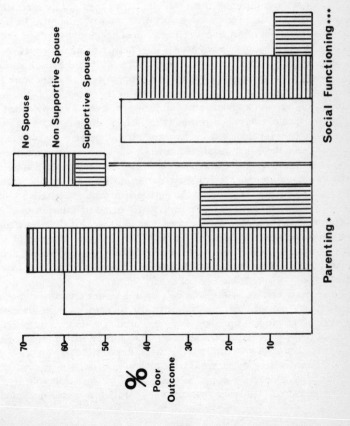

No Spouse

Non Supportive Spouse

Supportive Spouse

Parenting*

Social Functioning***

% Poor Outcome

*Figure 11.5 Marital support and outcome*

reflected the women's own characteristics. Perhaps the girls who were non-deviant themselves during childhood and adolescence were the ones to choose better functioning supportive men to marry. This probability was tested using the houseparent and teacher questionnaire measures of emotional/behavioural problems in childhood. The women were subdivided into 'deviant' and 'non-deviant' groups according to their questionnaire scores. As shown already, those women deviant on one or other (or both) of these questionnaires had a substantially worse outcome. However, the presence of behavioural deviance did not predict the women's spouses' characteristics. Nearly two-fifths of both the deviant and non-deviant groups were without a cohabiting partner at the time of follow-up. About half the spouses of the remainder showed substantial personal problems of one sort or another involving current psychiatric disorder, criminality or alcohol or drug abuse, but there was no evidence that the deviant women more often selected men with problems as their spouses (34 per cent v. 30 per cent). The lack of assortative mating within the ex-care group may be a function of the fact that, on leaving the institution, the girls were scattered to a variety of settings different from those in which they had been reared – a circumstance that contrasts sharply with that of girls brought up in their own families and one likely to introduce a greater degree of randomness in the pool of men available. Whether or not this was the case, the findings indicate that it is most unlikely that the association between spouse characteristics and the women's adult functioning was merely an artefact resulting from biases in the choice of marriage partner. Rather, it appears that the presence of a non-deviant, supportive spouse exerted a protective effect making it more likely that women from a deprived background would be able to function effectively. On the other hand, although there was no indication that the ex-care women's behaviour matched that of their male spouses, there was a marked tendency for the group of institution-reared women as a whole to be more likely than the comparison group to set up home with men with problems (51 per cent v. 13 per cent), a statistically significant difference. Moreover, the ex-care women with children were much more likely at follow-up to be without a spouse (22 per cent v. 0 per cent). For both these reasons, the ex-care women were much less likely than the comparison sample to experience the protective effect of a supportive spouse (27 per cent v. 74 per cent).

The separate effects of the women's own deviance and her spouse's characteristics are seen more easily with the measure of overall social functioning at follow-up, as that is based on larger numbers. Figure 11.6 shows that the women who were non-deviant in childhood had better outcomes than those who were deviant; but also that the outcome was better for women who had spouses who were free of significant psychosocial problems, regardless of the woman's own earlier adjustment. However, the women without a spouse included

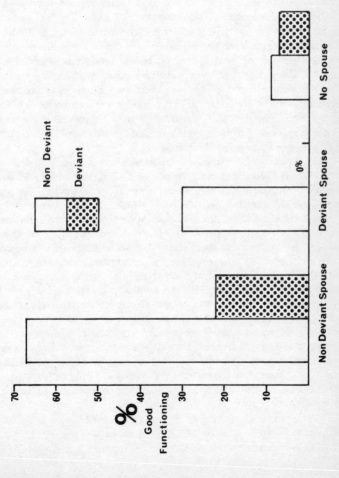

Figure 11.6  *Deviance on questionnaires, spouse's deviance and good social functioning*

few with good social functioning even when they had not shown emotional or behavioural problems in adolescence. This suggests that the effects of adverse characteristics in the spouse may involve an interaction between stressors and the women's ability to cope reflecting some more general consequence of their adverse childhood experiences than the emotional or behavioural problems recorded on the question-naires.

*Planning for a good outcome*   The data presented in the previous section show that assortative mating had not occurred with respect to the women's early teenage deviance. But it is important to consider whether the choice of spouse is merely a matter of chance and circum-stances or whether the women played a more active part in considering or 'planning' their own futures. No direct measures were available of their intentions in mate selection but the matter can be approached by considering the length of time the woman knew her first spouse before she began to live with him, together with the reasons for the cohabitation. In this analysis 'planning' is rated if the woman knew her future husband for over six months before cohabitation and if the reasons for living together were positive — that is, involving a clear positive decision without pregnancy, their own home circumstances, the need for somewhere to live or other pressures affecting their choice or timing. 'Non-planners', on the other hand, include all those who knew their spouses for six months or less and/or who had clearly negative pressure influencing their decision.

The first question is whether 'planners' do choose less deviant spouses. That is indeed the case: 76 per cent of them had non-deviant first spouses compared with only 35 per cent of 'non-planners'. Nor was planning merely a reflection of earlier adjustment: 47 per cent of 'planners' were previously rated as deviant on one or both question-naires compared with 64 per cent of 'non-planners'. Both of these differences are statistically significant. The second question concerns the outcome for those in both groups according to the kind of marital support that they were currently experiencing. This is a test both of whether 'planning' simply stands for a generally better level of adjust-ment prior to cohabitation and of the effects of marital support on later psychosocial functioning and parenting. For this analysis lack of marital support was rated if the woman was single, had an overtly discordant marriage, or if her husband had psychiatric, drink or drug problems or current criminality. This wider definition of marital support was chosen in preference to the narrower rating of 'supportive spouse' because of the findings on single women and deviant spouses presented above.

The results of this analysis are given in Figure 11.7 and in a linear logistic analysis in Appendix E. The findings are clear-cut. Both planners and non-planners without marital support had substantially

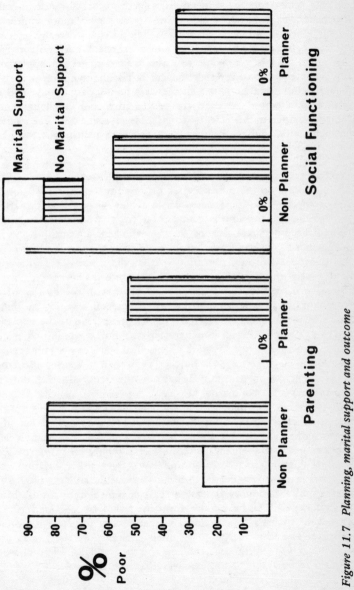

*Figure 11.7  Planning, marital support and outcome*

increased rates of problems in parenting and in social functioning compared with those in supportive relationships. Unsupported non-planners had the highest rates of problems on both outcome measures. This may imply that lack of planning is associated both with generally poorer psychosocial adjustment in the late teens and early twenties and also with persisting vulnerabilities. If this is so, however, it makes the beneficial impacts of supportive spouses even more impressive.

The extent to which the factors used in this analysis really represent a more considered plan for the future cannot be determined from these data. Nor is it possible to assess the extent to which 'planning' was a consequence of foresight on the part of the spouse. However, we may conclude that both the choice of a non-deviant spouse and the chance of a better outcome are related to a courtship long enough for the couple to be able to form some assessment of each others' characteristics, and to a decision to cohabit which is not forced by circumstances.

### The effects of spouses: Direction of causal influences

These findings on the positive effects of supportive marital relationship are of considerable importance because they suggest that the effects of prolonged institutionalisation are far from immutable. However, a number of other explanations for these findings are possible and it is necessary to consider these before concluding that the 'spouse effect' is a real one. The first possibility is that the findings are an artefact of the social functioning measure. This might be so because features of the women's psychosocial histories together with the quality of the current marriage were among the criteria used in creating the index. However, the effects of marital support proved not to be explained by this. Even when all the items in the index relating to marital circumstances and history were removed, the effect was still apparent (see Quinton *et al.*, 1984). Further evidence, of course, also comes from the effect on parenting behaviour, the rating of which does not depend on features of marital history.

The second possibility is that the direction of influence is not of a beneficial effect from a supportive spouse to the woman, but of an adverse one from a woman to her husband. That is, that 'lack of support' was a consequence of the effect of poorly functioning women on their husbands. This seemed unlikely because the associations were as strong with spouse deviance as they were with support — suggesting that a lack of support at least in part stemmed from the husband's characteristics. This was more formally tested by considering those aspects of spouse's functioning apparent at a time before he met the subject. Here the analysis concerned spouse's teenage drink, drug, delinquent and psychiatric problems and the woman's full psychosocial rating (because the hypothesis was that the effect was from her to him).

Once again the data support the view that there was a significant spouse effect: 15 per cent of those with a non-deviant spouse had poor functioning currently compared with 46 per cent with a spouse who showed deviance in his teens. It will be remembered that the choice of a spouse with these characteristics was not related to the woman's emotional/behavioural problems when in care.

Finally, it is necessary to examine whether the association between marital circumstances and outcome confounds the effect of a non-supportive or deviant spouse with the effect of single-parent status. Analysis confined to those currently cohabiting showed that this was not the case. Only 7 per cent of currently cohabiting women with non-deviant spouses showed poor social functioning compared with 36 per cent of those with deviant spouses. Multivariate analyses confirmed that this was not simply a function of the women's poor adjustment or planning (Appendix E).

We may conclude that a supportive marital relationship had a markedly positive effect on the social functioning of the ex-care women even when they had been showing emotional or behavioural problems in their earlier years. The choices or changes that lead to more satisfactory circumstances in adulthood are major breakpoints in the continuity of adversity across generations. However, as noted earlier, the ex-care women were much less likely than the comparison group to experience the beneficial effects of a supportive relationship with a non-deviant spouse. It is likely that this was partly due to the restricted range of potential spouses with whom the ex-care women come into contact. On leaving care, the majority of girls either went into hostels or lodging or returned to unsatisfactory family conditions and relationships — circumstances in which they were much more likely to meet men from similarly deprived backgrounds. Their lower educational attainments and poorer job records may also have had the same effect with respect to the working environment. Finally, a lack of role models of adequate marital partners is likely to have limited their expectations. Whether the pool of available spouses was more satisfactory than might have been available if they had spent their childhoods with their own families remains an open question.

## Planning for work and early work experience

The planning measure used in the above analyses was derived inferentially from the women's behaviour during their teenage years. A more direct measure of deliberate planning or foresight concerns their work intentions prior to leaving secondary school. Subjects were asked in detail about the transition from school to work, including the help and assistance they obtained from family, school and career advisers, and the extent to which they had a clear-cut idea about what they wanted to do. These plans need not have included long-term career objectives but simply concerned whether they had made a choice or decision about the kind of work they would like to do. Grandiose or unrealistic ideas were not considered to represent plans (e.g. to be a film-star or a racing driver) nor were preferences for occupations for which the person was completely unqualified (e.g. to become a vet, when the subject had not demonstrated any relevant academic capability). On the other hand, clearly expressed preferences in broad categories such as shop or secretarial work rated as occupational planning.

There was a significant difference between the ex-care and comparison groups in the extent to which such preferences were expressed (20 per cent v. 51 per cent), but, as with the planning for marriage measure, lack of planning within the ex-care group was not related to deviance on the teachers' questionnaire: 18 per cent of the non-deviant had definite work plans compared with 14 per cent of those showing behavioural deviance. (Only one comparison subject scored above the cut-off on the teachers' questionnaire and therefore the association could not be tested.) Figure 11.8 gives the relationship between planning for work and the two main outcome measures. For both parenting and overall social functioning planning is strongly related to good outcomes in the ex-care subjects but not amongst the comparison women where, indeed, the relationship is in the opposite direction. Most strikingly, none of the ex-care women who showed occupational planning were poor parents whereas, if subjects not currently parenting because of parenting breakdown are included — over half of the non-planners had a poor parenting outcome. In addition this group were approximately twice as likely as both ex-care planners and the comparison group to have children.

Since this work intention measure is a more direct assessment of a disposition to plan the question arises as to whether this reflects a general disposition or one confined to occupational aspirations. Two pieces of evidence suggest that this represents a more general characteristic. First, amongst the ex-care group lack of planning for work is strongly related to an increased risk of early pregnancy (Figure 11.9): 48 per cent of non-work planners became pregnant before their 19th birthday compared with 19 per cent of the planners. Moreover, one half of the latter group had had no pregnancies by the time of follow-up, a rate comparable to that in the comparison sample. This is not explained by a reduced likelihood of having a spouse. A similar proportion of both planners and non-planners had or previously had had a spouse (87 per cent v. 86 per cent). However, non-planners amongst the ex-care group were much more likely to have had a deviant first spouse (65 per cent v. 15 per cent), a significant difference. Secondly, planning for work was significantly related to the marital planning measure such that 93 per cent of work planners with spouses were rated as planners on that measure as well compared with 48 per cent of those without occupational plans when at school.

Finally, the importance of work planning can be assessed by

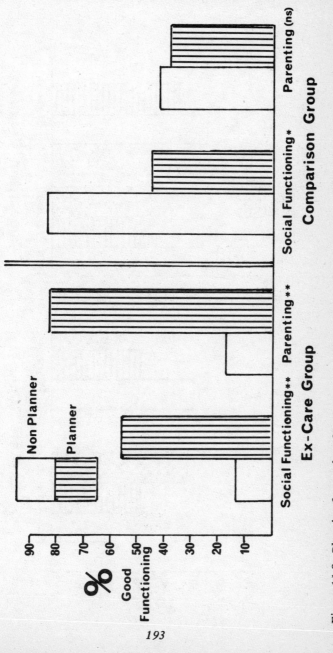

Figure 11.8 *Planning for work and outcome*

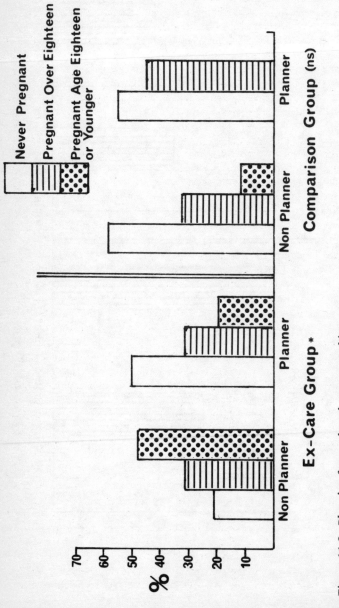

Figure 11.9 Planning for work and pregnancy history

considering the extent to which it was related to stable and positive work experiences. These were rated if the subject described predominantly mildly or definitely positive work experiences in their later teens, and if they had some definitely rewarding occupations in the sense of giving them pleasure or improving their self-esteem, and if they had a job in or starting in their teens lasting for at least two years. Thirty-one ex-care subjects had such experiences. This was strongly related to work planning such that 75 per cent of planners had positive experiences with work compared with only 27 per cent of non-planners. As with the planning measures, positive work experiences were not related to school deviance as rated on the teachers' questionnaire: 36 per cent of girls rated as non-deviant at school had later positive work experiences compared with 43 per cent of the previously deviant.

The data on planning show that the ex-care girls were by no means at the mercy of fate but that they were much less likely than the comparison group to plan either with respect to work or marriage. Thus, 44 per cent of the ex-care group were non-planners for marriage compared with 19 per cent of the comparison sample (exact test p=0.02). The lack of association with behavioural deviance show that the continuities that occur are not simply continuities of personal functioning. However, since planners fared markedly better in their choice of spouse and in work than non-planners, it follows that lack of planning amongst the ex-care group was an additional major risk.

One important finding that requires comment is the lack of an association between school experience and planning measures with outcome in the comparison sample. The data show that the difference in their case arises because lack of positive experiences or planning does not constitute an additional risk. This is clearly demonstrated by the lack of any association in the comparison group between either of the planning measures and the probability of having a non-deviant spouse (Figure 11.10). This suggests that there are factors in their later teenage environments that are strongly protective in the face of the girls' lack of foresight. Although there are no direct measures of this it seems likely that their own families exercised this role. The comparison girls all stayed with their parents until after the age of 18 and in the great majority of cases until they left home to marry. This protective function may have operated both by influencing spouse selection (only 18 per cent of comparison women had deviant first spouses compared with 53 per cent of the ex-care subjects), and by providing advice and social control. In addition the stable family experiences of the majority of the comparison group meant that they were less vulnerable to adverse social circumstances. That stable family relationships probably played this role is indicated by the markedly better outcomes for ex-care women who returned to non-discordant family homes. Only 30 per cent of this group had started their families by

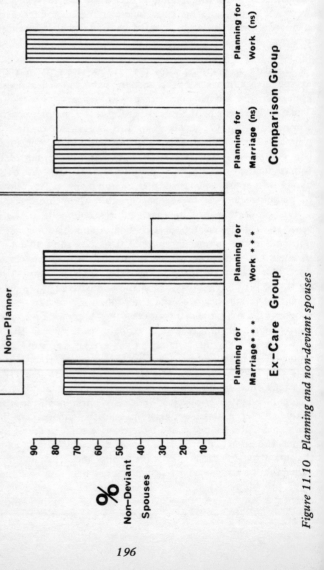

*Figure 11.10  Planning and non-deviant spouses*

the time of follow-up, a rate comparable to that in the comparison group.

## Factors leading to planning

Since the data presented above show that planning in the ex-care sample was not simply a lack of behavioural deviance, the question arises concerning what it was that enabled some of them to plan their lives whereas others seemed just to drift from adversity to adversity without any systematic attempt to alter their life-circumstances.

A clue to this is provided by the linkage between positive school experiences and the planning measures. Ex-care girls who reported such experiences were more likely to have shown forethought in considering their working futures and also to have planned their marriages (as operationally defined) than those who did not (77 per cent v. 47 per cent) and hence more likely to have made a harmonious relationship with a non-deviant spouse. Similarly, 42 per cent of those with positive school experiences were work planners compared with only 11 per cent of those without, a significant difference.

Again, this effect was not found in the control group. Obviously, we cannot know precisely how this link came about, but other research has suggested the importance of feelings of self-esteem and self-efficacy (Bandura, 1977; Harter, 1983) and it may be that the girls acquired a sense of their own worth and of their ability to control their destinies as a result of their pleasure, success and accomplishments in a few specific areas of their lives. Certainly, it is a common observation that many people with multiple psychosocial problems feel at the mercy of fate and hence do not act in any decisive way to resolve their difficulties even when they are able to do so. The findings suggest that the experience of some form of success, accomplishment, or even just pleasure in activities may be important, not because it dilutes the impact of unpleasant or stressful happenings, but because it serves to enhance confidence and competence to deal with the hazards and with the dilemmas of life.

## Current material circumstances

The final section in this chapter is concerned with the effects of the women's current housing condition and material resources. Usually the ex-care women were living in worse social circumstances than the comparison group women at the time of follow-up (44 per cent v. 24 per cent living in intermediate/poor circumstances, operationally defined in terms of a score based on lack of facilities such as a washing machine or telephone, the children having to share a bed or sleep in the parents' room, or overcrowding). Accordingly, it is necessary to determine the extent to which their poorer parenting was a consequence of their inadequate living conditions.

Figure 11.11 summarises the main findings with respect to both

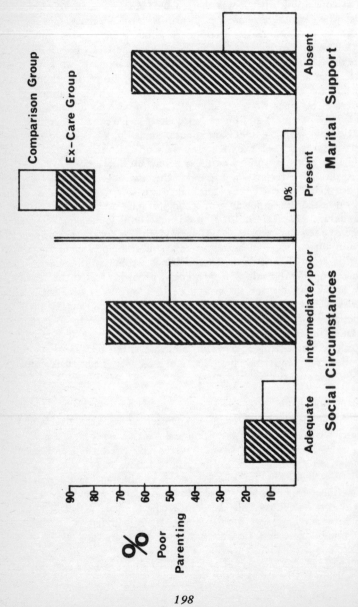

Figure 11.11 Current parenting, social circumstances and marital support

social circumstances and marital support and a multivariate analysis is given in the tables in Appendix E. It is clear that poor parenting was substantially less likely to occur in adequate social circumstances in both the ex-care group (20 per cent v. 75 per cent) and the comparison group (8 per cent v. 50 per cent). However, also, poor parenting was more likely to occur in the ex-care women, irrespective of social circumstances. Thus, for those in adequate social circumstances in the two groups the difference in poor parenting was between 20 and 8 per cent. The inference is that rearing patterns were associated with parenting independently of social circumstances, but that social conditions exerted an additional effect. However, because institutional rearing was associated with an increased likelihood of poor social circumstances, part of the effect of poor living conditions was an indirect outcome of the pattern of upbringing. The effect of marital support was greater than that of living conditions, but a comparable pattern of indirect links was evident. Nevertheless, there were differences. Three main features warrant attention. First, almost all instances (17 out of 20) of poor parenting occurred in the ex-care group, but this was largely the result of the prior association with marital support. Thus, of the 33 instances of lack of support, 26 occurred in the ex-care group. Secondly, provided marital support was available, poor parenting was a rare occurrence (3 per cent of cases), irrespective of the pattern of rearing. The inference to be drawn is that childhood adversities had a powerful indirect influence on parenting as a result of their effect on the choice of spouse, but very little direct influence provided that there was marital support.

## Summary

The overall pattern of findings suggest that childhood adversities lead to poor parenting through two main mechanisms. The first concerns the process by which they set in motion a train of events that predispose the woman to the experience of poor social circumstances and lack of marital support. This arises through various happenings that limit opportunities — by virtue of teenage pregnancies, early marriage to someone from an equally disadvantaged background, lack of educational qualifications for occupational advancement and other features of a similar kind. The second mechanism concerns some type of increased vulnerability or decreased coping skills which make it more likely that the women will succumb when faced with poor social circumstances or lack of marital support. Only a minority of women with a stable harmonious pattern of upbringing exhibited poor parenting when subjected to chronic stress and disadvantage in adult life, but a majority of those who lacked good rearing in childhood did so. It seemed that the experience of childhood adversities had no necessary effect on parenting (as shown by the good parenting of the institutional women with supportive spouses) but it left the individuals less well prepared to deal with adult adversities.

# 12 Conclusions

In Chapter 2 the issues in the study of inter-generational continuities to which these two studies were addressed were set out as a number of specific research questions. We can now review the empirical findings and assess the extent to which they answer those research questions and the implications they have for the study of inter-generational links. The research questions were: first, are current severe parenting problems usually related to the experience of poor parenting in childhood, or do they occur anew in each generation because of current social disadvantage? Secondly, how strong is the link looking forwards: that is, what proportion of children who experience poor parenting in their own childhood are themselves poor parents when they have children? And finally, what are the processes involved in continuities and discontinuities?

Within the limits provided by the samples studied the first question seems readily answered: serious parenting problems as evidenced by parenting breakdowns very seldom occur in the absence of the experience of poor parenting or marked family disruption in childhood. In the first study when the childhoods of both parents were considered, inter-generational continuities looking backwards were virtually complete. In the second study all the instances for parenting breakdown occurred amongst the ex-care women. Moreover, there were breakdowns for over a third of mothers. If the overall ratings of parenting are considered over two-fifths of the ex-care women had a poor outcome. It is tempting to translate these findings into some general statement about the effects of the experience of poor parenting on the parenting of the current generation; for example, to say that over a third of women who have been in care will be poor parents, or that women's parenting capacities are seriously damaged by adverse early experiences. But such conclusions would be seriously misleading. This is because the extent of continuity in personal functioning is heavily dependent on the extent of continuities in circumstances and environments so that the proportion in the second generation showing the problems they experienced in childhood will depend on the extent to which there is continuity in the contexts in which such problems are expressed (Quinton, 1985). On the other hand, this does not imply that the links are merely a consequence of chance and the social structure. The story is more interesting than that. The links are forged both through life-chances that are outside the control of individuals and through the actions of the people themselves, which serve either to perpetuate adversity or to break the vicious cycle of continuing disadvantage.

We can now examine the evidence for these general conclusions, but first a brief overview of the empirical findings is in order.

## Overview of the findings

### Parenting problems and reception of children into care

The findings from both studies justify the use of admission of children into care as an index of parenting difficulties. In the retrospective study the in-care mothers were approximately twice as likely as the comparison sample to have two or more parenting problems in relationships and/or control, and in the prospective study ex-care mothers who had had children taken into care were significantly more likely than those who had not to be rated as poor in their current parenting. Further, there can be little doubt that the experience of reception into care was associated with a much increased risk of parenting breakdown in the next generation. In the retrospective study 25 per cent of mothers had themselves been in care compared with 7 per cent in the comparison sample and in the prospective study parenting breakdowns were confined to the ex-care group. But although strong, these associations were far from inevitable. In the prospective study nearly two-thirds of mothers had had no parenting breakdowns or other separations at all and about one quarter showed good current parenting — a rate comparable to that in the comparison mothers. In addition, it would be wrong to see these continuities as applying specifically to parenting. It is clear from the data on the childhood backgrounds of the subjects in both of the studies, as well as from the correlates of marked current parenting problems or parenting breakdown for both the in-care and ex-care mothers that these samples differ from their comparison groups as much on other psychosocial problems as they do on parenting. Thus the parents in both generations were much more likely also to be experiencing psychiatric disturbance and marital discord and disruption as well as a number of material disadvantages. It is apparent, therefore, that these two studies were concerned with parenting problems that occurred in the context of multiple psychosocial problems. It would be unwarranted to assume that the antecedents or causes of parenting problems arising in the absence of similar psychosocial difficulties are the same. Indeed, the finding of a lack of association between the (mostly moderate) parenting problems and psychosocial difficulties in the prospective comparison sample suggests that the explanation will be different in this case. These studies were not designed to investigate parenting problems within this range and the comparison groups were too small to allow further analysis of this question.

It is, of course, also the case that no conclusions can be drawn from these data concerning the consequences of other kinds of substitute care such as fostering. Nor will the correlates of institutional care necessarily be the same for other groups excluded from these samples such as those from New Commonwealth backgrounds.

### Inter-generational continuities in parenting problems

In the retrospective study one or both parents in almost all the families with children taken into care reported marked adversities in their childhood families involving receptions into care, parental deviance or disorder, severe marital discord, and harsh parental discipline. An important inference from these data was that such experiences might be necessary antecedents of parenting breakdown in the next generation. This conclusion was supported in the prospective study where parenting breakdown was confined to the ex-care group. This does not imply that the influence is directly from adverse childhood experiences to parenting, or that breakdowns are an inevitable consequence of such adversities. The prospective study confirms the conclusion that inter-generational continuities looking forward are much weaker than continuities viewed retrospectively (Rutter and Madge, 1976). That is, the experience of poor parenting in childhood does *not* usually lead to marked parenting problems or to parenting breakdown in the next generation. This is supported by the data from the retrospective study *comparison* sample where one or both parents in two-fifths of families reported childhood family adversities as defined, without ever having children taken into care. On the other hand the in-care parents showed a much greater overlap of family and social adversities in childhood as well as a much greater probability that both of them had had such experiences. This overlap may increase the risk of later parenting problems and breakdown both through impacts on personality development and through increasing the probability of later adverse material circumstances and restricted opportunities. We can now consider the nature of these inter-generational continuities.

### The nature of inter-generational links

#### Genetic or experiential influences

Before discussing the impacts of childhood experiences and the nature of linking processes, it is necessary to deal, as far as the data will allow, with the possibility that neither experiential nor social processes are responsible for continuities. That is, whether the links are provided by biological factors and in particular genetic influences. Little is known about genetic influences on parenting (Rutter and Madge, 1976) but since mild and isolated parenting problems are not associated in these two studies with other psychosocial difficulties, it seems unlikely that genetic factors are important in explaining mild difficulties in parenting. On the other hand, recent studies have begun to delineate the effects of maternal depression on parenting qualities, and although genetic influences are not strong for such disorders, the possibility of some influence must remain open. The position is different with respect to the major personality and alcoholic problems shown to be associated with parenting breakdown in both studies, where the evidence for genetic influences is stronger.

Although genetic influences may be responsible for some increased disposition to maladaptive functioning in adulthood (including parenting), the evidence is against the conclusion that they account for most of the variance in outcomes. First, the data from the retrospective study showed that parental deviance seemed of little importance for parenting breakdown in the absence of experiences of poor parenting and disrupted family relationships. Secondly, in the prospective study, deviance in the biological parents showed little relationship to overall psychosocial functioning in adulthood once its impact through generating disrupted parenting experiences in childhood was taken into account. On the other hand, amongst the ex-care women parental deviance was related to personality disorder in adulthood even when the effect of disrupted parenting was controlled. (Low numbers did not allow a similar analysis of the relationship between deviance in the biological parents and the parenting of the ex-care subjects, so it is not known whether the pattern would have been like that for overall psychosocial functioning or for personality disorder.) It is safest to conclude that genetic factors probably played some part in the transmission of parenting difficulties. However, it is unlikely that these influences were direct. Several studies have shown that genetic factors act in part by increasing individual vulnerabilities to environmental stressors. Thus, whether genetically-based predispositions are translated into behaviours probably depends on environmental variables. In this regard it is important to note that parental deviance was not related at all to the major ameliorating influence – the presence of a non-deviant supportive spouse in adulthood.

The data discussed in this section clearly suggest the importance of experiential factors even when genetic loadings are apparently high. This inference is supported by Roy's (1983) study of the behaviour of fostered and institutionalised children from backgrounds equally high in parental deviance. Here the children in the institution-reared group were much more likely than those fostered by families to show over-active, socially disruptive behaviour. Taken together, the findings from these studies provide a strong indication of the likely importance of adverse early experiences, especially disrupted parenting, in the early years of childhood in increasing the risk of later parenting problems.

### The specific impacts of institutional experience
The findings from the retrospective study make clear the importance of major adverse experiences within the family in increasing the risk of

later parenting problems. This is in keeping with numerous studies that show the deleterious impacts of family hostility and disruption in childhood. The importance of early disrupted parenting is also clear for the ex-care sample, but it is more difficult to determine the role of the institutional upbringing *per se*. Many studies (e.g. Wolkind, 1974; Tizard and Hodges, 1978; Roy, 1983; Hodges and Tizard, submitted) have detailed the behavioural features common in institutional children including over-friendly, demanding or attention-seeking behaviour. Although such behaviours have been shown to occur in relatively well-run or 'good' institutions, it is not clear whether these are inevitable consequences of institutional care or related to specific characteristics such as multiple caretaking that are potentially remediable. In addition, it is not known whether the long-term implications of these experiences are worse than those of the adverse family circumstances from which the reception into care was usually designed to protect the children. The ex-care sample included a small group of women who were admitted to care in infancy and remained there for the rest of their upbringing. Therefore, although they had only the briefest exposure to family discord, most of them experienced multiple caretaking, and relationships that lacked closeness and meaning. These children had outcomes in adult life as bad as those who experienced extensive family discord and disruption. It is clear from other studies that institutionalisation from infancy has deleterious effects on development in childhood, and it may be that its harm lies in what it lacks in the way of stable positive influences.

Nevertheless it should not yet be concluded that an institutional upbringing as such is as damaging as a seriously discordant environment, or that the continuities occur primarily through the effects of early institutionalisation on personal functioning. In the first place, the data show that the experience of serious disruption in the first two years of life had a stronger association with later psychosocial problems than did age at admission *per se*. Secondly, those suffering adverse early experiences tended to suffer later adversities as well, and it is therefore difficult to separate the effects of early and later stresses. What evidence there is tends to suggest that most adversities that are strictly restricted to infancy have relatively few long-term sequelae provided that later environments are consistently good (Rutter, 1981c; in press c). Finally, the data from the prospective study — although limited in quality with respect to parental deviance — suggested that parental deviance and disorder were greater both among those admitted in infancy and among those admitted from severely disrupted homes. Thus, the poorer outcomes may have resulted from increased genetically-based vulnerabilities. It cannot be assumed that institutional experiences would have an equally deleterious effect if children's backgrounds were free of biological or psychosocial risks.

The ex-care children with the best outcomes were those admitted after the age of two from non-disrupted backgrounds, and it seems reasonable to conclude that adverse experiences before the age of two may have had particularly marked effects. These early experiences may operate by increasing susceptibility both to institutional rearing itself and also to later environmental stresses. However, it is also the case that the factors that create the adverse early circumstances — early admission and family disruption — are also partly responsible for the later adverse environments — staying in care or lack of family support in the teens — and thus that the adverse consequences of early and disrupted admissions cannot be explained simply by the impact of these experiences on development. This point is considered further in the next section.

*Impacts on individual functioning*
The data discussed above might seem consistent with the view that continuities are brought about by the impact of adverse early experiences on personality development, with some contribution through their interaction with genetically based vulnerabilities. As a partial explanation for continuities this model seems to have some validity. Behaviour during childhood and adolescence predicts adult functioning, and the rate of personality disorders in the ex-care sample is high. Since a designation of personality disorder requires evidence of persistent maladaptive behaviour across a variety of situations and relationships such disorders are very unlikely to be explained solely through persisting misfortune. On the other hand, poor outcomes are also associated with situational adversities. In consequence if the impact of early adversities on personality development is the principal reason for continuity, maladaptive personality characteristics should be responsible for the selection or creation of these situational difficulties.

The evidence from the prospective study is firmly against this. First, marriage to a non-deviant or supportive spouse was not related to the women's deviant behaviour in early adolescence. Secondly, marital support had a powerful ameliorating effect even for previously deviant women. Finally, institution-reared mothers who had good marital support showed, like the comparison group, no deficits in parenting despite the fact that they had *all* experienced marked early hardships. This finding constitutes strong evidence for the view that parenting behaviours are so greatly influenced by current circumstances that it would be wrong to regard them as only, or even primarily, aspects of personality functioning.

On the other hand, a quality of parenting similar to that in the comparison sample was evident for the ex-care mothers *only* when they were in supportive marital relationships. Poor parenting was significantly more frequent in the ex-care than in the comparison group when marital support was absent (65 per cent v. 29 per cent). These data go against the conclusion that poor parenting was just a matter of circumstances and that the greater problems in the ex-care group arose primarily through social factors influencing the availability of satisfactory spouses. It seems probable that their earlier experiences left them more vulnerable to stresses or difficult life-circumstances but that their parenting abilities were not seriously affected unless they encountered such problems. But the experience of parenting may also be a source of inter-generational discontinuity through the exposure of mothers to new influences and experiences. For example, the observational study of the ex-care and comparison group mothers suggested that positive changes in behaviour occurred through the experience of parenting. This inference seems warranted because the mothers' handling of second-born children showed significantly fewer problems than with first-borns (Dowdney *et al.*, 1985b). However, the interview evidence — based on parenting in the full family context and not on the one-to-one parenting situation in the observational study — did not confirm this improvement in the parenting of second or subsequent children.

The conclusion to be drawn from findings discussed in this section is that there is little evidence for a direct impact of the experience of adverse parenting in childhood on parenting capacities skills in later life. However, two final points should be raised concerning continuities through effects on personal functioning. First, these conclusions apply to young mothers whose predominant childhood experience was of the absence of normal parenting rather than the presence of severely abnormal parental behaviour (although the majority had some experience of this sort). Direct effects may still occur following prolonged exposure to deviant parenting as in the case of child abuse. This point remains to be explored. Secondly, the biggest single difference between ex-care mothers and the comparison sample involved deficits in parental sensitivity in the handling of issues of both control and distress. This difference occurred in both the retrospective and prospective studies and was confirmed in the direct observations (Dowdney *et al.*, 1985b). It was not possible to know whether this was a general feature of the women's behaviour that showed in relationships with adults as well as with their children, but it may represent an effect of adverse experiences on personality functioning of a persistent kind. Only a further follow-up of the ex-care women can resolve this point.

In conclusion these studies suggest that although the effects of early adverse experiences were clearly detectable in early adulthood, there was little evidence for direct effects on specific parenting qualities or for any immutable effect on personality development that made good parenting impossible. Where continuities arose it was through the conjunction of experiential and possibly genetically-based vulnerabilities and later stressful social circumstances. Nevertheless, the perpetuation of adverse experiences was much more common in the ex-care group and it is next necessary to consider how this might have arisen.

## The linking of environments

The linking of adverse environments refers to the likelihood of one adverse experience or environment leading to another, not necessarily of the same kind, but with a similar capacity to impede beneficial developmental changes or to restrict life-chances. It is apparent that much of the explanation for inter-generational continuities lies in the nature of these linking processes. Many sociologists have argued that these links are a consequence of social structural forces and that explanations through individual functioning are unnecessary. However, the problem with this view rests in the difficulty in explaining why continuities apply to only a minority of those from particular adverse circumstances. It seems clear that it is necessary to investigate at least three kinds of link between adverse circumstances: those occurring independently of individual behaviour; those made as a consequence of individual behaviour; and those produced through it.

### Independent links

A number of independent links can be illustrated in the data from the prospective study. It has been shown that the initial reception into care was, for the most part, from disrupted family homes with a high frequency of parental psychiatric disorder and deviant behaviour, and that the referrals resulted from these rather than from problems in the child. The joining of disruptive home life with later institutional experiences is the first linking of adverse developmental circumstances independent of the children's behaviour. The children admitted in infancy or from disrupted parenting backgrounds have a poorer adult outcome but this is not simply a consequence of the impact on the child's personality development of these two linked prior adversities. The likelihood of poorer environment in the teenage years is, in part, linked to the circumstances surrounding admission independent of their effects on the child's behaviour. For example, girls admitted from disrupted family circumstances were more likely to return to discordant families in their teens irrespective of whether they were showing overt behavioural deviance or not. These circumstances on return home were then related to leaving home for negative reasons, to early pregnancy and the consequent restriction of life-chances that this entailed. Similarly, the children admitted in infancy were less likely to return to a family experience of any kind, and consequently more likely to be placed in lodgings or hostels on leaving care — environments in which they often lacked any adult supervision or guidance and which contained many deviant peers. Conversely, girls admitted after the age of two from non-discordant or non-disrupted parenting experiences were more likely to have parents who maintained contact through their time in care, more likely to return to non-discordant family homes and substantially less at risk for early pregnancy.

A rather different kind of independent link concerns the choice of spouse. In this case the ex-care women as a whole were much more likely than the comparison sample to have deviant first spouses or to lack supportive marital relationships at interview, but these later experiences were uncorrelated with the earlier pattern of admission into care. In this case the risk of non-supportive marital circumstances applies to the group as a whole. Since choice of spouse was not related to teenage deviance this link is likely to be due to the environmental limitations affecting the social milieu of these young women and the men they were likely to meet. On the other hand, their circumstances on discharge from care did influence the probability of early co-habitation for negative reasons and therefore the restriction of life circumstances in other ways.

### The selection of environments

The selection of environments occurs both through choice and through the unintended consequences of individual actions. One of the most important conclusions from the prospective study is that the institutionalised girls often actively changed their lives for the better, especially through their selection of marital partner and control of their own fertility. Although the evidence is indirect, it seemed likely that their range of choice of partner was less than that for girls raised in unproblematic families and that the field contained many more potential pitfalls. Moreover, their chances of making such beneficial life-course decisions were lessened by the negative impact of their earlier experiences, or the degree to which they viewed their lives as controllable.

The lack of any association in the prospective comparison sample between the two outcome measures and planning for work or for marriage suggests that this group were protected from the extreme consequences of certain aspects of their behaviour in ways that the ex-care group was not. This protection may come from their families in their later teens. This view is substantiated by lower rates of teenage pregnancy and the better outcomes for the ex-care women who went home to non-discordant families.

A further important finding concerning linkage through selection of environments is that the continuities are not simply explained by better adjusted ex-care girls making the right choices and also having the better outcomes in adulthood. This is shown both by the lack of an association between behavioural deviance in the girls' teens and the selection of a supportive and non-deviant spouse, and by the finding that those who were not rated as 'planners' but nevertheless had a supportive spouse had considerably better outcomes than those who had a non-supportive one. Conversely, those who 'planned' but made a 'wrong' choice had poorer outcomes than those who did not plan but got things right.

One further link between an institutional upbringing and poorer outcomes forged through the selection of environments, concerns the consequences of early pregnancy and child-bearing. Over half of the ex-care women first became pregnant under the age of 19 compared with just over one-quarter of the comparison mothers. More importantly, a quarter of first ex-care pregnancies were unplanned and unwanted compared with none in the comparison sample. The majority of these unwelcome pregnancies occurred in the under-19 age group. It seems likely that the causes and correlates of early pregnancies were different in the two samples, those in the comparison group occurring predominantly in the context of stable relationships, whilst those in the ex-care group often arising as a result of temporary liaisons or occurring in unsupportive relationships established for negative reasons. The psychological dispositions associated with such pregnancies is not known, although they were not related to earlier behavioural deviance. However, a lack of planning for pregnancy was much more common in the ex-care group (74 per cent v. 33 per cent).

Recent studies have documented the adverse impacts of early pregnancy on women's later life-circumstances through effects on education, employment and income (Hofferth and Moore, 1979; McCluskey *et al.*, 1983). The prospective study shows also that early pregnancy may have a long-term impact on parenting under certain circumstances. Although unrelated to teenage behavioural deviance in the ex-care sample it was related to a lack of marital support and to poor parenting in the mid-twenties. These data are consistent with Kruk and Wolkind's (1983) finding that early pregnancy appeared in a working-class population to have no long-term sequelae for child development or parenting providing that the young mothers had good social support.

In sum, the ex-care women's early experience led to environments that 'encouraged' sexual activity in a group of girls less equipped to deter pregnancy, less able to cope with the demands of child-rearing and more likely to be channelled into unsatisfactory and unsupported parenting circumstances. In this way continuities are promoted by the linking of environments both independently of individual behaviour and as a consequence of individual actions, whether deliberate or unintended. In the ex-care sample the consequence of many early independent links was probably greatly to increase vulnerability to later adversities and to reduce the probability of positive circumstances later in life.

## *The production of environments*

The third form of environmental linkage to be discussed concerns the way in which individuals can alter their environments through their behaviour. This process involves transactions between them and their surroundings (Rutter, 1983a) and not just the selection of environments discussed in the previous section. For example, the ex-care subjects showed a much higher rate of behavioural disturbance than the comparison group. In their teens their greater interpersonal difficulties were associated with a greater likelihood of frequent job changes and this increased the probability of their experiencing socio-economic hardships. The same is true of their peer and marital relationships; because they were more likely to create tension and discord, they were to this extent more likely to experience discordant and disruptive relationships. The likelihood of adverse experiences was further increased as a consequence of their behaviours by the linking of other adverse circumstances — for example, their school achievements were lower so the probability of rewarding work experiences was reduced; and in turn, their own response to working conditions decreased the likelihood of positive experiences still further.

In parenting, too, their own behaviour increased the probability of a stressful parenting environment. For example, the observational data showed that reduced sensitivity to the child's needs generated problems. Thus disciplinary confrontations often arose from interactions not initially involving issues of discipline (Dowdney *et al.*, 1985b). These problems occurred through inadequate action to prevent disruptive behaviour arising, rather than from intervention after it occurred. These difficulties in parenting predisposed the children to show more disruptive behaviour, which in turn created more stresses for parents already vulnerable to stress.

## Individual life-histories

The processes of continuity and discontinuity discussed above can be illustrated by life-histories chosen to illustrate some of the main themes that have emerged from the statistical analyses of the data. Unlike the case examples used in previous chapters, which were selected on a random basis to illustrate particular measures, these examples have been deliberately chosen to highlight the interplay between life-history, development and outcome. All the case histories were taken from the sample of ex-care women for whom we had both interview and observational data. All personal details have been disguised or altered to preserve confidentiality.

### *Case 1: Carol*

Carol, her husband and three children lived in a pleasant rented cottage in the Warwickshire countryside near Banbury. The cottage had a nice homely feel about it. It was furnished with secondhand furniture and the walls were hung with many of Carol's own photographs and paintings. Her husband was a university graduate in electronics and was at the beginning of a promising career in that industry following some months of unemployment subsequent to his graduation. The couple were hoping to buy their own house in the near future. They were a settled, happy and socially active family with a bright future. But, as her history shows this had partly come about because of the favourable circumstances surrounding certain key breakpoints in Carol's life.

Carol's memories of admission to home 'A' were vivid. Her mother had pushed her three children out of a taxi on the steps of her Social Services office and abandoned them. She has only ever been seen on one or two occasions subsequently. The children were all together in the same cottage. Carol's early experiences were unhappy ones. She remembers the persistent teasing and scapegoating of backward and disturbed children. In addition, her first houseparents were strict and petty, punishing minor disobedience with prolonged punishments. For example, if the children laughed at the dinner table they were sent to bed early after school for a month. She also felt that she was given responsibilities beyond her years. Thus, on Sundays she had to take about ten children out to play for two hours so that her housemother could have a rest. Carol had no particular friends in this early period but was not bullied or picked on either. She remained close to her brother and regarded this relationship as important.

At some point towards the end of her primary school years — which she regarded neutrally — her houseparents retired and were replaced by a much more positive woman. Carol and her brother have a very high regard for 'Sadie' and are still in touch with her. This change enabled Carol to feel more settled in the cottage and happily it preceded her transfer to secondary school — an event which caused much unhappiness to many of the children. At this time of her life Carol was rated as being without emotional or behavioural problems on both the teachers' and the houseparents' questionnaires.

The secondary school experiences were happy although she felt the school was poor academically and that they were too lenient with her because she came from a home. She was very good at art and sport and was in nearly every school team. She also made friends with a crowd which included a cousin of her future husband, an important chance link in her positive life-history.

Carol left the home shortly before she was 16. For teenagers without family support and guidance this is a particularly 'dangerous' time in their lives. She took a flat with a friend from the same home but maintained her contact with Sadie and her school peer group. Her first serious boyfriend was another ex-care teenager but this relationship did not last. Through her school contacts she got to know her present husband and they started going out seriously when she was 16. Paul was from a stable and happy working-class family in south

London. However, things got off to a potentially bad start because despite taking contraceptive precautions, Carol became pregnant when she was still 16. A key factor at this point was the continuing support and commitment from Paul and the accepting and helpful attitude of his family. The couple married when she was 17, but she maintains that this was a free choice not forced by her pregnancy.

Support from Paul's family enabled him to go to university and for their marriage to consolidate without too much pressure. Indeed Carol herself began to catch up on her own education by taking some 'O' levels during this time. Her two subsequent pregnancies were planned. After completing his degree Paul was unemployed for nearly a year before joining his present firm.

It is clear that Carol's life could have taken a very different course if a number of life-history factors had not gone her way: poor house-parents gave way to good ones; stable school peer groups led to contacts with a different range of influences and potential spouses; her early relationship with another ex-care boy was not long-lasting, her early pregnancy was well supported and had no adverse effects. Undoubtedly, her own attractiveness and personality played a part in this probably by increasing the chance of this positive chain.

Carol came easily into the top groups on parenting for both the interview and observational assessments. She was warm, sensitive and firm but not aggressive in her style of control. Her earlier experiences left her with a 'no nonsense' view of child-rearing, but her interactions with her children were positive.

### Case 2: Sandra

It took over 2½ years to trace and interview Sandra after a number of her contacts had told us that she was not interested. When finally contacted she was friendly and helpful. A plump, attractive and cheerful girl, she said, 'You've been looking for me for a long time haven't you?' When contacted she, her husband Frank (who is 15 years her senior) and four children had been living in their new council property in south-east London for ten months. Prior to this they had spent several years in unsatisfactory part III accommodation or in bed and breakfast lodgings. Frank was a lorry dirver. Early in their relationship they had two other children who were adopted because of their parents' unsettled life at the time.

Sandra's household was friendly but chaotic. She was not a fastidious person and usually appeared rather unkempt and shoeless. Her life seemed to be conducted from her kitchen, the floor of which generally looked in need of a scrub. However, her family life seemed happy and supportive and she was coping well with her children. Although not highly sensitive in her responses, she was generally warm and practical in her parenting.

Sandra came from a large family of eleven children, seven of whom were her full siblings. The children were taken into care when she was about four years of age, following desertion by her mother who 'went off with the bloke next door'. This event followed years of violence and abuse from her husband who was frequently in prison. Violence characterised parent–child relationships as well. As Sandra put it, 'We knew when we was getting a good hiding because he used to put the dogs out in the garden 'cos if he hadn't they would have bit him.' Following her mother's desertion, her eldest sister tried to cope for a while but could not. The family were a'l taken into care 'by the court' and spent the predominant part of their childhoods in home 'B'. Her memories of her time in this home were rather vague but she felt that her own houseparents were satisfactory, 'the best of the bunch'. Some of them were 'old-fashioned' (i.e. strict) but she had no bad memories. She was fond of one of the housemothers but not strongly attached to her. She did, however, form a stronger relationship with a visiting teacher and was still in touch with her. Her peer relationships were good from her point of view, and she had a regular crowd with whom she went around. On the other hand, her relationships with her brothers were very poor, they fought constantly and had no positive feelings for each other. During her early secondary school years she remembered being prone to violent tempers and chasing her brothers with a kitchen knife. This evidence for behavioural disturbance was confirmed by the teacher and houseparent questionnaires.

Unlike Carol, our first example, Sandra's secondary schooling was unhappy. She went to a large comprehensive school some way from the home and never settled. She got progressively behind with her lessons and by the fourth year was truanting regularly. She made two friends at school but these contacts did not continue when she finally stopped attending some months before her 15th birthday.

Sandra's behaviour during her last few years in care was difficult. She was moved to another cottage at 13 years of age where she continued to get in trouble because of her quick temper and her minor pilfering such as 'nicking fags from the housemother'. When she was 15 the authorities wanted her to live in a hostel but she asked to return to her father (with whom she had had minimal contact) and this was arranged. They moved from flat to flat for several weeks until she was introduced to Frank (her future husband) and a prostitute called Angie by whose daughter Frank already had a child. Sandra began to live with them. When she was 16 she had her first child who was adopted after eight months. She and Frank stayed with Angie for four years until they left to live on their own. For the next 5½ years they lived in four separate homeless family units, in bed and breakfast accommodation and, for a short period, with Sandra's mother. During this time four more children were born, one of whom was adopted following what Sandra believed was a temporary placement. Their present accommodation was by far the most satisfactory.

Despite this unsatisfactory life-history and the two parenting break-downs, Sandra's cohabitee Frank has been a steady and supportive influence on her life. He himself had a stable but rather severe child-hood with a strict ex-army father who used the strap on him. His family was not discordant, however, and there was no suggestion of psychiatric problems or criminality in his family or his own history. He had been married previously; this had broken up when he was in the navy. Sandra described their relationship as very important to her. Because they began living together when she was so young, she had no peer group of her own age in her teens. She told Frank everything and had no other confidants. There were occasional arguments, the continuation of her tendency to be very quick tempered, but she stressed how much she had calmed down since her days in care.

Sandra's life-history is interesting from a number of points of view. Admitted to care after the age of two from disrupted parenting experiences she showed emotional and behavioural problems in care and was discharged to unsatisfactory circumstances. This led her into generally unfavourable social and environmental conditions and in her case the early pregnancy was not associated with the maternal and family support enjoyed by Carol. The continuity of adverse circum-stances continued until very recently and there have been two parenting breakdowns. Nevertheless, her husband has proved a stable and supportive figure and her current parenting had many positive features despite some continuing problems. One general area of concern lies in the paucity of her social contacts generally and her great reliance on Frank. This may render her vulnerable if any problems should occur in this relationship.

Sandra came in the middle group on the overall current parenting assessments on both interviews and observations. Her life centred on her children and although low on sensitivity she was warm and practical. Her main method of control was shouting but the children were not intimidated by her and were quick to make approaches to her to say they were sorry and to make up. She always accepted these approaches. She cuddled the children a great deal and would play pretend games with them. In general she was seen as a competent and caring parent who had done particularly well given the markedly rejecting experiences she had had with her own parents.

## Case 3: Liz

Liz's life and her current parenting qualities are an example of the triumph of human adaptability and resilience in the face of major persisting adversities. At the time of interview she was living with her two children aged seven and two in an old council flat in Charlton. She was unmarried and lived on social security. At first guarded in her response to the request to take part in the research, she relaxed during the interview and talked altogether for 6–7 hours. Her flat was very nicely appointed and decorated due entirely to her skill in shepherding her meagre resources. The children's room was described as being like a Hampstead primary school with all manner of educational aids. Both interviewer and observer commented on the superior quality of her parenting. She was in the top group on both assessments.

Liz was admitted to long-term care at about the age of seven, but she had had at least one shorter admission when she was three. She was the middle of three children. Her parents separated when she was about 1½ and her mother remarried. Her early years were spent in a variety of accommodations, including a caravan, in different parts of the country. At some point the family returned to London and shared a property which, in retrospect, Liz says was a brothel. She shared a bed with four other children and the house was often raided by police. Her mother's husband was one of a number of men she had at this time, apart from the regular clients. She was described as a sly and heartless person and a hopeless mother. Liz only remembered going out with her once when she was about four, to meet a client and being told: 'Keep your mouth shut or you'll get it.' About this time her mother was on probation for committing grievous bodily harm.

The reception into care followed a police raid. 'I remember the police coming. I was sitting on Jimmy's mum's lap at the time. I remember the policeman carrying me. His nose was bleeding, I thought I had done it, then my mother said someone had pushed him. We were taken to the police station and given some toys.'

Liz and her brother went first to a short-stay home and then to home 'B'. Her mother visited infrequently and used to make excuses. Liz remembers her housemother dressing them up for the occasion and they used to sit waiting, only to be disappointed. Contacts with her mother remained sporadic at about monthly intervals. Her time in the home was unhappy. One member of staff was strict and used to punish her by making her stand in the cold bathroom after everyone had gone to bed. She remembers few friends but was always fighting with her brother. They used to tell tales to get each other into trouble. She began to run away and was transferred to a boarding school for maladjusted children when she was eleven. She hated it there. The children were spiteful and she herself became a bully. She was part of a gang that used to terrorise the teachers. She had some attachments amongst the staff but in general made many enemies. She was discharged home to her mother at age 13 after, as she remembers it, threatening to burn the school down.

Her mother was not pleased to see her and wanted to appropriate her new school uniform. Liz went on to a local comprehensive and her disruptive behaviour continued. She truanted a great deal and had no close friends. Her home life was discordant and unhappy. Her mother showed no interest and she fought a lot with her younger sister. Her mother had a series of cohabitees but seems to have finally settled down and has been with the same man for eight years.

Liz left school at 15, already pregnant with her eldest child. She was living with her mother and there were frequent rows. They had a fight when she was five months pregnant. Following the birth she tried to get work but could never keep jobs because of her temper; she became pregnant again. Physical fights with her mother, who was trying to take over the parenting of the child, continued. Liz had twins both of whom died and she returned to a job which she managed to keep for two years. She became pregnant in her late teens with her youngest child and has not worked since.

Because of her early pregnancy the parents of her schoolfriends forbade them to see her. Her mother refused to let her go on seeing her child's father after she had let them cohabit in her house prior to the birth. Her mother always interfered jealously in her relationships. She left home at the age of 18 and started squatting. Liz had three separate cohabitations in her late teens, the last of which was with a young man with a long history of criminal and drink problems. The one prior to that was a drug addict. Her relationship with her most recent cohabitee had finished about three years previously and Liz had been in a homeless families unit before being given her present council flat.

There were few positive features in Liz's life until quite recently. The birth of her first child was a very significant event psychologically — 'I really wanted Sarah. It was the longest year of my life' — but the early history of parenting was unhappy. On occasions Sarah was primarily parented by her grandmother whilst Liz lived elsewhere. This finally resulted in a court case for custody which Liz won. The most recent significant event was a conversion to Christianity a year previously. Liz reviews her life of promiscuity, drinking and going to discos, 'I've tried that way of life and now I'm trying another. Things work out better this way. Problems work out, praying has helped me. I've changed for good. I try to do what He wants.'

The church provides Liz with much social and emotional support. It was hoped that this would allow her to become more secure and trusting in her relationships and to continue the personal development which is evident in the quality of her parenting.

## Theoretical implications

### Sociological considerations

The sociological criticism of the use of family or individual behaviour to explain inter-generational continuities in deprivation was discussed in Chapter 1. However, without some such focus it is difficult to explain why the outcome of apparently similar levels of disadvantage varies so greatly. A point well illustrated in the retrospective study by the way that the childhoods of the in-care and comparison samples were similar on social or structural characteristics but were markedly different in the quality of family life. It is clear that the impact of family behaviour on personality development must be taken into account since such behaviour has been shown to be the main mediator of the impact of the wider environment on the child (Rutter and Quinton, 1977). On the other hand, sociologists are correct in stressing the role of multiple disadvantage and the overlap of psychosocial problems in leading to marked parenting problems and to parenting breakdown. For example, receptions into care seldom occur from families of higher social status. Other parenting failures such as child abuse are similarly associated with a lack of material as well as personal resources (Garbarino, 1979). A simple explanation would be that the marital and psychological problems are caused by social disadvantage and that this is the reason for overlap. Although social factors beyond the control of the individual have been shown to be related to psychiatric problems (Brown and Harris, 1978), such forces cannot on their own be an adequate explanation of family and psychological problems since the direction of influence is not always from environment to functioning as is shown by the downward social mobility of schizophrenic patients (Goldberg and Morrison, 1963), and since marital problems relate strongly to social class in some populations but not in others (Rutter and Madge, 1976). Clearly the degree of overlap of family problems with environmental disadvantage will depend on the level of resources available to society as a whole and the way the social structure determines their allocation. Given this, the persistence of material disadvantage is predominantly a question of social structure, but this alone is not an adequate explanation of the transmission of disadvantage. This requires the actions of individuals within the particular social structure to be taken into account.

Recent advances in life-history research have begun to set out a conceptual and analytic approach that enables the links between social forces and individual actions to be studied (Baltes and Brim, 1979; Elder, 1974, 1979). This approach has been exploited effectively by Brown and his colleagues with respect to the consequences of loss of a parent in childhood for depression in adulthood (Brown *et al.*, 1986). Their work highlights the pattern of linkages working both independently of individual behaviour and as a consequence of it in a way very similar to the processes demonstrated in the prospective study described in this book.

A major conclusion from these studies must be that a consideration of individual actions and the psychological processes underlying them is entirely consistent with the study of the role of wider social forces in the explanation of social phenomena, and indeed that the inclusion of both is often essential. This may seem neither new nor controversial with respect to the impact of society upon its members, but its status has been much more in dispute in sociology with respect to the central question of the nature of inter-generational continuities for a variety of social problems.

### Continuities in development

Some current issues relating to the study of development were outlined in Chapter 1 and a number of relevant findings have been discussed earlier in this chapter. As was clear from the evidence reviewed in Chapter 1 there are abundant data to counter the view that early adverse experiences inevitably have long-lasting sequelae for personality development (Clarke and Clarke, 1976). Equally, within the range of normal behaviour, findings from many studies have demonstrated rather low correlations over time for behavioural characteristics of many types (Brim and Kagan, 1980) and it has become accepted by many that there is little behavioural continuity over the course of development from infancy to adulthood (Kohlberg *et al.*, 1972). However, other research evidence has shown substantial continuity for some deviant behaviours such as aggression (Robins, 1978; Olweus, 1979). It is clear, therefore, that theoretical models of development have to account for both continuity and discontinuity and this is demonstrated in the data from the prospective study. The first issue is whether the persistence of particular behaviours simply represents the persistence of adverse environments. This would be in keeping with situationist views that postulate that most variations in behaviour are due to the immediate effects of environmental forces and that there is no need to invoke either developmental processes or personality as mediating variables (Mischel, 1968). While the findings concerning the protective effects of a supportive spouse is perhaps evidence for this position, in other ways the data are inconsistent with it. In particular, the fact that the ex-care women showed worse functioning than the comparison sample when exposed to adverse current marital circumstances and housing conditions implies a difference between the two groups in their capacity to cope with stress. This suggests that environmental continuities are not a sufficient explanation for behavioural continuities and that developmental processes need to be taken into account.

The resolution of some of these issues lies, as Rutter (1984a) has pointed out, in distinguishing the notion of stability or constancy in behaviour from the idea of continuity in development. The former concepts imply a lack of change in behavioural functioning — a view that is at variance with much empirical evidence. The concept of continuity does not imply such constancies in behaviour, nor that earlier life-experiences necessarily have enduring consequences for personality development. Rather, the concept of continuity concerns the existence of meaningful links over time, with continuities in development lying within the environment as well as in the individual.

Evidence for both kinds of continuity has been presented in the analysis of data from the prospective study.

## Self-concepts as a mediating mechanism

The evidence pointing to the increased vulnerability to life stresses of the ex-care women has been reviewed. A central question involves the basis of this vulnerability. A related issue concerns the nature of the relationship between positive experiences in the teenage and early adult years and better psychosocial outcomes later. It was hypothesised that this association arose through the effect of positive and rewarding experiences in increasing the women's sense of worth and personal efficacy (Bandura, 1977; Harter, 1983). This conclusion was supported by the finding that positive experiences at school were not simply a reflection of better functioning at that time, and were associated with evidence of forethought concerning employment and marriage later. However, this conclusion must remain speculative both because there were no direct measures of self-esteem or self-efficacy and because the reports of planning involved long-term recall.

There are powerful arguments for the role of self-concepts in the aetiology of adult depression (Brown and Harris, 1976; Brown *et al.*, 1986), but the nature of the links between positive or negative self-evaluations in the teenage years and later psychological vulnerabilities remains unclear. For example, Brown *et al.* found that premarital pregnancy (a risk factor for depression in their Walthamstow sample) was associated with feelings of helplessness that pre-dated the pregnancy. However, this feeling of helplessness did not predict depression in adulthood unless associated with a marked lack of parental care in childhood. Moreover, this combination of antecedent factors was as strong a predictor of later depression in the absence of premarital pregnancy as when such an event had occurred. This finding parallels that reported above for the retrospective study in which marked unhappiness in the teenage years in the absence of childhood adversities was not related to later parenting breakdown but was a strong predictor in the presence of earlier adversities.

No firm conclusions can be drawn from Brown's data concerning the role of self-concepts as a mediating mechanism between childhood experiences and adult psychosocial problems. On their own, the measures of self are not predictive, but it may be that other important dimensions of self-concepts related to markedly adverse family experiences have not been distinguished. Alternatively, the problem may lie in retrospective measures of teenage self-image more generally. A lack of association may arise because the relatively common feeling of helplessness in the teens has not adequately been separated from a more profound or widespread feeling of lack of control over the individual's life. As Harter's recent review of the literature on the self-system (1983) admirably demonstrates, this topic involves a number of distinct concepts including core notions of the self, self-esteem, mastery and self-control. There is a need for both a clearer theoretical delineation of these concepts and a more sophisticated approach to measurement in order that research in this area can advance. On the other hand, her review shows the great fluidity of self-concepts in adolescence. For this reason the possibility that the positive experiences of the ex-care girls at this time had their impact through changes in self-esteem or feelings of mastery remains plausible.

### Specificity of the findings

This research has been concerned with the inter-generational transmission of marked family problems through parenting experiences and behaviour. For this reason the focus has been on parenting breakdown or marked difficulties in handling and responding to children. Evidence has been presented concerning the antecedents and consequences of parenting breakdown as shown by receptions of children into care. The retrospective study showed that one of the biggest differences between the in-care and comparison samples involved the occurrence of marked childhood adversities in both parents. In the comparison sample such adversities were common in the childhoods of one or other parent (but not both). In the prospective study, likewise, parenting breakdown and marked current parenting difficulties were virtually confined to the ex-care group but occurred predominantly when the mother lacked marital support or had a deviant spouse.

Does this, then, imply that childhood experiences are of little consequence for parenting unless both parents bring these experiences to marriage? It seems probable that this conjunction of adverse backgrounds is a very powerful factor in relation to parenting breakdown, but it would be quite wrong to conclude that marked parenting problems will not arise unless this or meeting of childhood adversities occurs, or conversely that current more mild difficulties are simply a response to current circumstances. For example, in the retrospective study, although the in-care parents were showing many more current problems in handling their children, such difficulties also occurred with surprising frequency in the comparison group. This sample had also experienced many childhood adversities and it would be surprising if these were not related to their current parenting in some way. This could not be investigated for two reasons. First, the sample was too small for statistical analysis, and secondly, the parenting measures were of insufficient range to allow distinctions to be made at the 'good' end of each dimension. Studies of larger samples at high risk for particular childhood adversities but without a history of parenting breakdown will be necessary to examine further the antecedents and correlates of parenting problems and qualities.

*Clinical implications*

Finally, some comments on the clinical and practical implications of these findings are necessary. At first sight our conclusions might seem to offer little of direct practical importance. The current trend is strongly against large children's homes and long-term residential care, so is it not the case that our evidence relates to a set of experiences that will soon no longer exist? Unfortunately, this seems not to be the case. Although a rather different group of children are now being placed in children's homes this is still a very common form of placement (Berridge, 1985). Moreover, the history of the girls in the prospective study points not only to the consequences of early and prolonged institutionalisation but also to the consequences of prolonged exposure to discordant and disrupted family relationships. Both of these kinds of experience have deleterious effects. Indeed, the findings raise concern by the fact that exposure to the first of these experiences was as a result of Social Services action designed to protect children from the second. We therefore need to ask whether this implies that a 'good' institution was as harmful as a 'bad' family.

A degree of caution is needed before drawing such a conclusion. In the first place we cannot know what would have happened if the girls had remained with their own families — perhaps they would have fared even worse. Also, it is necessary to recognise that the girls had both an institutional rearing *and* an adverse genetic background. It would not be warranted to assume that an institutional upbringing would lead to an equally unfortunate outcome if the children were otherwise normal — say those orphaned as a result of a parental car accident. It may be that the ill-effects of an institutional rearing largely apply when the children are constitutionally disadvantaged as well. In addition, we cannot be sure that the poor outcome derived from the institutional rearing rather than from the girls' experiences in infancy before admission. Nevertheless, the findings from other studies strongly indicate that it is unlikely that adverse experiences in the first year or so *per se* could influence adult behaviour in the absence of other adversities later in childhood (Rutter, 1981a). On the other hand, it is quite possible that the disrupted parenting in the girls' own families during the first two years predisposed them to be more susceptible to the ill-effects of an institutional upbringing. Finally, if institutions are harmful, there should be some identifiable features of institutional life that constitute the adverse influences. The one feature of many institutions that stands out as different from ordinary family life is the very high turnover of caretakers (see also, Tizard, 1975, 1977; Tizard and Hodges, 1978) and it may be this that constitutes the risk. If this supposition is accepted, two implications for practice follow. First, we need to seek to change the arrangements in residential nurseries so that there can be much greater stability in parenting. Of course, there are practical difficulties in ensuring that just one or two staff provide personalised care for the child. Nevertheless, it should be possible to arrange that one or other of a small number of staff is always available to care for the child at key times (such as getting up, meal-times, going to bed, times of sickness, etc.). Probably children can cope with three, four or five caregivers; what very young children find very unsettling is a roster of ever-changing caregivers so that there is no one on whom they can rely at times of distress. Secondly, Roy's (1983) findings on the better outcome for family-fostered children suggests that foster-care may be preferential to residential nurseries for very young children, provided that the child can stay throughout with the same foster-parents.

However, it would be quite misleading to see the effects of institutional care solely, or even mainly, in terms of what happens during the early years of childhood. Our findings show that the experience of disrupted parenting in infancy predicted what happened when the girls left care in adolescence. Moreover, the data strikingly demonstrated the importance of the period of transition when leaving the institution — in terms of family experiences at that time, working life, and whom they married. All too often the girls returned to an unhappy and discordant home, to parents with whom they had largely lost touch and with whom they did not get on. Both our interviews with the women and the Social Services case notes showed that very few of the girls had much advice or support after they left the children's home in spite of that being the time when they experienced the greatest change of environment and when they were most in need of help. Of course, it may well be that some would not have been very receptive to help at that time but still there is a clear implication from our findings that much more needs to be done to provide social work support and guidance during the critical period of transition during the few years after leaving the institution.

A second feature of the findings that is of relevance to practice is the dramatic demonstration of the ameliorating effect on adult social functioning of a harmonious marriage. This finding is of importance because of its indication both that experiences in *adult* life can have a massive effect on social functioning, and also that marital relationships constitute an environmental factor of major importance. The first conclusion shows that the process of development continues well past the childhood years and that good experiences in adulthood can do much to reduce the ill-effects of serious and prolonged adversities in childhood. Clearly, the potential for change remains for a long time; notions that it is 'too late to do any good' are rarely justified.

It might be thought that the findings on marriage have few implications for services. But that constitutes too narrow a view of the matter. This is because the longitudinal data show the importance of factors associated with a good marriage. One of the features of a deprived unhappy upbringing, and perhaps even more so of an institutional rearing, is that it is likely to engender the feeling that one is at the mercy of fate with key life decisions always being taken by somebody else. The data suggest that where this is the case poorer life decisions will be made and the gloomy prophesy will be fulfilled. However, things were substantially different when, as teenagers, the girls took some control of their lives and planned for their futures. This tendency to plan seemed to be related to experiences that engendered some feeling of worth. It would seem to be helpful to do all possible to ensure that young people acquire the belief that they *can* control what happens to them (see Bandura, 1977) and that they gain the social problem-solving skills to enable them to do so (Pellegrini, 1984). This has implications both for the ways in which children's homes are run and for the goals and approaches used in psychological and social therapies more generally (see Rutter, 1982b).

A further aspect of preparation for a successful marriage, however, concerns the range of opportunities available. One consequence of a deprived childhood seems to be a restriction of social contacts to friends from a similar background together with a tendency to set up home, and to have children early, perhaps to compensate for the earlier lack of affection. The implication is that experiences that widen people's horizons and social opportunities are likely to be helpful (the benefits of scholastic success to some extent operate in this fashion) and it may be advantageous for young people to postpone both marriage and child-bearing until they are able to cope with it. Contraceptive advice is necessary but that is not likely to be sufficient in itself. Many unwanted pregnancies arise against a background of a general feeling of hopelessness and inevitability, a pervasive lack of foresight and planning in all aspects of life. Family planning must form part of a wider community service that is educational in the broadest and best sense.

The findings on the positive effects of schooling are related to this issue. The finding that positive experiences at school did not predict outcome in the control group may be a consequence of the fact that the girls in that group had ample *other* sources of self-esteem in their families and friends. The data also suggest that, for the ex-care girls, good experiences *outside* the family may go a long way to ameliorate adverse experiences within the home. Moreover, most of the protective experiences at school for the ex-care girls did *not* involve academic successes. This serves to remind us that schooling constitutes a rich source of *social* experiences as well as an instrument for academic instruction.

Finally, it is necessary to emphasise again that the data show that continuities in development involve linkages within the environment as well as within the individual (see Rutter, 1983a, 1984a). In some circumstances the indirect effects of early adverse experiences may be quite long-lasting. Even so, such long-term effects are far from independent of intervening circumstances. The continuities stem from a multitude of links over time. Because each link is incomplete, subject to marked individual variation and open to modification there are many opportunities to break the chain. Such opportunities continue right into adult life.

# Appendix A   Sample selection

## The retrospective study

### The in-care sample

The in-care sample consisted of a consecutive series of 48 families living in one Inner London borough, who had had children admitted into residential care during a continuous eight-month period. Only those families for whom this was at least the second time a child (either the same or a different one) had been taken into care were included in the sample, in order to exclude those cases in which admission occurred because of some single, short-term crisis. In addition, selection was further restricted to families with a child between the ages of five and eight years living at home in order that comparable assessments of parenting could be made in all families. Families in which either of the parents of the children had been born abroad were excluded as it could not be assumed that their childhood experiences would be comparable with those of parents born in Great Britain. Families with mentally or physically handicapped children were also excluded as the presence of such handicaps might make the assessment of parenting skills not comparable with those of families with non-handicapped children.

### The comparison sample

The comparison sample consisted of 47 families with a child in the same age group living at home with its mother, but in which no child in the family had ever been taken into the care of the local authority. The sample was drawn randomly from the age–sex registers of two group general practices in the same Inner London borough as the one from which the in-care sample was taken. These practices were chosen because they served the more socially disadvantaged part of the area and thus the two groups could be expected to be roughly comparable in socio-economic level and environmental circumstances. However, precise matching was not undertaken because the relevant variables on which to match could not be known in advance.

### Checks on sample completeness

All possible care was taken to ensure that no cases in either sample fitting the criteria were missed. The in-care sample were initially identified from the borough's 'reception into care' forms. Missing information was always checked with the family's social worker unless the form gave definite information that ruled the family out on other grounds. For example, cases with no clear information about previous admissions into care were always checked before they were excluded.

Problems in collecting the comparison sample arose principally because addresses were out-of-date, or because delays in administrative machinery meant that the initial list of families included some who were no longer registered with the practices. In addition, since the general practitioners could not reveal family details for reasons of confidentiality, a larger number had to be screened in order to get a sample fitting the criteria. Thus in order to obtain the sample of 47, 76 families had to be contacted. There were no families from the original list who remained untraced or whose inclusion in the sample remained in doubt.

### Interview rates

As shown in Table A.1 the mothers in both samples were interviewed in the great majority of cases. The refusal rates were similar to those obtained in other epidemiological surveys (Rutter *et al.*, 1975a). The success in interviewing such high proportions of the mothers — especially in the in-care sample — often depended on making many visits to the families, in order to build relationships of trust and in order not to add further complications to the problems of social work management. Thus, in several cases between six and eight months elapsed between a case being identified and a final complete interview. On other occasions up to 30 visits were necessary before the family felt confident enough to discuss their situation.

*Table A.1   Retrospective study: Interview rates*

|  | In-care group | Comparison group |
| --- | --- | --- |
| Total number of eligible families | 48 | 47 |
| Mother or father interviewed | 92% | 91% |
| Mother interviewed | 89% | 91% |
| Cohabitee of mother interviewed* | 71% | 90% |
| Basic data on first cohabitee* | 82% | 90% |

* Percentage based on the N of mothers interviewed.

Most of the cohabitees in the comparison group were interviewed, but the success rate for cohabitees in the in-care group was substantially lower. In four of the six uninterviewed cases, the wife refused permission for the husband to be contacted on the grounds that it might cause serious family disruption. Since only about half of the mothers in the in-care group were currently cohabiting, the resulting number of interviewed cohabitees (15) was low.

## The prospective study

### *The ex-care group*

The study by King *et al.* (1971), conducted in 1964, provided an epidemiologically-based sample of Inner London children experiencing one form of long-term substitute care. The follow-up samples from the two homes were defined as all children coded as 'white' on the record sheets from the original study (King *et al.*, 1971) who were aged between 21 and 27 years on 1 January 1978 and for whom Rutter 'B' scales had been completed by their schools. The age criterion was applied in the hope of obtaining a high proportion of subjects with young children. Selection was further restricted to those with teacher questionnaire data ('B' scales) because of the importance of this independent measure of functioning during the children's time in care. However, in order to increase the sample of sibling pairs in the study, the sibs of those chosen on the main selection critieria but for whom 'B' scales were missing were also included. The totals in care and the totals selected are given in Table A.2.

*Table A.2  Sampling from the children's homes*

|  | Total in age group | Total with B scale | Selected because a sib | Total selected |
|---|---|---|---|---|
| Home 'A' | 47 | 42 | 2 | 44 |
| Home 'B' | 56 | 37 | 12 | 49 |

### *The comparison sample*

The comparison group of 51 comprised a quasi-random general population sample of young women of the same age, never admitted into care, living in childhood with their families in Inner London, and whose behaviour at school was assessed at approximately the same age by means of the same questionnaire ('B' scale). The group was originally chosen because it constituted the control group in a study of the children of parents with some form of psychiatric disorder (Rutter and Quinton, 1981). This sample was similarly followed to age 21–27 years using assessments identical to those used for the ex-care sample. The group departs from a truly random sample only in so far as it is restricted to children in the same school classes as the children of mentally-ill parents. The available data show that this introduced no relevant distortions or biases.

## Tracing

The follow-up of the institutionalised children presented major problems in tracing. Only a minority of children returned home to their parents for any length of time, and for those who did so relationships were often very poor. As a consequence, in many cases even when parents themselves could be traced, they did not know the current whereabouts of their children.

Initially it had been hoped to make extensive use of social service records as a tracing source but in general these did not prove to be very useful. In the first place between 3 and 15 years had elapsed since the child's final discharge from care so that existing addresses were quite out-of-date. Secondly, a substantial proportion of case notes was missing or could not be found. Thirdly, of the ten boroughs holding case files, five waited over one year from the beginning of the study before agreeing to allow access to the notes. Fourthly, two boroughs felt that the notes could only be seen with the written permission of the subjects we wished to contact. In all cases, once contacted, the subjects freely gave permission but, of course, this procedure meant that the notes were of no use for tracing purposes.

In the early stages some contacts were made using last known addresses from the social services notes or from the current or past staff of the homes who were still in contact with some of our sample. However, the single most useful tracing source was the National Health Service Central Register, the local Family Practitioner Committee (FPC) and the subjects' own general practitioner. The procedure used was for the Central Register to provide details of the local FPC areas in which the subjects were last known to have been registered. The FPCs were then contacted for the names and addresses of general practitioners. Finally, the doctors were asked if they would help us get in touch with the subjects either by forwarding a letter or by providing us with their names and addresses. These techniques proved very successful for tracing both cases and the comparison sample so that approximately 70 per cent of each group was located by these means.

Interviews were conducted both with the subjects and their current spouses. The interviewing rates are given in Table A.3. In all 91 per cent of the ex-care women were traced and all of those were interviewed. The tracing losses for the controls were somewhat higher, but 89 per cent of those traced were interviewed, giving an overall success rate of 80 per cent.

*Table A.3 Prospective study: Interview rates*

|  | Home 'A'<br>N=44 | Home 'B'<br>N=49 | Total<br>ex-care<br>N=93 | Comparison<br>group<br>N=51 |
|---|---|---|---|---|
|  | % | % | % | % |
| Traced | 89 | 98 | 91 | 90 |
| Interviewed | 88[a] | 94[a] | 91[a] | 80 |
| % interviewed of those traced | 100[a] | 100[a] | 100[a] | 89 |
| Spouse interviewed | 45[b] | 75 | 63 | 73 |

a  Four dead subjects not included in the calculation.
b  Two husbands were in Australia and so although the women were interviewed it was not possible to interview their spouses.

# Appendix B    Retrospective study: Reasons for admission

The reasons stated on the RIC forms are given for the first four families in each category.

## Group 1. Non-Psychiatric parental hospital admissions and satisfactory parenting

1  Mother going into hospital ? cancer. Marital problems. Father has left family with debts.
2  Mother's confinement. Good mother. Child previously abandoned at Social Services because electricity cut off. Similar action threatened again.
3  Mother's confinement. Unsupported mother coping well with stress. Similar previous admissions. (Mother actually had a spouse but wanted rehousing.)
4  To give mother a rest. Reasonable mother.

## Group 2. Family and psychiatric problems but no mention of problems in parenting

1  Admission requested by mother claiming that she cannot look after the children. Reports of very poor school attendance. Mother on drugs.
2  Serious marital problems. Father alcoholic, mother has made several recent suicide attempts. Admission to give parents a chance to sort problems out.
3  A mother of very limited intelligence and in poor health. Admission to give mother a break.
4  Gross family problems. Violence to mother by spouse. Admission because mother has left the family home.

## Group 3. Admissions mentioning parenting problems

1  No electricity or heating. Mother unable to cope and has little patience with the children. A potential batterer.
2  Family under intensive support. Admission following mother's suicide attempts. One child already in care through failure to thrive.
3  Section 2 admission. Neglect and abuse.

4 Section 2 admission. Husband imprisoned for abuse of the children. Children never go to school and set fire to the home. Mother beats children with a stick.

# Appendix C1   Retrospective study: Childhoods of 'no adversity' families included in Table 3.7

| Mother | Father |
|---|---|
| **In-care group** | |
| 1 5 Sibs. Fractured skull aged 5, strict father hit her with a belt. A brother went to live with grandmother because of ? abuse. | Parental marital discord. |
| 2 Parental marital discord. Long hospitalisation for rheumatic fever. | Sib group of 5 and single-parent family. |
| 3 Parental divorce at age 7. Lived with grandmother. Sister in care. Diphtheria aged 4. Went to father and step-mother aged 10. Very bad relationship with father. | Parental marital discord. Evacuated. |
| **Comparison group** | |
| 1 No early problems. Separations from parents in teens. | No problems. |
| 2 No problems. | Evacuated with mother. |
| 3 Mother psychiatric problems, no family discord. | No problems. |
| 4 Parental marital discord. Many short hospitalisations. Generally unhappy. | No problems. |
| 5 No problems. | Long hospitalisation at age 8–11 with rheumatic fever. |
| 6 Separations through parental marital discord. | No problems. |

|  | Mother | Father |
|---|---|---|
| 7 | Evacuation with school for one year. | No problems. |
| 8 | Evacuated – happy experience. | No problems. |
| 9 | No problems. | Father died when subject 7. Not disrupted but not a warm home. |
| 10 | Long hospitalisations because 'run down'. | Mother psychiatric disorder. Home happy. |
| 11 | Hard discipline by father. | No problems. |
| 12 | No problems. | Discord with parents and very poor parental control. |
| 13 | Parental marital discord. Lax but aggressive mother. Went to 'open air' school. | Family of 9. Serious discord with one brother. |
| 14 | Many minor hospitalisations. In convent school one year because of parental marital discord. | Mother ? psychiatric disorder. Brother abused. |
| 15 | No problems. | Discord with mother. Very lax discipline. |
| 16 | No problems. | Mother with psychiatric disorder, not a non-discordant home. |
| 17 | Father with a criminal record. Non-discordant home. | No problems. |
| 18 | Discord with mother. Lax discipline. | No problems. |
| 19–23 | No problems. | No problems. |

# Appendix C2  Retrospective study: Known data on childhoods of parents excluded from Table 3.7

|  | Mother | Father |
|---|---|---|
| **In-care group** | | |
| 1 | Very unhappy childhood. Long-term fostering. Harsh discipline. Parental marital discord. | Nothing known. |
| 2 | In psychiatric hospital at age 17. Mother with phobic disorder. Very poor but not discordant parental marriage. | Little known. Previously a psychiatric patient. |
| 3 | In psychiatric hospital at age 10. Beyond parental control and ? abused. Marked violent parental marital discord. | Nothing known. History of drug abuse. |
| 4 | Cold and harshly punitive mother. | Nothing known. |
| 5 | Brought up by grandmother from age six months. No known problems. | Nothing known. |
| 6 | Parents separated when she was 8. No remembered discord. Harsh discipline by mother. | Nothing known. |
| 7 | In residential care throughout childhood. | Little known, but from a discordant home. |
| 8 | Marked discord between parents and children. | Nothing known. |
| 9 | Persecuted by jealous older sister. Parental marital discord. Step-mother very cold. Very unhappy. | Nothing known. |

|    | Mother | Father |
|----|--------|--------|
| 10 | Parental divorce in infancy. Step-father alcoholic. Harsh parental discipline and parental marital discord. | Nothing known. |
| 11 | Harsh discipline. Parental marital discord. In care for one year at age 5. | Parents separated when age 3. ? Unhappy in childhood. |
| 12 | Father alcoholic. Harsh discipline by mother. Parental marital discord. | Father very strict, mother very lax. All sibs in trouble with the police for aggressive behaviour. |
| 13 | Lived with grandparents until age 7 then with own parents. Parental marital discord and harsh maternal discipline. | Satisfactory. Parental deviance and disorder not known. |
| 14 | Harsh discipline. Mother frequently used a cane. | Did not get on with parents. Left home to live with relatives at age 15. |
| 15 | No problems. | Multiple hospitalisations. Marked discord with parents. |
| 16 | Parental marital discord. Vary scared as a child. Parental deviance and disorder not known. | Evacuated to a woman who hit him with a belt. Harsh parenting from own father. Multiple hospitalisations. |
| 17 | Abuse by father. In care aged 11 to 15. Mother psychiatric disorder. Parental marital discord. | Satisfactory but parental deviance and disorder not known. |

## Comparison group

|   | Mother | Father |
|---|--------|--------|
| 1 | Mother psychiatric problems. | Never cohabited. |
| 2 | No problems. Warm home. | Nothing known. |
| 3 | No problems. Warm home. | Nothing known. |
| 4 | Mother psychiatric problems and very unstable but no discord and father supportive. | Very little known. |

# Appendix D    The validity of the interview data

Evidence for the validity of the assessments of current circumstances and functioning has been presented in previous studies (Brown and Rutter, 1966; Rutter and Brown, 1966; Quinton *et al.*, 1976), and data concerning the validity of the parenting assessments is presented in Chapter 8. In this appendix the principal concern is with the problems of validity for the long-term recall of life-history events. But first, three further analyses are presented concerning the validity of the ratings of current functioning.

## Agreement between self-ratings of malaise and psychiatric assessments

All subjects were asked to complete a 24-item questionnaire before being questioned on current psychiatric symptomatology. This 'malaise' inventory has been shown to be an effective screening instrument in identifying adults with symptoms of anxiety or depression (Rutter *et al.*, 1970). A comparison between the self-ratings and the interview assessments of current handicapping psychiatric problems is given in Table D.1.

*Table D.1    Current psychiatric disorder and self-ratings of malaise*

|         |              | Interview rating of disorder | | | |
|---------|--------------|-------------|--------------------------------------|------------------------------|------|
|         |              | No disorder | Anxious/ depressive disorder only | Personality disorder only | Both |
| Malaise | No problems  | 143 | 3 | 13 | 3 |
|         | Problems     | 15  | 7 | 13 | 12 |

Table based on subjects and spouses in the follow-ups of women *and* men.

The agreement between the two measures was generally satisfactory: 76 per cent of those who rated themselves as having anxious/depressive symptomatology were considered to have similar psychiatric problems on the basis of the interview accounts, but the agreement fell to 50 per cent for those considered predominantly to have personality disorders. This is not surprising since the questionnaire was not designed to identify such problems. Only 4 per cent of subjects who rated themselves below the cut-off point were assessed as having anxious/depressed symptoms.

**Agreement between self-reports of criminality and official records**
Criminal records were provided through the Home Office Research Unit on all subjects. It is therefore possible to compare their own reports of criminal activities with these records. It is evident that agreement was very high (Table D.2). The percentage agreement on the existence of a criminal record was 90 per cent. Moreover, where discrepancies occurred subjects were as likely to report that they had been convicted for an indictable offence when this did not appear in the records, as they were to deny the existence of known offences. It is almost certain that some discrepancies occurred because of problems of matching official records with identifying information on our subjects.

*Table D.2   Official and self-reports of criminality*

|  |  | Official report | |
|---|---|---|---|
|  |  | None known | Criminal record |
| Self-report | No criminality | 145 | 11 |
|  | Criminality | 10 | 50 |

Table based on subjects and spouses in the follow-ups of women *and* men.

% Agreement on occurrence = 83%
% Agreement on official record = 90%

**Official criminality and personality disorders**
One further methodological issue that could be explored using the official criminal records was the relationship between interview ratings of personality problems and an independent record of behaviour (Table D.3). We may conclude from these data that an interview rating of antisocial personality disorder is strongly supported by official criminal records with 73 per cent of those thus rated having a record of persistent criminality. The frequency of criminal activity was also raised for those with other types of personality problem. On the other hand, only half of the subjects (52 per cent) with more than one court appearance were rated as having this kind of psychiatric disorder.

*Table D.3   Persistent criminality and personality disorder*

| | | Criminal record | |
|---|---|---|---|
| | | None or one court appearance only | Two or more court appearances |
| Personality | No disorder | 154 | 16 |
| disorder | Antisocial | 3 | 8 |
| rating | Other type | 25 | 9 |

Table based on the follow-ups of women *and* men.
Figures are numbers of subjects.

## The validity of long-term recall

The methodological problems of long-term recall have been discussed in Chapter 2. Our approach to these problems involved encouraging the respondents' recall of their earlier lives by focusing on well-defined life-history periods bounded by major events determined externally. In principle this meant questioning about and placing events in relation to the subjects' schooling history or changes in institution. For example, they were asked to remember if they first went away before they started school or later; if their father left home after they went to a particular school or before, etc. The interviewer then tried to build a coherent picture of the subject's life by relating remembered events to each other and to major external happenings in a 'before or after' fashion. Most of the ex-care subjects became very involved in this task since this was often the first time they had ever had the opportunity to put together memories of their lives in a coherent way. In addition to this temporal placing technique, we tried to minimise the problems of distorted recall by concentrating on major events or severe disturbances in the subjects' lives. With regard to relationships, the focus was on *clearly* positive or negative features with persistence in time *and* intensity of feeling illustrated by recall of specific characteristics or happenings.

In considering the problems that arise in recall it is important to distinguish between *inaccuracies* and *systematic biases*. It is only the latter may lead to false conclusions concerning a causal relationship between earlier events and later outcome. Random inaccuracies in recall may lead to false negative conclusions of no associations when in reality associations do exist. That is, the failure to detect processes intervening between childhood experiences and later functioning. The possibility of false positive conclusions (i.e. the creation of associations through systematic bias when in reality no such associations exist) is a more serious problem in investigating the factors involved in the inter-generational transmission of parenting problems. A thoroughgoing investigation of these issues was not possible in this study because of the lack of systematic and reliable criterion data from each subject's childhood. However, those analyses that could be performed are presented below because of the importance of the reliability of retrospective accounts.

## Agreement on early experience between interview reports and official records

First we can compare the subjects' account of a number of key variables with the evidence that could be abstracted from case notes. The most satisfactory estimates of the accuracy of reporting may be made by examining the extent of agreement between the subjects and the case notes where the latter give positive evidence for the presence of a particular problem. Because the notes were not compiled systematically, no conclusions can be drawn concerning the positive reports by subjects when these items are not mentioned in the records. However, we may have more confidence in the degree of agreement shown when positive case note evidence is presented. As Table D.4 shows, the accuracy of reporting of major family characteristics as assessed on this basis was best with respect to maternal psychiatric problems and to marital problems (92 and 85 per cent agreement on positives respectively) but lower with respect to paternal characteristics and parenting features. There appear to be two reasons for this. First, fathers were much less likely to remain regularly in contact with their children and were thus much more shadowy figures. Secondly, problems associated with very poor parenting were more often associated with early admission to care, so that the subjects' knowledge relied more on hearsay evidence than on recall. This can be illustrated by examining the levels of agreement according to the child's age at admission to long-term care.

As is clear from Table D.5 the proportion of 'correct' reporting of both marital discord or separations and of parenting deficits rises with age at long-term admission. Thus the percentage agreement on the definite occurrence of marital problems was only 22 per cent for those admitted under the age of two, compared with 61 per cent for those admitted between age two and five and 73 per cent of those admitted at age five or later. For poor parenting, clear reporting ('recall') only became satisfactory for those in the oldest admission group, where the agreement with the case note evidence was 68 per cent.

Finally, the accuracy of reporting of the age at first admission to care and the age at admission to either home 'A' or 'B' can be considered. These data were consistently recorded in the King *et al.* data and also constitute the 'hardest' measure against which to assess reporting. It is apparent (Table D.6) that the accuracy of reports was substantially better for the (later) time of admission to the two

*Table D.4  Family characteristics prior to admission: Comparison of subjects' reports and official records*

|  | Agree | Reported by subject only | Reported in notes only | Agree | %<br>Agreement on occurrence | %<br>Agreement with notes |
|---|---|---|---|---|---|---|
| *Mother* |  |  |  |  |  |  |
| Psychiatric disorder | 31 | 13 | 4 | 22 | 72 | 92 |
| Criminality | 42 | 6 | 9 | 13 | 63 | 74 |
| *Father* |  |  |  |  |  |  |
| Psychiatric disorder | 39 | 16 | 5 | 10 | 49 | 80 |
| Criminality | 32 | 19 | 7 | 12 | 48 | 77 |
| Marital discord or separations | 9 | 11 | 12 | 37 | 76 | 86 |
| Neglect/abuse/ bad parenting | 22 | 10 | 15 | 23 | 65 | 75 |

Table based on the follow-ups of women *and* men.
Figures are numbers of subjects.

240

*Table D.5 Official and reported family discord and poor parenting by admission group*

**Marital discord and separations**

| | Admitted under age 2 Reported occurrence | | | Admitted age 2–4.11 Reported occurrence | | | Admitted age 5 or over Reported occurrence | | |
|---|---|---|---|---|---|---|---|---|---|
| | None | Possible | Definite | None | Possible | Definite | None | Possible | Definite |
| Official None | 2 | 2 | 1 | 3 | 1 | 0 | 4 | 3 | 4 |
| records Possible | 4 | 0 | 0 | 0 | 0 | 0 | 1 | 0 | 0 |
| Definite | 2 | 4 | 1 | 3 | 6 | 7 | 2 | 5 | 15 |
| % agreement on occurrence | 22% | | | 61% | | | 73% | | |

**Poor parenting, neglect or abuse**

| | Reported occurrence | | | Reported occurrence | | | Reported occurrence | | |
|---|---|---|---|---|---|---|---|---|---|
| | None | Possible | Definite | None | Possible | Definite | None | Possible | Definite |
| Official None | 9 | 0 | 0 | 6 | 0 | 3 | 7 | 1 | 6 |
| records Possible | 1 | 0 | 0 | 1 | 0 | 0 | 1 | 0 | 1 |
| Definite | 3 | 2 | 1 | 6 | 3 | 1 | 3 | 2 | 13 |
| % agreement on occurrence | 29% | | | 14% | | | 68% | | |

children's homes — nearly always the beginning of long-term care. Thus the reports of those first admitted under the age of two were correct in only 57 per cent of cases, whereas this rose to 71 per cent for those whose first admissions were at age five or later. Only two children from whom records were available were admitted to home 'A' or 'B' under two years of age.

Table D.6   *Reported and official ages at admission to care*

|  |  | Reported age at admission | | |
|---|---|---|---|---|
|  |  | Under 2 | 2–4.11 | 5 or over |
| Official first | Under 2 | 26 | 15 | 5 |
| admission | 2–4.11 | 9 | 26 | 5 |
|  | 5 or over | 0 | 12 | 29 |

28% full agreement, 59% within one year, 77% within two years

| Official | Under 2 | 1 | 1 | 0 |
|---|---|---|---|---|
| admission to | 2–4.11 | 5 | 27 | 0 |
| home A or B | 5 or over | 0 | 15 | 82 |

44% full agreement, 74% within one year, 87% within two years

*Note:*   The large 5 or over v. 2–4.11 cell on admission to homes A or B may be due to a confusion between age at admission *including* homes A or B and actual transfer to the institution.

Table based on the follow-ups of women *and* men.

The accuracy of reporting of admissions to the two homes for those admitted later was substantially better, with those admitted between two and five correct in 82 per cent of cases, and those admitted at five or later correct in 85 per cent. The extent to which these levels of reporting can be considered as satisfactory depend on the use to be made of the information. Thus 44 per cent of subjects are correct to the year concerning their later admission, 74 per cent are correct to one year and 87 per cent within two years. This final level of reporting is good. If, however, the placing of subjects into groups with respect to a particular age of admission is required — under two, for example — reliance on self-reports would not be sufficient.

### Agreement between sibs
The inconsistencies in the case notes make it difficult to judge the accuracy of those positive reports of family characteristics that were not officially recorded. An alternative way of examining this is to

compare the accounts of sibs on the same set of variables (Table D.7). For this analysis all pairs of sibs were included. Thus, for example, a sib group of three provided three pairs. Sibling agreement was better than the agreement between individuals and official records. Percentage agreement on occurrence ranged from 69 per cent for paternal psychiatric disorder to 91 per cent for marital discord and separations. It will be appreciated that these accounts were given to different interviewers who did not exchange information on a subject's reports prior to interviews with other members of the family. In that these descriptions are refering to characteristics and events, the great majority of which were experienced at not later than the age of six or seven, the level of agreement is impressive. This does not necessarily provide evidence for the accuracy of *recall* since such information may have come to the subjects from other sources later in their lives or from discussion between themselves. Nevertheless both the comparisons with official records and the comparison between sib accounts give confidence in the quality or reporting of the major features of the subjects' childhoods.

*Table D.7   Agreement between sibs on family characteristics*

|  | Agree none | One sib only | Both | % Agree present |
|---|---|---|---|---|
| *Mother* | | | | |
| Psychiatric disorder | 24 | 14 | 24 | 77 |
| Criminality | 40 | 9 | 13 | 74 |
| *Father* | | | | |
| Psychiatric disorder | 30 | 15 | 17 | 69 |
| Criminality | 30 | 14 | 18 | 72 |
| Marital discord/ separation | 8 | 9 | 43 | 91 |
| Neglect/abuse/ poor parenting | 24 | 17 | 21 | 71 |
| Contacts with parents[a] whilst in care | 32 | 8 | 22 | 85 |

a   Contacts more than three-monthly before the age of 11.

Table based on the follow-ups of women *and* men.

**Biases in reporting: Long-term recall**

*Overlap between accounts of relationships*

Assessing the degree of systematic bias in long-term recall is problematic. For example, poorer current adjustment might be associated with unhappier earlier experiences which are accurately recalled or alternatively might lead to distorted negative reporting of events in childhood. Evidence for systematic biases can be assessed in these data by considering the extent to which relationships with different groups of persons — for example, care staff, sibs and peers — are reported in the same way, or conversely the extent to which subjects differentiate between these relationships. These reports both for earlier and later childhood are given in Table D.8A and B.

The data show that although there was a tendency for those with the unhappiest experiences to report poor relationships with different categories of people, there was great heterogeneity in the accounts. Moreover, the patterns of reporting vary with the age under consideration. Thus, relationships with sibs, peers and staff were generally seen as worse in the infants and primary school years than in later early adolescence, but the data show that subjects did not tend to report all early relationships in the same way.

**Current functioning and accounts of early experiences**

A further test of possible biases in reporting can be applied by examining the association between current functioning and earlier experiences. Here the question is not whether those currently functioning more poorly reported worse early experiences, but whether they consistently saw the majority of earlier experiences in the same light.

Table D.9 shows the association between overall psychosocial outcome and reports of relationships with staff and peers in the two main childhood periods. For both these times, subjects with currently poor functioning were more likely to assess their earlier relationships as poor, although this trend became much more pronounced in the teenage years. The proportion of well-functioning adults who reported poor relationships with staff in the earlier age period was not significantly different from the reports of those currently with problems. The association between psychosocial outcome and the reporting of good relationships was by no means as consistent. Those with good psychosocial outcome were not significantly more likely to report their in-care relationships as positive than those with current difficulties, except as regards relationships with care staff in their teens. It seems probable that these patterns of association reflect true variations in in-care experiences since they differ by time-period and by the type of relationship under consideration. This conclusion can be further supported by the data presented in Chapter 10 which show substantial variations in the kinds of experiences and relationships that are

Table D.8A  *Overlap between accounts of relationships*

| | Relationships with peers | | | | | | | |
| | Years 0–11 | | | | Years 11–16 | | | |
| | Good | Neutral | Mixed | Poor | Good | Neutral | Mixed | Poor |
|---|---|---|---|---|---|---|---|---|
| Relationships with staff | | | | | | | | |
| Good | 5 | 10 | 1 | 4 | 19 | 13 | 2 | 1 |
| Neutral | 0 | 44 | 1 | 8 | 11 | 22 | 0 | 0 |
| Mixed | 1 | 9 | 2 | 2 | 6 | 6 | 2 | 2 |
| Poor | 1 | 23 | 0 | 25 | 3 | 18 | 1 | 9 |
| | Tau(b) 0.31 | | | | Tau(b) 0.37 | | | |

Table D.8B

| | Relationships with peers | | | | | | | |
| | Years 0–11 | | | | Years 11–16 | | | |
| | Good | Neutral | Mixed | Poor | Good | Neutral | Mixed | Poor |
|---|---|---|---|---|---|---|---|---|
| Relationships with sibs | | | | | | | | |
| Good | 2 | 17 | 0 | 5 | 16 | 13 | 0 | 6 |
| Neutral | 2 | 42 | 0 | 17 | 10 | 32 | 3 | 6 |
| Mixed | 0 | 5 | 2 | 2 | 2 | 2 | 0 | 0 |
| Poor | 1 | 15 | 0 | 13 | 6 | 4 | 0 | 4 |
| | Tau(b) 0.17 | | | | Tau(b) 0.17 | | | |

Table based on the follow-ups of women *and* men.

245

*Table D.9 Psychosocial outcome and accounts of relationships with staff*

| Social functioning | Years 0–11 | | | | Years 11–16 | | | |
|---|---|---|---|---|---|---|---|---|
| | Good | Neutral | Mixed | Poor | Good | Neutral | Mixed | Poor |
| Good | 5 | 15 | 0 | 8 | 10 | 5 | 4 | 1 |
| History only | 3 | 13 | 5 | 3 | 9 | 6 | 3 | 1 |
| Some problems | 9 | 11 | 3 | 15 | 11 | 11 | 1 | 9 |
| Poor | 3 | 14 | 6 | 23 | 6 | 12 | 8 | 20 |
| | Good v. rest (ns) | | | | Good v. rest ** | | | |
| | Poor v. rest* | | | | Poor v. rest ** | | | |

*Psychosocial outcome and accounts of relationships with peers*

| Social functioning | Years 0–11 | | | | Years 11–16 | | | |
|---|---|---|---|---|---|---|---|---|
| | Good | Neutral | Mixed | Poor | Good | Neutral | Mixed | Poor |
| Good | 1 | 25 | 0 | 2 | 8 | 10 | 2 | 0 |
| History only | 3 | 14 | 1 | 6 | 9 | 9 | 0 | 0 |
| Some problems | 2 | 20 | 1 | 15 | 12 | 17 | 2 | 1 |
| Poor | 1 | 27 | 2 | 16 | 11 | 21 | 2 | 12 |
| | Good v. rest (ns) | | | | Good v. rest (ns) | | | |
| | Poor v. rest * | | | | Poor v. rest *** | | | |

Table based on the follow-ups of women *and* men.
Figures are ns.

associated with parenting problems and psychosocial outcome. However, the absence of consistent and independent contemporary evidence on the subjects' childhood relationships inevitably means that this assessment of the extent of systematic reporting biases has limitations.

# Appendix E  Multivariate analyses

The numbers given at the head of each of these multivariate analyses are the numbers of the figures to which they refer.

*Figure 11.2  Parental deviance, disrupted parenting, age at admission and personality disorder: Linear logistic analysis*

| Model | Model fitted | | | Comparison of models | | | |
|---|---|---|---|---|---|---|---|
| | Deviance | df | P | Term added | Improvement in fit | df | P |
| A. Constant | 16.05 | 5 | 0.01 | B to A | 5.32 | 1 | 0.05 |
| B. Parental deviance only | 10.73 | 4 | 0.05 | C to A | 7.49 | 1 | 0.01 |
| C. Disrupted parenting only | 8.56 | 4 | 0.10 | D to A | 3.39 | 1 | 0.01 |
| D. Age at admission only | 12.66 | 4 | 0.02 | C to B | 4.70 | 1 | 0.05 |
| | | | | D to B | 4.08 | 1 | 0.05 |
| | | | | C+D to B | 7.24 | 1 | 0.01 |
| | | | | D to B+C | 2.54 | 1 | ns |

*Figure 11.2  Parental deviance, disrupted parenting and personality disorder: Linear logistic analysis*

| Model | Model fitted | | | Comparison of models | | | |
|---|---|---|---|---|---|---|---|
| | Deviance | df | P | Term added | Improvement in fit | df | P |
| A. Constant | 10.02 | 3 | 0.02 | | | | |
| B. Disrupted parenting | 2.54 | 2 | ns | B to A | 7.48 | 1 | 0.01 |
| C. Parental deviance | 4.70 | 2 | ns | C to A | 5.32 | 1 | 0.05 |
| D. Disruption and deviance | 0.0007 | 1 | ns | C to B | 2.53 | 1 | ns |
| | | | | B to C | 4.69 | 1 | 0.05 |

*Figure 11.2  Parental deviance, disrupted parenting and poor social functioning: Linear logistic analysis*

| Model | Model fitted | | | Comparison of models | | | |
|---|---|---|---|---|---|---|---|
| | Deviance | df | P | Term added | Improvement in fit | df | P |
| A. Constant | 9.13 | 3 | 0.05 | | | | |
| B. Disrupted parenting | 0.02 | 2 | ns | B to A | 9.11 | 1 | 0.01 |
| C. Parental deviance | 7.88 | 2 | 0.02 | C to A | 2.25 | 1 | ns |
| D. Disruption and deviance | 0.0007 | 1 | ns | C to B | 0.01 | 1 | ns |
| | | | | B to C | 7.87 | 1 | 0.01 |

*Figure 11.7  Planning marital support and outcome: Linear logistic analysis*

| Model | Model fitted | | | Term added | Comparison of models | | |
|---|---|---|---|---|---|---|---|
| | Deviance | df | P | | Improvement in fit | df | P |
| A. Constant | 23.69 | 3 | 0.001 | | | | |
| B. Planning only | 15.68 | 2 | 0.001 | B to A | 8.01 | 1 | 0.01 |
| C. Marital support only | 6.24 | 2 | 0.05 | C to A | 17.45 | 1 | 0.001 |
| D. Planning and support | 0.97 | 1 | ns | D to A | 22.72 | 2 | 0.001 |

*Figure 11.7  Planning marital support and social functioning: Linear logistic analysis*

| Model | Model fitted | | | Term added | Comparison of models | | |
|---|---|---|---|---|---|---|---|
| | Deviance | df | P | | Improvement in fit | df | P |
| A. Constant | 26.72 | 3 | 0.001 | | | | |
| B. Planning only | 20.93 | 2 | 0.001 | B to A | 5.79 | 2 | 0.025 |
| C. Marital support only | 2.46 | 2 | ns | C to A | 24.26 | 1 | 0.001 |
| D. Planning and support | 0.0008 | 1 | ns | D to A | 26.71 | 2 | 0.001 |

*Figure 11.11  Current parenting, social circumstances and marital support: Linear logistic analysis*

| | Model fitted | | | Comparison of models | | | |
|---|---|---|---|---|---|---|---|
| Model | Deviance | df | P | Term added | Improvement in fit | df | P |
| A. Constant | 41.36 | 7 | 0.001 | | | | |
| B. Sample selection | 33.45 | 6 | 0.001 | B to A | 7.91 | 1 | 0.01 |
| C. Sample + circumstances | 18.70 | 5 | 0.01 | C to B | 14.79 | 1 | 0.01 |
| D. Sample + marital support | 11.44 | 5 | 0.05 | D to B | 22.01 | 1 | 0.001 |
| E. Sample + support + circumstances | 3.75 | 4 | ns | E to D | 7.69 | 1 | 0.01 |

# References

Altemeier III, W.A., O'Connor, S., Vietze, P.M., Sandler, H.M. and Sherrod, K.B. (1982), Antecedents of child abuse, *Journal of Pediatrics*, 100, 823–9.

——(1984), Prediction of child abuse: A prospective study of feasability, *Journal of Child Abuse*, 8, 393–400.

Anthony, E.J. (1984), The syndrome of the psychologically invulnerable child, in Anthony, E.J. and Koupernick, C. (eds), *The Child in His Family: Children at Psychiatric Risk*, New York: Wiley.

Arling, S.L. and Harlow, H.F. (1967), Effects of social deprivation on maternal behaviour of rhesus monkeys, *Journal of Comparative Physiology and Psychology*, 64, 371–8.

Atkinson, A.R., Maynard, A.R. and Trinder, C.G. (1983), *Parents and Children: Incomes in two generations*, London: Heinemann Educational Books.

Baddeley, A. (1979), The limitations of human memory: Implications for the design of retrospective surveys, in Moss, L. and Goldstein, H. (eds), *The Recall Method in Social Surveys*, University of London Institute of Education: Studies in Education No. 9.

Baltes, P.B. and Brim, O.G. Jnr (1979), *Life Span Development and Behaviour, Vol.2*, New York: Academic Press.

Bandura, A. (1977), Self-efficacy: towards a unifying theory of behavioural change, *Psychological Review*, 84, 191–215.

Bartlett, F.C. (1932), *Remembering*, Cambridge: Cambridge University Press.

Bean, J.A., Leeper, D.P., Wallace, R.B., Sherman, B.M. and Jagger, H. (1979), Variations in the reporting of menstrual histories, *American Journal of Epidemiology*, 109, 181–5.

Belsky, J. (1984), The determinants of parenting: A process model, *Child Development*, 55, 83–96.

Berridge, D. (1985), *Children's Homes*, Oxford: Basil Blackwell.

Berthoud, R. (1983), Who suffers social disadvantage?, in Brown, M. (ed.), *The Structure of Disadvantage*, London: Heinemann Educational Books.

Blurton-Jones, N. (1972), *Ethological Studies of Child Behaviour*, Cambridge: Cambridge University Press.

Bohman, M., Sigvardsson, S. and Cloninger, R. (1981), Maternal inheritance of alcohol abuse: cross-fostering analysis of adopted women, *Archives of General Psychiatry*, 38, 965–9.

Bretherton, I. and Waters, E. (1985), Growing points of attachment theory and research, *Monographs of the Society for Research in Child Development*, Serial no.209, 50, nos 1–2.

Brim, O.G. and Kagan, J. (eds) (1980), *Constancy and Change in Human Development*, Cambridge, Mass.: Harvard University Press.

Bronfenbrenner, U. (1979), *The Ecology of Human Development: Experiments by Nature and Design*, Cambridge, Mass.: Harvard University Press.

Brown, G.W. and Harris, T. (1978), *The Social Origins of Depression*, London: Tavistock Publications.

Brown, M. and Madge, N. (1982), *Despite the Welfare State*, SRC/DHSS Studies in Deprivation and Disadvantage, London: Heinemann Educational Books.

Brown, G.W. and Rutter, M. (1966), The measurement of family activities and relationships: a methodological study, *Human Relations*, 19, 241–63.

Brown, G.W., Bhrolchain, N.M. and Harris, T. (1975), Social class and psychiatric disturbance among women in an urban working class population, *Sociology*, 9, 225–54.

Brown, G.W., Harris, T. and Bifulco, A. (1986), Long-term effects of early loss of parent, in Rutter, M., Izard, C. and Read, P. (eds), *Depression in Young People*, New York: Guilford Press.

Cannell, C.F. (1977), A summary of studies of interviewing methodology, *Vital and Health Statistics*, series 2, No.69.

Cannell, C.F., Fisher, G. and Bakker, T. (1961), Reporting of hospitalization in the health interview survey, *Vital and Health Statistics*, series 2, No.6.

Clarke, A.M. and Clarke, A.D.B. (eds) (1976), *Early Experience: Myth and Evidence*, London: Open Books.

Clarke-Stewart, K.A. (1978), And daddy makes three: the father's impact on mother and young child, *Child Development*, 49, 446–78.

Cloninger, C.R., Bohman, M. and Sigvardsson, S. (1981), Inheritance of alcohol abuse: cross-fostering analysis of adopted men, *Archives of General Psychiatry*, 38, 861–8.

Cohen, S. and Syme, L.S. (1985), *Social Support and Health*, New York: Academic Press.

Cox, A. and Rutter, M. (1985), Diagnostic appraisal and interviewing, in Rutter, M. and Hersov, L. (eds), *Child and Adolescent Psychiatry: Modern Approaches* (2nd edn), Oxford: Blackwell Scientific Publications.

Cox, A., Rutter, M., Yule, W. and Quinton, D. (1977), Bias resulting from missing information: some epidemiological findings, *Journal of Preventive and Social Medicine*, 31, 131–6.

Creighton, S.J. (1984), *Trends in Child Abuse*, London: NSPCC.

Crnic, K., Greenbert, M.T., Ragozin, A., Robinson, N. and Basham, R. (1983), Effects of stress and social support on mothers and premature and full-term infants, *Child Development*, 54, 209—17.

Crockenberg, S. (1981), Infant irritability, mother responsiveness, and social support: influences on the security of infant–mother attachment, *Child Development*, 52, 857—65.

Crowe, R.R. (1972), The adopted offspring of women criminal offenders, *Archives of General Psychiatry*, 31, 785—91.

Crowe, R.R. (1974), An adoption study of antisocial personality, *Archives of General Psychiatry*, 31, 785—91.

Crowe, R.R. (1983), Antisocial personality disorders, in Tarter, R.E. (ed.), *The Child at Psychiatric Risk*, Oxford: Oxford University Press.

Davenport, Y.B., Zahn-Waxler, C., Adland, M.L. and Mayfield, A. (1984), Early child-rearing practices in families with a manic-depressive parent, *American Journal of Psychiatry*, 141, 230—5.

Davie, R., Butler, N. and Goldstein, H. (1972), *From Birth to Seven: A Report on the National Child Development Study*, London: Longman.

Dowdney, L., Mrazek, D., Quinton, D. and Rutter, M. (1984), Observation of parent–child interaction with two- to three-year-olds', *Journal of Child Psychology and Psychiatry*, 25, 379—407.

Dowdney, L., Skuse, D., Rutter, M. and Mrazek, D. (1985a), Parenting qualities: concepts, measures and origins, in Stevenson, J. (ed.), *Recent Research in Developmental Psychopathology. Journal of Child Psychology and Psychiatry* book supplement no.4, Oxford: Pergamon Press.

Dowdney, L., Skuse, D., Rutter, M., Quinton, D. and Mrazek, D. (1985b), The nature and quality of parenting provided by women raised in institutions, *Journal of Child Psychology and Psychiatry*, 26, 599—625.

Dunn, G. (1981), The role of linear models in psychiatric epidemiology, *Psychological Medicine*, 11, 179—84.

Dunn, J. and Kendrick, C. (1982), *Siblings: Love, Envy and Understanding*, London: Grant McIntyre.

Egeland, B., Jacobvitz, D. and Papatola, K. (1984), Intergenerational Continuity in Abuse, paper presented at the Social Science Research Council Conference on Child Abuse and Neglect, York, Maine, 20—23 May 1984.

Elder, G. (1974), *Children of the Great Depression*, Chicago: University of Chicago Press.

Elder, G.H., Caspi, A. and Downey, G. (1985), Problem behaviour and family relationships: Life course and intergenerational themes, in Sorensen, A., Weinert, F. and Sherrod, L. (eds), *Human Development: Multidisciplinary Perspectives*, Hillsdale, N.J.: Erlbaum.

Everitt, B.S. (1977), *The Analysis of Contingency Tables*, London: Chapman and Hall.

Feinberg, S.E. (1977), *The Analysis of Cross-Classified Categorical Data*, Cambridge, Mass.: MIT Press.

Finkelhor, D., Gelles, R.J., Hotaling, G.T. and Straus, M. (eds) (1983), *The Dark Side of Families: Current Family Violence Research*, Beverly Hills, Calif.: Sage Publications.

Frommer, E. and O'Shea, G. (1973a), Antenatal identification of women liable to have problems in managing their infants, *British Journal of Psychiatry*, 123, 149–56.

Frommer, E.A. and O'Shea, G. (1973b), The importance of childhood experience in relation to problems of marriage and family-building, *British Journal of Psychiatry*, 123, 157–60.

Garbarino, J. (1979), An ecological approach to child maltreatment, in Pelton, L. (ed.), *The Social Context of Child Abuse and Neglect*, New York: Human Sciences Press.

Garmezy, N. (1974), The study of competence in children at risk for severe psychopathology, in Anthony, E. and Koupernick, C. (eds), *The Child in his Family*, Vol.3, Children at Psychiatric Risk, New York: Wiley.

Gershon, E. (1983), The genetics of affective disorders, in Grinspoon, L. (ed.), *Psychiatry Update*, Vol.II, Washington, D.C.: American Psychiatric Association.

Gibbens, T.N.C. and Walker, D. (1956), *Cruel parents: case studies of prisoners convicted of violence towards children*, Institute for the Study and Treatment of Delinquency.

Gilbert, G.N. (1981), *Modelling Society*, London: George Allen and Unwin.

Glenn, N.D. and Skelton, B.A. (1983), Pre-adult background variables and divorce: a note of caution about over-reliance on explained variance, *Journal of Marriage and the Family*, 45, 405–10.

Goldberg, E.M. and Morrison, S.L. (1963), Schizophrenia and social class, *British Journal of Psychiatry*, 109, 785–802.

Goldberg, S. (1983), Parent–infant bonding: another look, *Child Development*, 54, 1355–82.

Graham, P.J. and Rutter, M. (1968), The reliability and validity of the psychiatric assessment of the child II. Interview with the parent, *British Journal of Psychiatry*, 114, 581–92.

Gurin, G., Veroff, J. and Feld, S. (1960), *Americans view their Mental Health*, New York: Basic Books.

Harlow, H.F. (1965), Sexual behaviour in the rhesus monkey, in Beach, F.A. (ed.), *Sex and Behaviour*, New York: Wiley.

Harman, D. and Brim, O.G. (1980), *Learning to be Parents: Principles, Programs and Methods*, London: Sage Publications.

Harter, S. (1983), Developmental perspectives on the self-system, in Hetherington, E.M. (ed.), *Socialization, Personality and Social Development*, Vol.4, *Handbook of Child Psychology* (4th edn), New York: Wiley.

Hetherington, E.M., Cox, M. and Cox, R. (1982), Effects of divorce on parents and children, in Lamb, M.E. (ed.), *Non-Traditional Families*, Hillsdale, N.J.: Erlbaum.

Hodges, J. and Tizard, B., Family and peer relationships in adolescents who spent their early years in residential care (submitted for publication).

Hofferth, S.L. and Moore, K.A. (1979), Early childrearing and later economic wellbeing, *American Sociological Review*, 44, 784–815.

Hutchings, B. and Mednick, S.A. (1974), Registered criminality in the adoptive and biological parents of registered male criminal adoptees, in Fieve, R.R. and Zubin, J.A. (eds), *Genetics and Psychopathology*, Baltimore: Johns Hopkins University Press.

Ilsley, R. and Thompson, B. (1961), Women from broken homes, *Sociological Review*, 9, 27–54.

Joseph, Sir K. (1972), Speech to the Preschool Playgroups Association, 29 June 1972.

Kagan, J. (1980), Perspectives on continuity, in Brim, O.G. and Kagan, J. (eds), *Constancy and Change in Human Development*, Cambridge, Mass.: Harvard University Press.

Kendler, K.S. and Gruenberger, A.M. (1984), An independent analysis of the Danish Adoption Study of schizophrenia. VI: the relationship between psychiatric disorders as defined by DSM–III in the relatives and adoptees, *Archives of General Psychiatry*, 41, 555–64.

Kety, S., Rosenthal, D., Wender, P.H., Schulsinger, F. and Jacobsen, B. (1974), Mental illness in the biological and adoptive families of adoptive individuals who have become schizophrenic: a preliminary report based upon psychiatric interviews, in Fieve, R.R., Brill, H. and Rosenthal, D. (eds), *Genetics and Psychopathology*, Baltimore: Johns Hopkins University Press.

King, R.D., Raynes, N.V. and Tizard, J. (1971), *Patterns of Residential Care: Sociological Studies of Institutions for Handicapped Children*, London: Routledge and Kegan Paul.

Klaus, M.H. and Kennell, J.H. (1976), *Maternal–Infant Bonding: The impact of early separation or loss on family development*, Saint Louis: C.V. Mosby.

Kohlberg, L., LaCrosse, J. and Ricks, D. (1972), The predictability of adult mental health from childhood behaviour, in Wolman, B.B. (ed.), *Manual of Child Psychopathology*, New York: McGraw-Hill.

Krug, D. and Davis, P. (1981), Study Findings of the National Study of the Incidence and Severity of Child Abuse and Neglect, DHSS publication no.(OHDS)81-30325, 41–3.

Lambert, L., Essen, J. and Head, J. (1977), Variations in behaviour ratings of children who have been in care, *Journal of Child Psychology and Psychiatry*, 8, 335—46.

Langner, T.S. and Michael, S.T. (1963), *Life Stress and Mental Health*, London: Macmillan Press.

Lewis, H. (1954), *Deprived Children: A Social and Clinical Study*, London: Oxford University Press.

Longstreth, L.E. (1981), Revising Skeels' final study: a critique, *Developmental Psychology*, 17, 620—5.

Lukianowitz, N. (1971), Battered Children, *Psychiatrica Clinica*, 4, 257—80.

Lytton, H. (1971), Observation studies of parent–child interaction: a methodological review, *Child Development*, 42, 651—84.

Maccoby, E.E. and Jacklin, C.N. (1974), *The Psychology of Sex Differences*, Stanford, CA: Stanford University Press.

Maccoby, E.E. and Martin, J.A. (1983), Socialization in the context of the family: parent–child interaction, in Hetherington, E.M. (ed.), *Socialization, Personality and Social Development*, Vol.4, *Handbook of Child Psychology* (4th edn), New York: Wiley.

Mapstone, E. (1969), Children in Care, *Concern*, 3, 23—8.

McClusky, K.A., Killarney, J. and Papini, D.R. (1983), Adolescent pregnancy and parenthood: implications for development, in Callaghan, E.J. and McClusky, K.A. (eds), *Lifespan Development Psychology: Non-normative life events*, New York: Academic Press.

McDowell, L. (1983), Housing deprivation: an intergenerational approach, in Brown, M. (ed.), *The Structure of Disadvantage*, London: Heinemann Educational Books.

McGuffin, P., Farmer, A.E., Gotesman, I.I., Murray, R.M. and Reveley, A.M. (1985), Twin concordance for operationally defined schizophrenia, *Archives of General Psychiatry*, 41, 541—5.

Miller, F.J.W., Kolvin, I. and Fells, H. (1985), Becoming Deprived: A cross-generation study based on the Newcastle upon Tyne 1000-Family Study, in Nicol, A.R. (ed.), *Longitudinal Studies in Child Psychology and Psychiatry: Practical lessons from research experience*, Chichester: John Wiley.

Millham, S., Bullock, R., Hosie and Haak, M. (1986), *Children Lost in Care: the family contacts of children in care*, Aldershot: Gower.

Mills, M., Puckering, C., Pound, A. and Cox, A. (1985), What is it about depressed mothers that influences their children's functioning? in Stevenson, J. (ed.), *Recent Research in Developmental Psychopathology. Journal of Child Psychology and Psychiatry*, monograph supplement No.4, Oxford: Pergamon Press.

Mischel, W. (1968), *Personality and Assessment*, New York: Wiley.

Moustakas, C.E., Sigel, I.E. and Schalock, M.D. (1956), An objective measurement and analysis of child–adult interaction, *Child Development*, 27, 109—34.

Mrazek, D., Dowdney, L., Rutter, M. and Quinton, D. (1982), Mother and pre-school child interaction: A sequential approach, *Journal of the American Academy of Child Psychiatry*, 21, 453–64.

Naslund, B., Perssson-Blennow, I., McNeil, T., Kaij, L. and Malmquist-Larsson, A. (1984), Offspring of women with non-organic psychosis: infant attachment to the mother at one year of age, *Acta Psychiatrica Scandanavica*, 69, 321–41.

Newson, J. and Newson, E. (1968), *Four Years Old in an Urban Community*, London: Allen and Unwin.

Oliver, J.E. (1985), Successive generations of child maltreatment: social and medical disorders in parents, *British Journal of Psychiatry*, 147, 484–90.

Oliver, J.E. and Cox, J. (1973), A family kindred with ill-used children: the burden on the community, *British Journal of Psychiatry*, 123, 81–90.

Oliver, J.E. and Taylor, J. (1971), Five generations of ill-treated children in one family, *British Journal of Psychiatry*, 119, 473–80.

Oliver, J.E., Cox, J., Taylor, A. and Baldwin, J.A. (1974), Severely ill-treated young children in North-east Wiltshire, Oxford University Unit of Clinical Epidemiology, Research report no.4.

Olweus, D. (1979), The stability of aggressive reaction patterns in males: a review, *Psychological Bulletin*, 86, 852–75.

Packman, J. with Randall, J. and Jacques, N. (1986), *Who Needs Care? Social work decisions about children*, Oxford: Basil Blackwell.

Paganini-Hill, A. and Ross, A.K. (1982), Reliability of recall of drug use and other health-related information, *American Journal of Epidemiology*, 116, 114–22.

Patterson, G.R. (1982), *Coercive Family Process*, Eugene Oregon: Castalia Publishing Co.

Paykel, E.S. (1978), Contribution of life events to causation of psychiatric illness, *Psychological Medicine*, 8, 245–53.

Pellegrini, D. (1975), Training in Social Problem Solving, in Rutter, M. and Hersov, L. (eds), *Child and Adolescent Psychiatry: Modern Approaches*, 2nd edn, Oxford: Blackwell Scientific.

Plomin, R. (1983), Childhood temperament, in Lahey, B.B. and Kazdin, A.E. (eds), *Advances in Clinical Child Psychology*, Vol.6, New York: Plenum Press.

Pound, A., Cox, A., Puckering, C. and Mills, M. (1985), The impact of maternal depression on young children, in Stevenson, J. (ed.), *Recent Research in Developmental Psychology. Journal of Child Psychology and Psychiatry*, Monograph Supplement no.4, Oxford: Pergamon Press.

Quinton, D. (1985), Measuring intergenerational change: a view from developmental psychopathology, in Measuring socio-demographic change, OPCS Occasional Paper 34, London: Office of Population Censuses and Surveys.

Quinton, D. and Rutter, M. (1984a), Parents with children in care. I. Current circumstances and parenting skills, *Journal of Child Psychology and Psychiatry*, 25, 211—29.

Quinton, D. and Rutter, M. (1984b), Parents with children in care. II. Intergenerational continuities, *Journal of Child Psychology and Psychiatry*, 25, 231—50.

Quinton, D. and Rutter, M. (1985), Family pathology and child psychiatric disorder: A four-year prospective study, in Nicol, A.R. (ed.), *Longitudinal Studies in Child Psychology and Psychiatry: Practical Lessons from Research Experience*, Chichester: Wiley.

Quinton, D., Rutter, M. and Liddle, C. (1984), Institutional rearing, parenting difficulties and marital support, *Psychological Medicine*, 14, 107—24.

Quinton, D., Rutter, M. and Rowlands, O. (1976), An evaluation of an interview assessment of marriage, *Psychological Medicine*, 6, 577—86.

Radke-Yarrow, M. and Kuczynski, L. (1983), Perspectives and strategies in childrearing. Studies of rearing in normal and depressed mothers, in Magnusson, D. and Allen, V. (eds), *Human Development: Interactional Perspectives*, New York and London: Academic Press.

Robins, L.N. (1966), *Deviant Children Grown Up*, Baltimore: Williams and Wilkins.

Robins, L.N. (1978), Sturdy childhood predictors of adult antisocial behaviour: replications from longitudinal studies, *Psychological Medicine*, 8, 611—22.

Robins, L.N., Schoenberg, S.P., Holmes, S.J., Ratcliff, K.S., Behham, A. and Works, J. (1985), Early home environment and retrospective recall: a test of concordance between siblings with and without psychiatric disorders, *American Journal of Orthopsychiatry*, 55, 27—41.

Roy, P. (1983), Is continuity enough?: substitute care and socialization, paper presented at the Spring Scientific Meeting, Royal College of Psychiatrists, Child and Adolescent Psychiatry Specialist Section, March 1983.

Rowe, J. (1985), *Social Work Decisions in Child Care*, London: HMSO.

Rutter, M. (1967), A children's behaviour questionnaire for completion by teachers: preliminary findings, *Journal of Child Psychology and Psychiatry*, 8, 1—11.

Rutter, M. (1970), Sex differences in children's response to family stress, in Anthony, E.J. and Coupernick, C. (eds), *The Child in his Family*, New York: Wiley.

Rutter, M. (1975), *Helping Troubled Children*, Harmondsworth: Penguin Books.

Rutter, M. (1979), Protective factors in children's response to stress and disadvantage, in Kent, J.W. and Rolf, J.E. (eds), *Primary Prevention of Psychopathology*, vol.3, *Social Competence in Children*, Hanover: University Press of New England.

Rutter, M. (1981a), *Maternal Deprivation Reassessed*, Harmondsworth: Penguin Books.

Rutter, M. (1981b), Epidemiological/longitudinal strategies and causal research in child psychiatry, *Journal of American Academy of Child Psychiatry*, 20, 513—44.

Rutter, M. (1981c), Stress, coping and development: Some issues and some questions, *Journal of Child Psychology and Psychiatry*, 22, 323—56.

Rutter, M. (1982), Epidemiological-longitudinal approaches to the study of development, in Collins, W.A. (ed.), *The Concept of Development. Minnesota Symposia on Child Psychology*, vol.15, Hillsdale, N.J.: Erlbaum.

Rutter, M. (1983), Statistical and personal interactions: facets and perspectives, in Magnusson, D. and Allen, V. (eds), *Human Development: An interactional perspective*, New York: Academic Press.

Rutter, M. (1984a), Continuities and discontinuities in social-emotional development: empircal and conceptual perspectives, in Emde, R. and Harmon, R. (eds), *Continuities and Discontinuities in Development*, New York: Plenum Press.

Rutter, M. (1984b), Psychopathology and development: I. Childhood antecedents of adult psychiatric disorder, *Australian and New Zealand Journal of Psychiatry*, 18, 225—34.

Rutter, M. (1984c), Psychopathology and development: II. Childhood experiences and personality development, *Australian and New Zealand Journal of Psychiatry*, 18, 314—27.

Rutter, M. (1985a), Resilience in the face of adversity: protective factors and resistence to psychiatric disorder, *British Journal of Psychiatry*, 147, 598—611.

Rutter, M. (1985b), Family and school influences on behavioural development, *Journal of Child Psychology and Psychiatry*, 26, 349—68.

Rutter, M. (1985c), Family and school influences on cognitive development, *Journal of Child Psychology and Psychiatry*, 26, 683—704.

Rutter, M. (in press a), Intergenerational continuities and discontinuities in serious parenting difficulties, in Chicchetti, D. and Carlson, V. (eds), *Research on the Consequences of Child Maltreatment*, New York: Cambridge University Press.

Rutter, M. (in press b), Myerian Psychobiology: personality development and the role of life experiences, *American Journal of Psychiatry*.

Rutter, M. (in press c), Continuities and discontinuities from infancy, in Osofsky, J. (ed.), *Handbook of Infant Development* (2nd edn), New York: Wiley.

Rutter, M. (in press d), Psychosocial resilience and protective mechanisms, in Rolf, J., Masten, A., Chicchetti, D., Nuechterlein, K. and Weintraub, S. (eds), *Risk and Protective Factors in the Development of Psychopathology*, New York: Cambridge University Press.

Rutter, M. and Brown, G.W. (1966), The reliability and validity of measures of family life in families containing a psychiatric patient, *Social Psychiatry*, 1, 38–53.

Rutter, M. and Giller, H. (1983), *Juvenile Delinquency: Trends and Perspectives*, Harmondsworth: Penguin Books.

Rutter, M. and Madge, N. (1976), *Cycles of Disadvantage: A Review of Research*, London: Heinemann.

Rutter, M. and Quinton, D. (1977), Psychiatric disorder: ecological factors and concepts of causation, in McGurk, H. (ed.), *Ecological Factors in Human Development*, Amsterdam: North-Holland.

Rutter, M. and Quinton, D. (1981), Longitudinal studies of institutional children and children of mentally ill parents (United Kingdom), in Mednick, S.A. and Baert, A.E. (eds), *Prospective Longitudinal Research: An Empirical Basis for the Primary Prevention of Psychosocial Disorders*, Oxford: Oxford University Press.

Rutter, M. and Quinton, D. (1984), Parental psychiatric disorder: effects on children, *Psychological Medicine*, 14, 853–80.

Rutter, M. and Quinton, D. (1984), Long-term follow-up of women institutionalized in childhood: factors promoting good functioning in adult life, *British Journal of Developmental Psychology*, 18, 225–34.

Rutter, M., Quinton, D. and Liddle, C. (1983), Parenting in two generations: Looking backwards and looking forwards, in Madge, N. (ed.), *Families at Risk*, DHSS/SSRC Studies in Deprivation and Disadvantage, London: Heinemann Educational Books.

Rutter, M., Tizard, J. and Whitmore, K. (eds) (1970), *Education, Health and Behaviour*, London: Longmans.

Rutter, M., Cox, A., Tupling, C., Berger, M. and Yule, W. (1975a), Attainment and adjustment in two geographical areas: I. The prevalence of psychiatric disorder, *British Journal of Psychiatry*, 126, 493–509.

Rutter, M., Yule, B., Quinton, D., Rowlands, O., Yule, W. and Berger, M. (1975b), Attainment and adjustment in two geographical areas: III. Some factors accounting for area differences, *British Journal of Psychiatry*, 126, 520–33.

Sackett, G.P. and Ruppenthal, G.C. (1973), Development of monkeys after varied experiences during infancy, in Barrett, S.A. (ed.), *Ethology and Development. Clinics in Developmental Medicine*, no.47, London: Heinemann.

Scarr, S. and McCartney, K. (1983), How people make their own environments: a theory of genotype environmental effects, *Child Development*, 54, 424–35.

Schaffer, H.R. and Liddell, C. (1984), Adult–child interaction under dyadic and polyadic conditions, *British Journal of Developmental Psychology*, 2, 33–42.

Schaffer, H.R. and Schaffer, E.B. (1968), *Child Care and the Family*, Occasional Papers on Social Administration No.25, London: Bell.

Scott, P.D. (1973), Fatal Battered Baby Cases, *Medicine, Science and the Law*, 13, 197–206.

Seay, B., Alexander, B.K. and Harlow, H.F. (1964), Maternal behaviour of socially deprived monkeys, *Journal of Abnormal and Social Psychology*, 69, 345–54.

Shure, M.B. and Spivak, G. (1978), *Problem-Solving Techniques in Child Rearing*, San Francisco: Jossey-Bass.

Skeels, H.M. (1966), Adult status of children from contrasting early life experiences: a follow-up study, *Monographs of the Society for Research in Child Development*, 31, whole no.105.

Skuse, D. (1984a), Extreme deprivation in early childhood–I. Diverse outcomes for three siblings from an extraordinary family, *Journal of Child Psychology and Psychiatry*, 25, 523–41.

Skuse, D. (1984b), Extreme deprivation in early childhood–II. Theoretical issues and a comparative review, *Journal of Child Psychology and Psychiatry*, 25, 543–72.

Smith, S.M. (ed.) (1978), *The Maltreatment of Children*, Lancaster: M.T.P. Press.

Straus, M.A. (1979), Family patterns and child abuse in a nationally representative American sample, *Child Abuse and Neglect*, 3, 213–25.

Tienari, P. *et al.* (1985), Interaction of genetic and psychosocial factors in schizophrenia, *Acta Psychiatrica Scandinavica*, 71, 19–30.

Tilley, B.C. *et al.* (1985), A comparison of pregnancy history recall and medical records, *American Journal of Epidemiology*, 121, 269–81.

Tizard, B. and Hodges, J. (1978), The effects of early institutional rearing on the development of eight-year-old children, *Journal of Child Psychology and Psychiatry*, 19, 99–118.

Tizard, B. and Rees, J. (1974), A comparison of the effects of adoption, restoration to the natural mother, and continued institutionalization on the cognitive development of four-year-old children, *Child Development*, 45, 92–9.

Tizard, B. and Rees, J. (1975), The effects of early institutional rearing on the behavioural problems and affectional relationships of four-year-old children, *Journal of Child Psychology and Psychiatry*, 16, 61–73.

Torgersen, S. (1983), Genetics of neurosis: the effect of sampling variation on the twin concordance ratio, *British Journal of Psychiatry*, 142, 126–32.

Torgersen, S. (1985), Hereditary differentiation of anxiety and affective neuroses, *British Journal of Psychiatry*, 146, 530–4.

Troisi, A. and D'Amato, F.R. (1984), Ambivalence in monkey mothering: infant abuse combined with maternal possessiveness, *Journal of Nervous and Mental Diseases*, 172, 105—8.

Vernon, J. and Fruin, D. (1986), *In Care: a study of social work decision-making*, London: National Children's Bureau.

Wadsworth, J., Taylor, B., Osborn, A. and Butler, N. (1984), Teenage mothering: child development at five years, *Journal of Child Psychology and Psychiatry*, 25, 305—14.

Wadsworth, M.E.J. (1984), Early stress and associations with adult health, behaviour and parenting, in Butler, N.R. and Corner, B.D. (eds), *Stress and Disability in Childhood: The Long-Term Problems*, Bristol: Wright.

Wadsworth, M.E.J. (1985), Parenting skills and their transmission through generations, *Adoption and Fostering*, 9, 28—32.

Walker, L.G., Thomson, N. and Lindsay, W.R. (1984), Assessing family relationships. A multi-method, multi-situation approach, *British Journal of Psychiatry*, 144, 387—94.

Wallerstein, J. (1983), Children of divorce: Stress and developmental tasks, in Garmezy, N. and Rutter, M. (eds), *Stress, Coping and Development in Children*, New York: McGraw-Hill.

Wedge, P. and Prosser, N. (1973), *Born to Fail?*, London: Arrow Books.

Werner, E.E. and Smith, R.S. (1982), *Vulnerable but Invincible: A longitudinal study of resilient children and youth*, New York: McGraw-Hill.

Wilson, H. and Herbert, G.W. (1978), *Parents and Children in the Inner City*, London: Routledge and Kegan Paul.

Wohlwill, J.F. (1980), Cognitive development in childhood, in Brim, O.G. and Kagan, J. (eds), *Constancy and Change in Human Development*, Cambridge, Mass.: Harvard University Press.

Wolkind, S.N. (1974), The components of 'affectionless psychopathy' in institutionalized children, *Journal of Child Psychology and Psychiatry*, 15, 215—20.

Wolkind, S.N. (1977), Women who have been 'in care': psychological and social status during pregnancy, *Journal of Child Psychology and Psychiatry*, 18, 179—82.

Wolkind, S.N. and Coleman, E.Z. (1983), Adult psychiatric disorder and childhood experiences: the validity of retrospective data, *British Journal of Psychiatry*, 143, 188—91.

Wolkind, S.N. and Kruk, S. (1985), From child to parent: early separation and the adaptation to motherhood, in Nicol, A.R. (ed.), *Longitudinal Studies in Child Psychology and Psychiatry: Practical Lessons from Research Experience*, Chichester: Wiley.

Wolkind, S.N., Kruk, S. and Chaves, L. (1976), Childhood separation experiences and psychosocial status in primiparous women: preliminary findings, *British Journal of Psychiatry*, 15, 215—20.

Wolkind, S.N. and Rutter, M. (1973), Children who have been 'in care': an epidemiological study, *Journal of Child Psychology and Psychiatry*, 14, 97–105.

Wolkind, S.N. and Rutter, M. (1985), Sociocultural factors, in Rutter, M. and Hersov, L. (eds), *Child and Adolescent Psychiatry: Modern approaches* (2nd edn), Oxford: Blackwell Scientific Publications, 82–100.

Yarrow, M.R., Campbell, J.D. and Burton, R.V. (1964), Recollections of childhood: a study of the retrospective method, *Monographs of the Society for Research in Child Development*, 35, no.5.

Yule, W. and Raynes, N.V. (1972), Behavioural characteristics of children in residential care in relation to indices of separation, *Journal of Child Psychology and Psychiatry*, 13, 249–59.

# Index